Service-Learning as a New Paradigm in Higher Education of China

Service-Learning as a New Paradigm in Higher Education of China

Edited by Carol MA Hok-ka, Alfred CHAN Cheung-ming, Alice LIU Cheng, and Fanny MAK Mui-fong

Michigan State University Press | East Lansing

♾ The paper used in this publication meets the minimum requirements of ANSI/NISO Z39.48-1992 (R 1997) (Permanence of Paper).

Michigan State University Press
East Lansing, Michigan 48823-5245

Printed and bound in the United States of America.

27 26 25 24 23 22 21 20 19 18   1 2 3 4 5 6 7 8 9 10

LIBRARY OF CONGRESS CATALOGING-IN-PUBLICATION DATA
Names: MA Hok-ka, Carol, editor.
Title: Service-learning as a new paradigm in higher education of China / edited by Carol MA
Hok-ka, Alfred CHAN Cheung-ming, Alice LIU Cheng, and Fanny MAK Mui-fong.
Description: East Lansing : Michigan State University Press, 2018. | Series: Transformations in
higher education : scholarship of engagement | Includes bibliographical references.
Identifiers: LCCN 2017017684 | ISBN 9781611862713 (pbk. : alk. paper) | ISBN
9781609175535 (pdf) | ISBN 9781628953206 (epub) | ISBN 9781628963205 (kindle)
Subjects: LCSH: Service learning—China. | Community and college—China. | College student
development programs—China. | Education, Higher—Aims and objectives—China.
Classification: LCC LC221.4.C55 S47 2018 | DDC 361.3/70951—dc23 LC record available at
https://lccn.loc.gov/2017017684

Book design by Charlie Sharp, Sharp Des!gns, East Lansing, MI
Cover design by Shaun Allshouse, www.shaunallshouse.com

Michigan State University Press is a member of the Green Press Initiative and
is committed to developing and encouraging ecologically responsible publishing
practices. For more information about the Green Press Initiative and the use
of recycled paper in book publishing, please visit *www.greenpressinitiative.org.*

Visit Michigan State University Press at *www.msupress.org*

Transformations in Higher Education:
Scholarship of Engagement

The Transformations in Higher Education: Scholarship of Engagement book series is designed to provide a forum where scholars can address the diverse issues provoked by community-campus partnerships that are directed toward creating innovative solutions to societal problems. Numerous social critics and key national commissions have drawn attention to the pervasive and burgeoning problems of individuals, families, communities, economies, health services, and education in American society. Such issues as child and youth development, economic competitiveness, environmental quality, and health and health care require creative research and the design, deployment, and evaluation of innovative public policies and intervention programs. Similar problems and initiatives have been articulated in many other countries, apart from the devastating consequences of poverty that burdens economic and social change. As a consequence, there has been increasing societal pressure on universities to partner with communities to design and deliver knowledge applications that address these issues, and to co-create novel approaches to effect system changes that can lead to sustainable and evidence-based solutions. Knowledge generation and knowledge application are critical parts of the engagement process, but so too are knowledge dissemination and preservation. The Transformations in Higher Education: Scholarship of Engagement series was designed to meet one aspect of the dissemination/preservation dyad.

This series is sponsored by the National Collaborative for the Study of University Engagement (NCSUE) and is published in partnership with the Michigan State University Press. An external board of editors supports the NCSUE editorial staff in order to insure that all volumes in the series are peer reviewed throughout the publication process. Manuscripts embracing campus-community partnerships are invited from authors regardless of discipline, geographic place, or type of transformational change accomplished. Similarly, the series embraces all methodological approaches from rigorous randomized trials to narrative and ethnographic studies. Analyses may span the qualitative to quantitative continuum, with particular emphasis on mixed-model approaches. However, all manuscripts must attend to detailing critical aspects of partnership development, community involvement, and evidence of program changes or impacts. Monographs and books provide ample space for authors to address all facets of engaged scholarship thereby building a compendium of praxis that will facilitate replication and generalization, two of the cornerstones of evidence-based programs, practices, and policies. We invite you to submit your work for publication review and to fully participate in our effort to assist higher education to renew its covenant with society through engaged scholarship.

Hiram E. Fitzgerald
Burton Bargerstock
Laurie Van Egeren

Contents

Part 1. Service-Learning and Chinese Higher Education

Part 2. Disciplinary Perspectives

Part 3. Exemplary Practices

Preface

In 2006, when I first set up an Office of Service-Learning (OSL) at Lingnan University, many people thought that service-learning was merely a synonym for community service. After promotion and outreach to various faculty members, students, and community partners, they realized the power of service-learning and witnessed the transformation of our students. I never thought there would be a significant development resulting from service-learning within such a short time as a decade. Service-learning has become an emerging pedagogy in many higher education institutions in Asia because it provides students a plethora of positive outcomes related to their personal and civic development, giving them mature interpersonal and communication skills and enhancing their realized life satisfaction as well as their academic and professional development.

I have been asking myself how service-learning, volunteerism, community engagement, social practices, and community services differ. It seems that they are all similar terms, but with different forms, durations, purposes, and practices. When I first heard the term service-learning, it was at the 2004 "Service-Learning: Developing New Leadership for Communities, Nations and the World" conference organized by the International Partnership for Service-Learning and Leadership in Chiang Mei, Thailand. With the support of the Lingnan Foundation, Lingnan University was able to send a group of students and teachers to learn about service-learning and explore the possibilities for implementing it at Lingnan. In 2004–2005, Lingnan started the first service-learning and research scheme, which addressed the needs of the aging in society and worked with professors from the social sciences department to integrate service-learning into various courses, including "Social Gerontology," "Health Illness and Behaviors," and "Crime and Delinquency." After earning positive feedback from the community, Lingnan University received a donation in 2006 to establish the first OSL in Hong Kong. Within ten years, Lingnan has organized various regional conferences on service-learning, reactivated the Service-Learning Asia Network, set up the Service-Learning Higher Education Network in Hong Kong, developed the first service-learning training program in Mainland China, and published various service-learning manuals and articles. The Lingnan service-learning model serves as a reference for other universities to develop their own characteristic service-learning program.

Since 2006, Lingnan University, Lingnan Foundation, and the United Board for Christian Higher Education in Asia have organized various Asia-Pacific regional service-learning conferences which have attracted over 2,000 participants from all over the world to exchange ideas about coordinating service-learning. With this joint effort, the Service-Learning Asia Network serves to foster the collaborative work in the region. These landmark events and networks have demonstrated that service-learning has, in a sense, come of age in Asia. Indeed, many leading universities and colleges in the region have established service-learning centers or programs which support a dedicated core of faculty and serve an increasingly larger student population. In 2008, the Service-Learning Higher Education Network in Hong Kong created a platform among higher education institutions to exchange and support service-learning programs and research. Lingnan University was the first to set up an OSL in Hong Kong (2006) and to require service-learning for graduation (2016–2017). Hong Kong Polytechnic University and Chung Chi College at the Chinese University also established OSLs, in 2012 and 2013, respectively. Chung Chi College has organized service-learning conferences among Chinese since 2014 to enlighten people in Hong Kong, Mainland China, and Macau about various practices of service-learning. The Education University of Hong Kong introduced mandatory co-curricular and service-learning courses to all undergraduates in 2014. Service-learning in Hong Kong is not only a kind of experiential education, but also a way of echoing the government's knowledge-transfer initiative and addressing community needs through various educational programs.

In 1997, Hong Kong returned to Mainland China and officially became the Hong Kong Special Administrative Region of the People's Republic of China. Under the principle of "one country, two systems," Hong Kong has a separate political and social system. Though there are two systems, the government encourages dialogue between Hong Kong and Mainland China about relevant topics. Education is one of the areas where the two regions seek to learn from each other.

In 2010, there was a general education reform in China, and some higher education institutions have taken it as an opportunity to embed service-learning into different academic programs. In 2012 Lingnan University received a grant from the United Board for Christian Higher Education in Asia to work with different Chinese higher education institutions—including Sun Yat-sen University (SYSU), Guangxi Medical University, South China Normal University, South China University of Technology, Beijing Normal University-Hong Kong Baptist University United International College, and Zhuhai City Polytechnic—to conduct training, design service-learning curriculum, implement service-learning projects, and evaluate the outcomes of service-learning practices. The participating institutions showed enthusiasm to exchange the service-learning ideas and practices with other universities in Asia. They presented their service-learning experiences at the 4th Asia-Pacific Regional Conference on Service-Learning in 2013 and successfully raised the awareness of using service-learning as a pedagogy among Chinese universities, social enterprises, and business sectors.

Because of increasing interest in participating in service-learning in China, Lingnan University has organized a series of training programs for exploring the meaning of service-learning and promoting various practices of service-learning among Chinese faculty members and students. Universities in China were invited to join the training to understand the ideology and practice of service-learning. Teachers expressed great enthusiasm for the idea of further developing service-learning in the education system, and they have integrated service-learning into diverse academic courses or general education curricula. With these joint efforts and in-depth discussion with various stakeholders, we have consolidated stories and studied the concept of service-learning in Chinese context. The purpose of this book is to give a detailed introduction of service-learning to institutions in China and further analyze ways in which the concept benefits students, universities, communities, and the country as a whole. Case studies about how institutions integrate service-learning in various curricula will be presented as a new paradigm in Chinese higher education.

Though the concept of service-learning originated in Western society, the rationale behind it is rooted in Chinese society, its philosophy, history, languages, and culture. When service-learning is promoted in China, many people want to know how the Chinese interpret its meaning and the ways of teaching and learning in service-learning.

In the first two chapters in this book, the authors discuss the concept of service-learning and why it is a new paradigm in higher education. They note the rapid development of service-learning in the world and suggest why and how we should promote service-learning in China. In order to understand more about higher education in China, the authors also discuss its principles and status quo, as well as its concept of service-learning within traditional Chinese values. An analysis of the evolution of service and learning in Confucian culture in different periods with various key scholars is discussed for further understanding of the development of service and learning in China. In "Service-Learning and the Aims of Chinese Higher Education," Carol MA Hok-ka, Fanny MAK Mui-fong, and Alice LIU Cheng emphasize the importance of understanding the connections among service-learning, volunteerism, Confucian ideas, and the contemporary education objectives of China.

Part 2 presents various disciplinary perspectives including, liberal arts education, medical education, and philanthropy education. The authors from these chapters relate their experiences linking liberal arts education and service-learning and discuss how service-learning has positive effects on students, including how it helps to develop a sense of social responsibility in students.

Referencing these disciplinary perspectives provides us with concepts of how and what service-learning schemes are being used in Chinese higher education institutions. However, we still need exemplary practices and case studies to further illustrate the value of service-learning in China's higher education institutions. We thus invited professors to join a service-learning training program to share information about their pilot service-learning courses designed to address various societal issues, including tax evasion, waste, leprosy rehabilitation care, ethnic minority groups, aging, migrant kids, and civic society in China. Within one and a half years, teachers learned about service-learning curriculum design and integrated service elements into their courses. They not only enhanced their understanding of teaching, learning, and service-learning, but also developed their own professionalism and engagement with their communities. With support from the Lingnan team, they also reflected on what they learned about how to ensure the quality of a service-learning experience. For example, in "Serving the Community by Providing Tax Consultations," Long and Jiang mention that there are various ways to improve the quality of service-learning projects in a taxation management course by providing more professional training for students and developing a feedback mechanism and sharing platform. In "Waste Separation and Engaging in Civic Education,"

Lily Qi emphasizes the importance of the linkage between learning goals and service outcomes. In "Oral History of Sian Leprosy Rehabilitation Village," Han Yimin understands the values of service-learning, especially as an opportunity and important direction for education reform in China. Wang, Xiong, and Liu in "The Renewal of Earnest Practice" explain that service-learning is different from traditional Chinese voluntary modules such as *xue Lifung* (learning from Lifung), *Sanxiaxiang* (Three Downs to the Countryside) activity and voluntary teaching. They link service-learning to community-based research projects and write about the ethics of philanthropy and the preservation of rural culture. Finally, in "Service-Learning and Education Realization," Lin, Huang, and Huo mention that they have explored new ways to enhance students' citizenship and quality.

Universities such as Beijing Normal University–Hong Kong Baptist University United International College and SYSU have developed their own independent courses and general education core curricula, respectively, which are based on their university plans to integrate service-learning into the curriculum. This may serve as a possible model for other interested Chinese universities to pilot their own service-learning courses. More information can be found in "The Independent Service-Learning Course" and "Service-Learning in the General Education Core Curriculum."

Lingnan University, which serves as a pioneer in participating in service-learning in Hong Kong, also describes how an OSL is set up and what challenges and case-sharing from various departments the university faces. It is not easy to implement service-learning without institutionalization, committed professors, and a strong community network. Lingnan's experience of the institutionalization of service-learning is discussed in "Pioneer in Various Forms."

With the joint efforts from various teachers, we describe all our experiences in case studies, empirical data, and educational and institutional policies. This book provides an important resource for development of service-learning in China and fills a niche within the world-wide literature of service-learning. Our team would like to thank all of the involved stakeholders, including teachers, agency partners, students, translators, foundations, and institutions who supported this publication and help promote service-learning in China.

PART 1

Service-Learning and Chinese Higher Education

The Concept and Development of Service-Learning

Carol MA Hok-Ka

Definition and Background of Service-Learning

Pioneered by American higher education in the early twentieth century, service-learning is a teaching method that combines academic knowledge and community service. Service-learning first joined two complex concepts in the late 1960s: community action—the "service"—and efforts to learn from that action and connect what is learned to existing knowledge—the "learning" (Stanton, Giles, & Gruz, 1999). Defining the term *service-learning* relies on three key elements: (1) community service, (2) learning opportunities for students, and (3) critical reflection. Schools cooperate with the community to provide students with a variety of service opportunities through which students are encouraged to apply classroom knowledge in practice, think independently, and reflect critically. These actions not only deepen students' theoretical knowledge but also provide students with a holistic learning environment. In addition, service-learning practices aim to meet the needs of the community and strengthen the reciprocal cooperation between the university and community.

The concept of service-learning emphasizes the importance of "learning by doing." Through the process of going into the community, engaging with individuals, and serving others, students are often inspired to have in-depth individual reflections. It also enhances the civic consciousness and sense of social responsibility of students by encouraging them to be actively concerned about social issues, discover their communities' needs, and help groups who are in need. Contrary to general volunteer service, service-learning connects academic study and practical community experience. Through service-learning, students engage in experiential learning, which helps them gain a more comprehensive understanding of their academic knowledge and improve their ability to use this knowledge flexibly and reasonably. In addition to bettering student outcomes, service-learning also contributes to the betterment of society.

Unlike the traditional one-way teaching and learning method of *teachers teach, students learn*, service-learning requires cooperation and active communication among course instructors, students, and service agencies. The course instructor's role is to inspire students to link up theory and service practice. Additionally, through designing and preparing for service-learning activities, students are trained to take initiative, be creative, and think independently. Course instructors and students also need to continually hold in-depth conversations with service agencies in order to ensure that the service projects are in line with the actual needs of the community, respectful of the wishes and requirements of the community, and effective in improving the circumstances of the community. As a result of this comprehensive teaching model, schools are able to not only produce civic-minded individuals and academic scholars, but also enhance practical and moral education. Thus, the community is able to benefit from the knowledge and resources of the schools and students. Service-learning leads to a win-win-win situation for schools, students, and communities. In short, there are three core elements in service-learning: (1) to combine academic theories and community service; (2) to carry out active and in-depth reflection on the process of learning and serving; and (3) to enhance the students' sense of social responsibility and promote their whole-person development.

Since the early twentieth century, the education style and method of service-learning has continually and quickly spread throughout higher education in the United States with the support of university administrations, state and national government, and local communities. Subsequently, its influence has quickly extended to European, other North and South American, Asian, and African universities/colleges. Due to the dynamics and the flexible nature of service-learning, universities and colleges are able to adjust methods of service-learning implementation in accordance with their communities' and university customs. In recent years, this advanced-education method has been developing rapidly and is widely acclaimed by schools in the Asia Pacific region, especially in Hong Kong, Taiwan, Singapore, Japan, the Philippines, and beyond (Ma & Tandon, 2014).

Theoretical Basis of Service-Learning

From a scientific education approach, service-learning has a solid theoretical foundation and is one of the most influential and respected experiential learning approaches. The concept was first developed in 1938 by John Dewey (Lipka, Beane, & O'Connell, 1985; Clark & Welmers, 1994). Dewey thought that *experience* was the most basic and core component in education. He proposed experience as a center, education is a life, and school is a society as some important educational ideas (Dewey, 1990). The concept of combining community service practice and academic learning echoes Dewey's ideas, emphasizing and enhancing the relationship between learning and practice (Sheckley & Keeton, 1997). Furthermore, the purposes of service-learning are also highly consistent with the three objectives in experiential learning: (1) to enable students to become a more effective force for social change, (2) to develop their sense of belonging as community members, and (3) to develop their potential (Carter, 1997).

In 1984, Kolb proposed the Deweyian experiential learning model (see Figure 1), which has become a major theoretical basis for many educators, as well as an important reference for project or program design when carrying out service-learning.

This model divides the experiential learning process into four main phases and it stresses the importance of continuous learning and reflection. In the first phase, students gain concrete experience in community service. Then, in the second phase, they combine service experience with the knowledge learned in the classroom through critical thinking, continuous observation,

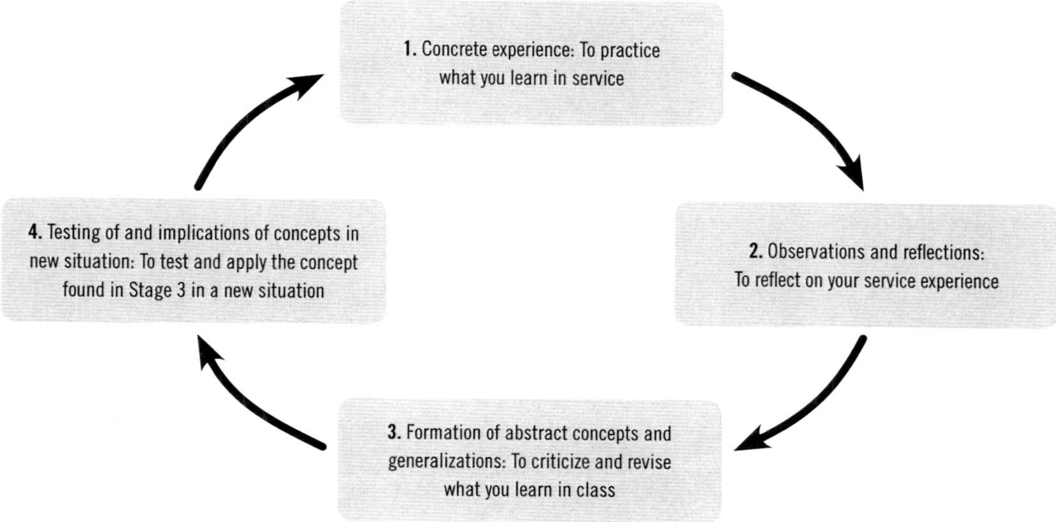

Figure 1. The Deweyian experiential learning model (adapted from Kolb, 1984).

and in-depth reflection. Based on their experiences, students are then able to revise and deepen their understanding of the approach, which becomes internalized into new abstractions during the third phase. Finally, in the fourth phase, the new concepts are converted and summarized to be new knowledge. The basic learning procedure of the Deweyian model starts from and ends with experience, making the process of learning a continuous cycle. Reflection is the fundamental driving force, since it ensures the continued development of the learning process and the core elements necessary for the learners to acquire new knowledge and skills.

In higher education, a wide range of theoretical knowledge is taught but the corresponding opportunity to practice is not provided in class, which greatly limits the inner learning circle. By advocating cooperation between schools and the community, service-learning creates a realistic and diverse experiential platform for students, which succeeds in effectively promoting learning and development of students.

Service-Learning Function in Contemporary Society

The recent emergence of service-learning and its expansion throughout Asia has been intentional. It has and continues to be an inevitable trend due to its alignment with contemporary characteristics and attributes of Asian society and its commitment to long-term societal development. Educational methods should keep pace with the times in order to remain current and relatable. In the past two decades, a new economic model has emerged in Asia, which has caused significant changes in the social environment, thus resulting in major shifts in education.

The new economy in Asia is characterized primarily by three aspects: digitization, globalization, and monopoly capitalism. The first aspect, digitization, refers to the fact that Asian societies are currently in an age of information and technological advancement. Due to the development of information technology and the dynamism of the electronics industry, predicting the future has become increasingly difficult; the only prediction that can be made for certain is change. Adapting to this rapidly changing society has become a major challenge for today's youth. Only by continuously improving their creativity, resilience, and social experience and by embracing the concept of lifelong learning can our youth comprehend the pulse of society and find their own suitable social positions.

Through the second aspect of the new economy, globalization, cross-regional and cross-border exchanges and cooperation in various fields have become a major practice of development. This trend is seen in almost every sphere of life, from the political sectors to the economic, cultural, and arts sectors. Education has been a primary catalyst for globalization, especially throughout Asia. For example, many Chinese universities have numerous foreign professors and staff members, and Chinese educators are also teaching and working in other countries. In addition, diversity in the student population is highly regarded in higher education, which is why many institutions have adopted international practices, such as exchange programs, that provide opportunities for foreign and local students to interact. This diversity helps students develop an international perspective, become global citizens, and enhance their cross-cultural communication skills, all of which have recently become important educational goals for higher education institutions.

In the last aspect of the new economy, monopoly capitalism, the society relies on capitalism. Modern society tends to lean toward materialism and hedonism as people focus more on material rewards than intrinsic values. Therefore, it is crucial to foster the development of positive values, high ethical standards, and a strong sense of social responsibility in young adults in order to eliminate these detrimental societal trends and replace them with healthy and sustainable ones.

Theoretical learning in schools is far from satisfying students' needs in terms of acquiring social knowledge and practical skills. As an advanced experiential education method, service-learning not only connects academic knowledge with service in the community, but also aids in the enhancement of students' social and practical skills. This is achieved by: (1) providing opportunities for students to engage in learning outside the confines of the traditional classroom, analyze social issues and use their expertise to seek ways to address societal needs, improve their problem solving skills, and understand their academic material and its application to real-world settings; (2) fostering students' character development, especially in terms of their commitment to serving and learning initiatives and their ability to work well with diverse groups of people to achieve community goals; and (3) by encouraging students to be open-minded, broaden their horizons, pursue social justice, eliminate discrimination and prejudice, develop a global-citizen consciousness, and see the world and their experiences through a cross-border and trans-regional lens.

In addition to character development, service-learning also has a direct and positive impact on social development. China and many other countries are facing a number of challenges, particularly in terms of economic disparities, global warming, energy supply, food shortages, and aging. Globalization is the driving force in the exchange of different countries, cultures, and ethnic groups. While these exchanges have helped establishing partnerships, they have also led to a number of conflicts and disagreements among groups. Conflict has become inevitable in the globalization process, since many social problems occur at the global level or at least have global consequences. Service-learning, however, can be a means to unite diverse groups of people and address these global social issues. Students, schools, communities, and even those in high-power positions within society can work together to encourage active global citizenship, alleviate social issues, and create a better global environment for all.

The New Idea of Service-Learning in Higher Education

The Responsibility of Contemporary Higher Education

Since the twentieth century, higher education institutions around the world have been significantly impacted by knowledge, economy, and globalization. A growing number of individuals and governments are recognizing that knowledge impacts one's future and that education creates success. Knowledge is beginning to play a key role in the process of promoting social development. There is also an increasing demand for talent with high cultural aptitude all over the world; however, the rapid expansion of higher education has produced several issues in regard to this increased demand.

In general, the primary aim of universities is to nurture talent, create knowledge, and serve the community. Although a greater number of people are receiving higher education degrees, the quality and social function of talents taught at universities are now being questioned. It is noted that contemporary university/college students' sense of responsibility, initiative, creativity, resilience, ability to learn, and team spirit needs to be strengthened. Universities have also been accused of failing to cultivate skills and abilities that contribute to addressing the needs of society. In addition, universities' performance in national cultural continuity, the construction of spiritual civilization, academic and technological innovation, and other aspects has also been unsatisfactory. Hence, the traditional higher education system can no longer achieve its fundamental objective of nurturing talents and promoting social progress (Wang, 1999). For the long-term development of society, it is imperative that educational reforms align with societal needs and trends.

Many countries recognize the important role of higher education in sustainable societal development; however, the methods of establishing and promoting this role are still debated. Since the 1980s, many education departments have actively developed higher education reform strategies at a variety of levels, each of which stresses the fundamental role and responsibilities of universities and urges re-emphasizing the goals of education.

Currently, there are three practices that promote the fundamental role and goals of higher education. The first practice includes closely relating systematic theoretical studies in class with experiential learning in daily practice and continually promoting lifelong learning. Within their time at university, students are only able to gain a limited amount of theoretical knowledge. Therefore, it is critical to nurture the spirit of active learning and practice. This will strengthen university graduates' understanding and application of knowledge gained in schools and enable them to constantly improve their knowledge and skills through active learning in both work and daily life. In this way, higher education is no longer the end of education but a starting point for lifelong learning. In 1998, the United Nations Educational, Scientific, and Cultural Organization (UNESCO) stated in the first World Conference on Higher Education, "The goal to deepen the reform of higher education systems throughout the world is to provide a favorable environment for lifelong learning, trigger cultural debate, maintain social diversity, as well as consolidate human wisdom and moral standards" (Education Bureau, 2002). Related educational policies and programmatic documents—including *Learning to Be: The World of Education Today and Tomorrow*, promulgated by Faure (2013); the Higher Education Guideline Law; the Lifelong Learning Act; and the "Towards a Learning Society" white paper enacted by France, the United States, Japan, Korea, Taiwan, as well as other countries and regions (Feng, 2010)—have also been put forward, emphasizing the importance of lifelong learning.

The second practice emphasizes integrated development and promotes holistic education. Nowadays, there is a rising demand for diverse talents. The once-elite candidates, which refers to individuals who excel only in particular academic subjects, no longer meet the current needs of the new world. Fields such as science, technology, economics, culture, and the arts require a variety of attributes that are often referred to as "soft skills," including but not limited to versatility, vision, a positive attitude, practical aptitude, responsibility, social skills, and civic awareness. Thus, these attributes are now being emphasized in the student's education. In addition to a mastery of their professional knowledge, people also need to have strong analytical minds and teamwork skills in order to address today's social issues, namely environmental problems, population issues, and the sustainable development of society and advanced technology on human-related issues, such as reproductive technology. In its first report, *Policy Paper for Change and Development in Higher Education*, UNESCO (1995) calls for countries to focus their education on cultivating well-rounded individuals with rich knowledge, sound ideas, good personalities, and positive values. The idea of a well-rounded student quickly swept the world and different countries and regions started to promote integrated education in different ways according to their characteristics. Some examples of integrated education practices include general education in the United States and France, holistic education in Taiwan and Hong Kong, character education in Singapore, and quality education in China. Although the names are different, the central ideas of each of these approaches are the same.

The third practice that promotes the fundamental role and goals of higher education includes implementing open and pluralistic teaching in practice. In a world that lacks consistency, teaching undergraduates to be open-minded, creative, and enthusiastic is not only critical, but also a major goal of higher education. Nevertheless, traditional one-way teaching places students in a passive position to absorb knowledge and cannot fully evoke their enthusiasm for learning. A single teaching platform, limited to the inside of the classroom, also hinders the development of students' creativity and practical abilities, and may even lead to social dislocation and failure to use their knowledge out of class after graduation. Even though some universities arrange for or encourage students to join internships before they graduate, preparation time is inadequate and the sudden change may lead to confusion. Therefore, many countries have significantly extended their educational platforms to give students a chance to see the world, learn from real-world experiences, and exercise their social skills, organizational skills, innovative thinking abilities, and so on. For example, in the 1960s, China began to organize community-service activities for university/college students on a large scale in order to encourage students' understanding of social problems and help those who are in need. The Massachusetts Institute of Technology in America also exemplifies this extension of education platforms. They work with leading companies and organizations to regularly arrange experiential learning opportunities for students, thus strengthening students' resilience, cooperativeness, and flexibility in the application of knowledge. In an era of new technology, there are a greater number of connections and collaborations in all subject areas. This requires universities to construct practical education platforms together with communities, enterprises, and governments, so students have the opportunity to not only exercise their social skills, but to also investigate and solve practical problems in society.

In an exploratory stage of education reform, various countries and regions are doing research on creating educational programs that are in line with contemporary societal characteristics and uphold the three major approaches of "lifelong learning," "holistic education," and "open learning." Service-learning has emerged as a new kind of experiential learning teaching method, creating possibilities for cooperation among schools, communities, and various enterprises. The combination of community service and academic learning increases students' engagement and facilitates teachers' operability in the teaching process, without ignoring the importance of the theoretical knowledge emphasized in traditional education. In addition, it helps universities practice three major educational approaches in the new era of education reform; hence, it quickly became incorporated into many universities.

Service-Learning Development Patterns in Different Countries and Regions

Though service-learning originated in the United States, it has been quickly spreading to different countries in Europe, the Americas, Asia, Africa, and other regions (Berry & Chisholm, 1999). In recent years, service-learning has received positive responses, which has allowed for its rapid development in the higher education sector in Asia Pacific region (Xing & Ma, 2010). With the flexibility of service-learning, universities and colleges in different countries are making adjustments throughout the implementation process according to their own characteristics and needs. In 1989, Honnett and Poulsen published a summary of good service-learning principles at the Wingspread Conference, hosted by the Johnson Foundation, which is widely used in the United States. (Honnett & Poulsen, 1989) However, some countries and universities do not refer to these practices as "service-learning." Instead, they use other terms, such as *service practicum, community engagement, social practice, civic engagement, civic education*, etc. In China, the term *social practice* has been used for more than twenty years. In Malaysia, using *community engagement* is more popular than using *service-learning*. In India, *community-based research* and *community engagement* are mostly used. But many more universities are using the term *service-learning* due to the rapid development of its philosophy and increased number of institutions participating in the Service-Learning Asia Network. Though the names differ, the purposes of these practices are similar; they all aim to strengthen partnerships between universities and communities by encouraging students to apply their knowledge and skills to service opportunities in order to address social issues. Universities in Asia focus on more action-oriented initiatives and use students as connectors between university and community.

The concept of service-learning is still relatively new to Chinese education; therefore, many universities are still exploring how to best initiate this nascent pedagogy. Successful service-learning examples might serve as references to bring new inspiration and thoughts to Chinese universities. Therefore, in the following, the typical pattern for conducting service-learning in universities in

South Africa, the United States, and Taiwan are cited, so that interested universities and colleges can comprehend the flexibility of service-learning and concrete ways to institutionalize it in different higher education systems.

The prevalent service-learning model in South Africa's higher education institutions is mainly based on the concept of community engagement, which refers to community building dedicated to meeting the needs of the community and improving social problems with services provided by university/college students. The education reform in South Africa's universities has also emphasized the integration of community involvement into teaching and research to strengthen young people's sense of social purpose. In order to assist in national reconstruction, teachers use their expertise to teach students to recognize the problems and contradictions associated with social change in South Africa. Thus, the South African government strongly advocates for the inclusion of service-learning in higher education systems. The government also standardizes and popularizes universities' community involvement by establishing partnerships among universities, communities, and organizations. This effectively unites all social forces to improve people's well-being and quality of life. Many universities and colleges have responded positively to this and students are encouraged to join by means of incorporating service-learning into regular curricula with academic credits (Moore & Lin, 2009). For instance, students majoring in education at the University of the Witwatersrand use their expertise to provide adult education for community residents, which addresses the insufficiency of elementary education, local illiteracy, and other issues. Moreover, a group of architecture students have lent their tangible skills to the local community by using limited resources to design and produce furniture and toys for orphanages (Community Higher Education Service Partnerships & Higher Education Quality Committee, 2007).

The service-learning model in the United States revolves around students' learning and growth by providing them experiential learning opportunities. Through the service-learning process, students improve their civic orientation, social competence, and lifelong skills. The linkage between university and community creates an additional learning platform for students beyond the classroom, allowing students to use a variety of learning methods to accumulate knowledge in the big social classroom, exercise their skills in observing and analyzing social issues during service, and apply what they have learned to solve problems. American colleges place special emphasis on assessing students' learning outcomes after participating in service-learning—from students' enhancement of various abilities to their understanding and application of theoretical knowledge, as well as their awareness of community issues and civic consciousness. American scholars in colleges are actively working on research related to the development of accurate and effective evaluation tools to improve the effectiveness of service-learning (Lan & Xu, 2011). For example, Stanford University is a prestigious college which offers service-learning courses in different academic departments. These courses include theory, skills training, seminars, and discussions, as well as community-service projects for students to enrich their practical experience in order to achieve the intended learning outcomes.

In Taiwan, the terms and concepts of service-learning are well-known and fully integrated into the education system. This is because the Ministry of Education (MOE) in Taiwan has actively promoted service-learning as an effective teaching strategy for helping students to have active learning and civic engagement awareness since 1990. The Taiwanese government started to promote volunteerism in 1980 and the National Youth Commission played a vital role to promote the transition from voluntary service to service learning. In 2007, the MOE announced the "Universities Service Learning Initiatives" and then follow by encouraging universities, colleges, primary and secondary schools to promote service-learning courses and activities in Taiwan.

All service-learning courses and programs have some common features, such as progressiveness, multiplicity, and expansiveness. For instance, Providence University requires all of its first-year students to complete one of their service-learning courses, including attending lectures (introduction of the values and theoretical knowledge of service-learning, ethics and regulations on volunteerism, methods of self-understanding and self-affirmation, service experience sharing from corporate volunteers and overseas volunteers), completing a certain number of community services hours, and sharing the outcomes of their service-learning experience. After completing the required service-learning course, sophomore students and above can choose to participate in professional courses with service-learning elements. In addition to local service opportunities, Providence University also offers international volunteer programs, providing opportunities for students to further expand their learning and services in different regions and cultures (Providence University, 2009).

Regardless of the service-learning model that a university adopts, the community and students must interact and benefit from one another through close communication and cooperation. The ultimate goal of service-learning is to achieve a win-win situation for both community building and students' learning; therefore, there is always room for improvement in the above models. Universities/colleges that focus on community participation and social problem solving can strengthen the ties of the community to theoretical studies which, in turn, enable students to learn through their service, contribute to the community, and improve service quality with their professional skills. Similarly, universities/colleges that emphasize student learning outcomes and capacity building can conduct more in-depth investigations of social problems in order to provide pertinent programs that cater to the needs of the community. If students' services can effectively address community issues, community partners will show greater initiative in cooperating with universities/colleges and expanding service-learning projects, which helps to ensure the continuity of close relations and cooperation. Moreover, universities/colleges that carry out service-learning on a large scale and incorporate it into core courses must pay close attention to student feedback and assessment methods to guarantee the teaching quality of service-learning curriculum. Furthermore, it is also important to increase the diversity of service-learning projects in order to encourage students to take an active role in the projects and to discourage the notion that service-learning is an academic burden.

Student learning and community service are core elements of the service-learning concept. They provide the fundamental differences between service-learning and traditional volunteer service experiences, which lack learning elements, and practicum experiences, which lack service elements. American scholar Barbara Jacoby and her team mention that the fundamental difference between service-learning and volunteer service is that the former focuses on "reflection and learning objectives set in advance" (Jacoby et.al, 1996, 20). Many Chinese universities conduct different types of volunteer projects, but these projects generally focus on service without incorporating components of learning enhancement. Service-learning is a modern teaching method in response to the trends, opportunities, and challenges currently confronting higher education in China. It can be a good way for countries, universities, communities, teachers, and students to make common progress and promote educational reform and development.

The Necessity of Promoting Service-Learning in China

The Current Situation of Higher Education in China

Chinese education has experienced large-scale historical changes since the founding of the People's Republic of China (PRC). In the 1950s and 1960s, over 80% of the population was illiterate. Currently, nine years of compulsory education is required, which implies that higher education in the PRC is flourishing. When university/college entrance examinations were reinstated and national policy in support of higher education was promoted, the university/college enrollment figures increased at the end of the 1970s. Thus, the scale of higher education has been growing and the government, people, and society now place more emphasis on education. While the scale and number of intakes of universities/colleges are rapidly expanding, the quality of education is not. With the rapid change in society and the beginning of an intellectual economy, improving the quality of education has become one of the core missions of contemporary China's development.

Since the reform and opening-up policies, China has been in line with international standards, and its education system has been greatly influenced by the situation in Asia and the world. Therefore, the reform of education according to the trends of our times has become an important measure to improve the quality of Chinese higher-education. First of all, the explosive growth of information technology has accelerated the dissemination and increase of new knowledge. Traditionally, the overuse of technology has been an ineffective way for teachers to give lectures. Students cannot absorb the new knowledge and information immediately, which results in the universities/colleges producing graduates who may lag behind the times. Not only is this a waste of national resources, but it is also a hindrance to the promising futures of students when universities/colleges fail to meet the social needs and nurture the talents of those who can work for the betterment of society. Therefore, universities/colleges need to enrich the social knowledge and strengthen the social abilities of the students when teaching theoretical knowledge. Secondly, the process of globalization has increased the pressure on China and its motivation to close the gap between its higher education and the rest of the world's advanced-education systems. Under the cooperation and competition of globalization, greater demands are being placed on the reform of Chinese higher education and the discussion and examples of the world's advanced teaching methods can provide the reference for Chinese universities. Thirdly, monopoly capitalism has fueled egoism and materialism around the world. When a country's economy develops rapidly and options significantly increase, as has recently occurred in China, young people tend to pursue material wealth blindly. They ignore the promotion of ethical progress, which results in the development of negative values. Hence, it is essential to nurture moral character and correct values in students.

The Chinese government and education department have promulgated many important documents and related policies that promote reforms in higher education. These documents and policies have included the *Suggestions on Strengthening the Teaching Work of Undergraduate Education in the University* in 2001, *Views on the Implementation of Undergraduate Teaching Quality and Teaching Reform Project in Universities* in 2007, *Outline of China National Plan for Medium and Long-term Education Reform and Development (2010–2020)* in 2010, the *12th Five-year Plan in National Education Development* in 2012, and so on. The policies point out the direction for China's higher education reform and development in the new era, as well as define the responsibility and purpose of universities, which are to promote students' all-around development; nurture practicing, pioneering, and innovative elites with profound knowledge who can serve the society well; cultivate correct moral values and noble character in students; and inculcate a feeling of citizenship and social responsibility in them.

Major universities have responded in accordance with the objectives and direction of education reform to develop appropriate school policies and curriculum reform programs. The quality-education and general-education concepts that have expanded rapidly in recent years primarily aim to cultivate "whole-person development" of talents. However, the reform is relatively slow, as many universities are still in the exploration stage. The concrete way to operationalize the new education ideas are still unknown. Service-learning, though, is a highly operable and flexible experiential teaching method and its basic concepts share the central ideas of whole-person development. Today, the concept of service-learning is spreading gradually in Mainland universities/colleges; some institutions have even begun to carry out respective projects that have produced positive results and are unanimously supported by both teachers and students. The purpose of this book is to give a detailed introduction of service-learning to institutions in China and to further analyze ways in which the concept benefits students, universities, communities, and the country as a whole.

Benefits of Promoting Service-Learning in China

While the reasons and emphasis of universities in different regions for implementing service-learning may differ slightly, the primary purpose is always to connect the university and the community. Through service-learning, students apply what they have learned from the class to practice and improve social issues. This matches the situation and needs in China as well as the requirements of higher education reform. Not only is the method of service-learning consistent with traditional Confucianism and contemporary higher education purposes, it also could potentially provide great benefits and advantages to the state's, communities', universities', and students' development.

Benefits to the Country

The corresponding ideas of the three major concepts in service-learning can be found in Confucianism, including: (1) learning by doing, (2) nurturing the spirit of dedication and noble character, and (3) establishing a sense of social responsibility. Therefore, service-learning is not a completely unfamiliar idea, because the great Chinese philosophers and educators have long raised these important educational concepts. The concept did not rouse enough attention because of the rapid development of Chinese society. The key is to integrate these concepts and apply them in the education system through service-learning. Confucianism and Chinese traditional virtues can be carried forward through service-learning. Service-learning can be a means to establish an education and exchange platform with developed countries and promote the integration of China with the world. The cooperation among countries, universities/colleges and society could be beneficial in building a harmonious socialist society.

Benefits to the Community

As a developing country, China has undergone major socioeconomic changes. China's rapid economic progress not only promotes the development of the society, but also carries some problems and challenges, including the growing inequality gap between the rich and poor, serious environmental damage, migrant workers' difficulty socially integrating due the imbalance between urban and rural development, and the problem of the education of abandoned children. In order to promote long-term sustainable development of the country while also strengthening its economy, China must promote social harmony, reduce discrimination and conflict, and take the needs of the community and the public seriously. Service-learning encourages teachers and students to have prolonged contact with the community, to observe the community, and to listen to the voices of people directly. Furthermore, they can even cooperate with enterprises and institutions to address community problems. As a result, the university, government, enterprises, and other forces are able to unite and overcome the difficulties associated with addressing social problems, such as limitations to human and resource capital. These new partnerships can also enhance people's understanding of the community dynamics and their needs. Macro-investigations of the state, combined with students' microstudies, provide information that is more comprehensive for the analysis of social problems.

Benefits to Schools and Teachers

The education reform in China has strengthened the intellectual economy, since universities are now facing higher requirements and challenges and are responsible for developing students academically, professionally, and personally. As the country strengthens academic research and teaching, it should also continue exploring and innovating, so as to complete the arduous task of contemporary higher education reform. Service-learning can help universities to achieve these goals. Teachers can expand the scope of research to larger communities where they carry out service-learning courses. Academic research that is closely related to social dynamics has very high application value, which can directly promote social progress. Since service-learning has become an important mode of higher education, the implementation of this teaching method can better align Chinese colleges with international standards, improve the reputation of the schools, and create more opportunities for academic exchanges and cooperation. In terms of personnel training, service-learning is a way to enrich colleges' teaching methods and teach in accordance with students' aptitude, thus maximizing their potential and talents. By connecting classroom teaching and community service, students can enhance their abilities by different aspects of theoretical or practical knowledge.

Benefits to Students

If college students want to be successful in this rapidly changing time, they need to comprehensively develop in personality, ability, and international vision. Service-learning breaks the traditional learning methods in Chinese universities, so that learning is not confined to only classrooms and books. By bridging schools and community, students can obtain knowledge from both environments. In service-learning courses, students are able to exercise and develop a variety of skills, such as team cooperation, organization and leadership, communication, research, problem solving, etc. Even more, service-learning strengthens students' understanding and application of subject-related knowledge and allows them to develop a better understanding of the dynamic world. Ultimately, this understanding builds up a solid foundation for the future when the students enter society and the workplace.

As an innovative experiential teaching method, service-learning brings about new power for university education in addition to supplementing Chinese quality education and burgeoning liberal education.

REFERENCES

Berry, H. A., & Chisholm, L. A. (1999). *Service-learning in higher education around the world: An initial look.* New York: Ford Foundation. http://files.eric.ed.gov/fulltext/ED439654.pdf.

Carver, R. L. (1997). Theoretical underpinnings of service learning. *Theory into Practice*, 36(3): 143–149.

Clark, S. N., & Welmers, M. J. (1994). Service learning: A natural link to interdisciplinary studies. *Schools in the Middle*, 4(1): 11–15.

Community Higher Education Service Partnerships & Higher Education Quality Committee. (2007). *Service-learning in the curriculum: Lessons from the field.* Pretoria: Community Higher Education Service Partnerships & Higher Education Quality Committee.

Dewey, J. (1990). *Min zhu zhu yi yu jiao yu* [Democracy and education]. (Wang, C. X., Trans.). Beijing: People's Education Press.

Education Bureau. (2002). *Motion on "Report on higher education in Hong Kong" to be moved by Hon YEUNG Yiu-chung at the Legislative Council meeting* [in Chinese]. http://www.edb.gov.hk/sc/about-edb/press/legco/speech/2012/20040117107349.html.

Faure, E., et al. (2013). *Learning to be: The world of education today and tomorrow.* 2nd. ed. Beijing: Educational Science Publishing House. Paris: International Commission on the Development of Education.

Feng, X. L. (2010). Zhong shen jiao yu zhan wang [Lifelong education prospects]. *University Academic* 9:43–45.

Jacoby, B., et al. (1996). *Service-learning in higher education: Concepts and practices.* San Francisco, CA: Jossey-Bass.

Kolb, D. (1984). *Experiential learning: Experience as the source of learning and development.* Englewood Cliffs, NJ: Prentice Hall.

Lan, C. F., & Xu, W. M. (2011). *Fu wu—xue xi zai gao deng jiao yu zhong de li lun yu shi jian* [Service-Learning: Theory and practice in higher education]. Hangzhou: Zhejiang University Press.

Lipka, R. P., Beane, J. A., & O'Connell, B. R. (1985). *Community service projects: Citizenship in action.* Bloomington, IN: Phi Delta Kappa Educational Foundation.

MA, H.-K. C., & Tandon, R. (2014). *Knowledge engagement and higher education in Asia and the Pacific.* London Palgrave: Macmillan UK.

Moore, M., & Lin, P. L. (2009). *Service-learning in higher education: Paradigms & challenges.* Indianapolis: University of Indianapolis Press.

Providence University. (2009). *Volunteering providence origin.* http://www.service-learning.pu.edu.tw/Webpage/03-01.aspx.

Sheckley, B. G., & Keeton, M. T. (1997). Service-learning: A theoretical model. In J. Schine (Ed.), *Service-learning: Ninety-sixth yearbook for the national society for the study of education,* 32–55. Chicago: University of Chicago Press.

Stanton, T. K., Giles, D. E., Jr., & Cruz, N. I. (1999). *Service-learning: A movement's pioneers reflect on its origins, practice, and future.* San Francisco: Jossey-Bass.

United Nations Educational, Scientific, and Cultural Organization (UNESCO). (1995). *Policy paper for change and development in higher education.* Paris: UNESCO.

Wang, Y. J. (1999). Tiao zhan yu ying da: Dang qian shi jie gao deng jiao yu fa zhan yu gai ge shu ping—jian tan 21 shi ji da xue de li xiang [Challenge and response: The current world higher education development and reform review—on the ideal 21st century university]. *Liaoning Education Research,* 1:35–37.

Xing, J., & MA, H.-K. C. (2010). *Service-learning in Asia: Curricular models and practices.* Hong Kong: Hong Kong University Press.

Service-Learning and the Aims of Chinese Higher Education

Carol MA Hok-ka, Fanny MAK Mui-fong, and Alice LIU Cheng

Aims and Current Situation of Chinese Higher Education

Since the implementation of reform and opening-up, China (officially the People's Republic of China [PRC]) has witnessed groundbreaking changes, particularly within its culture, economy, and education. Over the past two to three decades, the country has played a larger role in the international context. Now, the country is characterized by digitalization, globalization, and rapid economic development. In today's ever-changing society, new opportunities and challenges are constantly emerging. As a result, people are faced with the difficulty of meeting the high demands of this rapidly evolving environment. The traditional talents and singular disciplinary skills that were once recognized and highly valued are no longer advantageous in today's diverse and contemporary society in China. Rather, multidisciplinary perspectives, skills, and experiences equip individuals with the tools necessary to thrive in today's world. Youth are the future pillars of China. Therefore, the top priorities in Chinese education are to keep up with the demands of contemporary society and invest in youth development. The aim of higher education in China is to provide youth opportunities to acquire practical skills, noble-mindedness, and a sense of social responsibility.

As the base for educating future citizens, higher education imparts the mission of educating civically aware professionals, promoting social development, and preserving cultural achievements. The aim of higher education reform in China is to adapt teaching methods based on context and produce skilled citizens who can contribute to the betterment of China. By confronting modern changes and challenges, China has placed higher demands on its universities and colleges to make advancement in whole-person education. The mission of higher education is not limited to applying knowledge into practice and innovation, but also includes establishing the correct philosophy of life and values, demonstrating the spirit of dedication, and, most importantly, strengthening civic awareness in order to promote social development.

Developing Practical and Innovative Citizens

Confucius said, "Is it not pleasure, having learned something, to try it out at due intervals?" (Lau, 1979, 59). Zhu Xi (1992) of the Song Dynasty mentioned that both knowledge and action are equally important, and Wang Yangming (1992) of the Ming Dynasty also said that knowledge and action are as one. Traditional Chinese education emphasizes the importance of putting knowledge into practice. Modern Chinese society now lives in an era of the knowledge-based economy, where higher education is thriving. One of the main goals in Chinese education reform is to cultivate practical skills and innovation (MOE, 2012).

In 2002, Chinese higher education made the transition from meritocracy to popularization (MOE, 2011). In 1978, the gross enrollment ratio (GER) in Chinese universities and colleges was only 1.55%. GER, which refers to the total enrollment in tertiary education and corresponding school-age population from 18 to 22, signifies the scale of education and access to education, both of which are important indicators of education development. According to international standards, the popularization of higher education rests upon three stages based on GER: meritocratic education (GER below 15%); popularized education (GER 15%–50%), universal education (GER above 50%). Since the expansion of undergraduate enrollment in 1999, the ratio rose to 15% in 2002 and 26.9% in 2011. In 2010, the Ministry of Education of the People's Republic of China (MOE) predicted that the GER in Chinese higher education will reach 40% by the year 2020. Popularization of higher education demonstrates the masses' motivation to be cultured. The phenomenon also implies a need to modify existing pedagogy and training models with current circumstances in mind, so that recent graduates can find their places in China's modernization.

University graduates should not only devote their lives to theoretical research, but also address the needs of their communities. In reality, there is a strong demand in the workforce for acquiring not only knowledge but also social skills. University graduates are encouraged to be innovative, explore new ideas, and test out scientific principles in hopes of benefiting the community. After all, theory and application are complementary and mutually enforcing. Rich knowledge in theory can be conducive to the development of new ideas, and implementation of new ideas can in turn strengthen the application of theory. Furthermore, the application of theory can drive social development and social values can also be added to understand and explore theory. Famous curriculum theorist Ralph W. Tyler (1994, 28) once said, "Learners must have experiences that give them opportunity to practice the behavior(s) implied by the objective(s)." Therefore, "scholars engrossed in the books of sages" no longer fit the needs of modern society, which requires multiskilled and multiperspective individuals. Rather, education today aims to, as well as ought to, integrate learning and practice.

Since the PRC resumed the National Higher Education Entrance Examination (also known as *gaokao*) in 1977, many universities and colleges sought to strengthen students' research skills and theoretical competence. While scholarly research is well developed, Chinese higher education has thus far ignored the cultivation of practical skills. Hence, overemphasis on learning and ignorance of practices have come to the forefront (Gu & Xu, 2009). To tackle this issue, scholars suggest that tertiary institutes allocate their resources based on market and social indicators; thus, tertiary institutions should promote and increase the exchanges and cooperation between universities and colleges and society. Graduates will then be welcomed by corporations. In order to reach the goals of education reform in China, scholars suggest that the visions of universities and colleges should be market oriented. With optimized curriculum design and diversified field education, fresh graduates will be better prepared to acclimate and contribute to society.

In fact, the Chinese government pays great attention to the training of undergraduates' innovation and practical skills. In *Opinion on Implementing Reforms of the Undergraduate Program Quality*, the MOE (2007) and Ministry of Finance of the PRC stress the practical skills of university students. The ministries also call for the co-building of bases for practical education by tertiary institutions, scientific research institutions, sectors, corporations, and other relevant institutions. Numerous universities and colleges actively responded to the calls, and thus adjusted their curricula and teaching models. These adjustments have improved education for practical students. Meanwhile, over 100 representatives from more than thirty universities and colleges attended the "Seminar on Practical Undergraduate Programs in China" organized in Shanghai in 2007. The representative discussed and investigated the topic of practical education in higher education deeply and broadly. The *Outline of China's National Plan for Medium- and Long-Term Education Reform and Development (2010–2020)* proposed by the MOE (2010) thoroughly analyzes the major challenges to be tackled by Chinese education. The *Outline* suggests an expansion of practical, multidisciplinary and technical education in order to enhance students' capabilities in adapting to the society, employment and entrepreneurship. The *12th Five-Year Plan of National Education Development* once again emphasizes the importance of practical education (MOE, 2012). Universities and colleges should modify course structure by increasing the number of practice-based courses and strengthening the infrastructure for practice-based education. Reform measures and implementation are yet to be perfect, but, thankfully, educating practical and innovative students has become the major strategic policy in educational reform as well as the value orientation of higher education in China.

Moral Education for Undergraduates

From the past to the present, Chinese education has strived to equip students with Chinese virtues and the skills needed for success. Confucian master Han Yu says, "what the Great Learning teaches is to illustrate illustrious virtue; to renovate the people; and to rest in the highest excellence" (Markham & Lohr, 2009, 120). Similarly, socialist China promotes quality education and liberal education. University is the place where young adults form and develop their values and perspectives on life and the world. Correct and effective moral education is of utmost importance. Higher education should act as a beacon for undergraduates to choose their paths, and it should provide mentoring for the development of the whole person. Han (1958) points out the responsibilities of a teacher in *On Teaching*: "a teacher is one who transmits knowledge, provides for study and dispels confusion." Teachers must teach what is moral first. Only after that can teachers instruct students with theory and answer their questions. Since moral education is the basis for educating students, it should be prioritized in all educational activities.

However, there has been much social restraint and overemphasis on economic functions in education in recent years. Chinese universities and colleges focus primarily on instrumentality and practicality in hopes of promoting social, economic, political, and scientific development. As a result, moral education and humanistic development for students have been ignored. Famous Chinese educator Yang Shuzi (2001) questioned the role of universities seeking excellence in the move of the mass system. He believed that universities should educate people and train quality talents rather than just produce high-end equipment. In the rapidly developing market economy, the exaggeration on materialism and personal gains has influenced Chinese students in their goal setting and lifelong pursuits, creating a seedbed for pragmatism and hedonism. Wrong values, such as "money as aspiration" and "profits and gains equal prospects," are taking root in China. Since undergraduates are the mainstay of spiritual guidance and intelligence, they set moral examples for society to follow. Incorrect moral education will, therefore, bring repercussions to the moral foundations of society.

For a long time, the Chinese government has advocated moral education and promulgated related policies and pertinent documents (see The Central People's Government of the People's Republic of China & State Council of State Council of the People's Republic of China, 2004; MOE, 2012). "Moral education comes first. Fully implement quality education" is the main strategic theme in China's current education reform. Chinese universities and colleges have launched moral education in different classes, but they face certain limitations and challenges—programs have been overly ambitious, vague, disconnected from students' ideas, more theoretical rather than practical, and/or their assessment methods have been flawed (Wang, 2013). This, in turn, discourages students from participating in moral education and pursuing moralistic goals and aspirations. Moral education should incorporate real-world circumstances into classroom teachings, aid students in setting clear goals, and relate to the experiences of students. Instructional methods and approaches should be lively, diverse and practice-based. Moreover, it should stress the importance of paying close attention to students' spiritual development and emotional needs.

Students do not feel moved to make a change just by passively listening to teachers about moral education. This is because moral education is a dynamic process of introspection. To boost spiritual power through practice and to achieve "knowledge and action as one," students must actively participate in moral education activities and experience how their own power can serve society and help those less fortunate. Social service experience can help students observe society from a different standpoint and open their minds to understanding the needs and thoughts of others. When education helps students understand their inner worlds, positive morality—lending a hand and selfless dedication—is established. With the popularization of tertiary education, most graduates find jobs related to services to a certain extent. In modern China, where people come first and development is harmonious, it is indeed crucial to know how to serve society and deal with people with good virtues. Service-learning focuses on moral education and humanistic concerns. This new pedagogy can easily integrate with the existing moral education in China to provide students the skills, knowledge, social awareness, and compassion necessary for creating a more harmonious and prosperous Chinese society.

Civic Awareness and Social Responsibility in Undergraduates' Education

Educator Gu Xiancheng of the Ming Dynasty emphasized a good man should care for his family, country, and the world (Gu, 1988). Modern China also places the importance on civic awareness and community participation. Actually, even before the Ming Dynasty, China has believed in nurturing its youth to be socially responsible. Youth are expected to bear the nation's responsibilities and address social justice issues present in society. As Chinese citizens, youth are responsible for creating a foundation for the nation's future social development. As a result, undergraduate students must recognize this duty and have a grasp on social development through political, economic, and cultural perspectives. Furthermore, social responsibility implies moral responsibility shared by an individual to his/ her country, groups, etc. Moral responsibility and civic awareness are highly intertwined and mutually reinforcing. Detailed observation and profound understanding of society is the basis for acquiring civic awareness. To go one step further, an individual must acknowledge and understand social trends and think critically about how social issues relate and are interconnected. Civic awareness in action would then be implementing an idea and effectively promoting social progress or change.

In Hu Jintao's *Report to the Seventeenth National Congress of the Communist Party of China* (2007, 11), promoting civic awareness is included as a goal in the democratic and education development in China: "strengthen civic awareness education; establish the ideas of socialist democracy, rule of law, freedom, equality, fairness and justice." This, in addition to other developmental initiatives outlined by the Chinese government, indicates that civic awareness has become a top priority in Chinese education (MOE, 2010). In recent years, there is a growing trend of Chinese universities and colleges practicing and implementing civic education. Corresponding projects related to civic education are on the rise and gaining momentum. For example, Beijing Normal University established the Center for Citizenship and Moral Education in 2003 to encourage civic awareness among undergraduates. In July 2005, the MOE and Center for Civic Education from the United States co-hosted a symposium on "Practicing Civic Education," in which many universities and colleges from Beijing, Shanghai, Jiangsu, and Yunnan actively participated. While the presence of civic education has increased in both discourse and practice, there is still room for improvement in the system, integrity, and practice of civic education.

First of all, understanding social development and civic responsibility is a gradual process. Corresponding education should take students' psychological development and cognitive patterns into account and proceed from easy to difficult. However, even if civic education is introduced in schools at different levels, the curricula are generally unsystematic and incoherent. For example, students are taught social democracy and communism before they have a basic understanding or awareness of social issues. This inevitably causes difficulty in learning. General and vague civic education can neither reach students according to their aptitude nor provoke critical and analytical thought. Some scholars have also suggested that the ignorance and weakening of individuality in Chinese higher education is also a primary factor in the lack of social responsibility among university students (Yang, 2008).

Moreover, civic responsibility and society are intimately related. Mere theoretical training in civic education in tertiary education therefore will not suffice. Every facet of society, including the family and community, has a key role in setting an example, modeling social responsibility for youth. Negative social trends and family education can cause university students to develop a low sense of responsibility, impacting the effectiveness of civic education in universities and colleges. Today, society tends to overlook its role and social responsibility in promoting civic awareness among youth. Rather, it is seen as a task or responsibility of those involved in youth education. Only with participation in and commitment to civic education will Chinese society be able to effectively develop civically aware and responsible citizens.

The Central People's Government of the People's Republic of China (2001) declared in the *Program for Improving Civic Morality*, "the process of improving civic morality is about integrating education and practice" (para. 5). If civic education only contains theories without practice, undergraduate students are more likely to remain passive and less likely to take direct action to improve national affairs and engage in social change. Independence and innovation can only be stimulated by letting students practice their skills and knowledge in the real world. This opportunity enables students to study and observe society in-depth, experience both the positive and negatives aspects of the world, and, ultimately create solutions to improve society. Thus, it is imperative that practice-based education is present in higher education to encourage community action and societal progression.

By taking into account the aims of higher education and understanding the advantages and weaknesses in current education, Chinese universities and colleges are emphasizing education reform. It is hoped to cultivate well-rounded students who possess the qualities of innovation and practice, honorable virtues, and strong social responsibility. While it is still the initial period of reform, many universities and colleges are facing the absence of guiding and instrumental schemes. The current reform contains certain weaknesses and shortcomings, which slows down the progress of reform and social change. Service-learning, as an effective and instrumental practice-based pedagogy, can satisfy the demands of these universities and colleges. First of all, service-learning is flexible. Projects can be tailored in accordance with students' aptitudes. Furthermore, progressive educational activities, from introductory to advanced, can be designed to meet the psychological development and cognitive patterns of the students. Second, service-learning supports cooperation among schools, community, the government, and other institutions. This creates a favorable environment to foster social consciousness among university students in addition to inspiring the society to join efforts in boosting students' spiritual development. Third, service-learning encourages students to apply classroom knowledge in volunteering activities. Civic education, therefore, allows students to stay in touch with reality, and provides a platform and space for students to practice and gain experience in tackling society's social problems. In this way, students are motivated to initiate action and become passionate about taking social responsibility. Lastly and most importantly, the ideas of service-learning are very similar to those of Confucianism and traditional Chinese educational philosophy. As a result of the historical and cultural foundations for service-learning's development in China, the pedagogy is spreading and becoming more accepted nationwide.

The Connection between Service-Learning, Confucianism, and Contemporary Educational Goals in China

While service-learning originated in the United States, one can find its roots in Confucianism and modern Chinese educational philosophies. As a new pedagogy that advocates the integration of learning and service as well as the cooperation between community and universities, service-learning benefits all involved—teachers, students, universities, communities, etc. Therefore, service-learning is not a completely foreign pedagogy from the West that is incapable of becoming part of Chinese society. Chinese universities and colleges should adopt the practice of service-learning from the West, but in a manner that fits with Chinese characteristics, such as incorporating the ideas of Confucianism. This guarantees a sustainable and effective development of the socialist and modernized education. Actually, since the Spring and Autumn periods (722 BC–481 BC) and the Warring States period (fifth century BC–221 BC), many schools of thought have blossomed with the idea of moral education. When we study the concept of school, the ideas of service or learning are found. Various ruling thoughts and living values have developed rapidly. It was not until the Qin Dynasty (221 BC–207 BC) that the Constraint Spirit of Legalism emerged; its advocates opposed the idea that the constitution of political governance should be based on personal connections and relationships (or simply nepotism). They promoted the idea that moral standards and social constructions should be built with the assumption that human nature is essentially egoistic. Hence, they emphasized the rights of the despotic monarchy, in which the emperor possesses absolute authority over his subjects and the sovereign state, allowing him to centralize the state power and unify the world.

After the unification of the world, many people wanted to solve problems resulting from the tyranny of Qin. The pre-Han Dynasty adopted the ideology of *qing jing wu wei* (quietism and non-activity) following the belief of Daoism. This ideology enabled people to recover and rebuild what was destroyed by the Qin Dynasty. The Western Han Dynasty was a peaceful and prosperous period that also experienced political, economic and cultural development. Han Wudi (the sixth emperor of the Han Dynasty) adopted Confucianism, which encouraged the growth of active enterprise. By replacing Daoism with active enterprise as the supreme orthodox national philosophy, Han Wudi was able to strengthen his power. Additionally, under his rule, moral ethics, religion, law, and the ruling system were further developed. Confucianism had an enduring effect and an enormous influence on the existence of imperial China. Confucianism core virtues of human thought—such as *ren* (benevolence), *yi* (justice), *li* (propriety), *zhi* (wisdom), *xin* (integrity), *zhong* (loyalty), *xiao* (filial piety), *ti* (brotherhood), *jie* (regulation), *shu* (forgiveness), *yong* (courage), and *rang* (complaisant)—changed the future and development of China. These core values continue to exist today. The concepts of service and learning have been infused into the development of Confucianism. Western thoughts and ideas spread rapidly following the end of the Opium War. Bureaucrats and students were sent abroad to study Western thought and military strategies and, thus, greatly impacted the development of Chinese Confucianism. Facing the wave of Westernization, Chinese thought towards service and learning gradually were replaced and integrated. Tables 1 through 4 show the evolution of service and learning in Confucian culture in China in different periods with various key scholars.

Table 1. Background, Evolution Reasons, Service, and Learning in Confucius (Spring and Autumn, 551–479 BC) and Mencius (Spring and Autumn, 372–289 BC) Eras of China

DYNASTY	BACKGROUND	EVOLUTIONARY REASON
Confucius (Spring and Autumn, 551–479 BC)	The fundamental purpose of education is to nurture talent. Confucius, as the educator of ancient China, proposed "individualized learning," "integrated learning and thinking"; however, because of the chaos of the war in the Spring and Autumn periods, Confucius's thought was not well adopted. Yet, its objective attitude and realistic thinking brought enduring impacts on education, such as thoughts about cultural heritage.	Learning is only for feudal officials in the Western Zhou Dynasty and the Eastern Zhou Dynasty. In the Spring and Autumn periods, the monarchy declined and slavery was disintegrated. Also, feudal hegemony was serious and thus countries recruited talents by regime. Because of the increased population, land distribution became difficult and eventually social upheaval prevailed. During these periods, scholars and intellectuals proposed various solutions to address societal problems and life issues based on their philosophical thoughts and beliefs. Interests among individuals and countries were interrelated and influenced one another. Many different theories, doctrines and ideologies emerged and blossomed.
Mencius (Spring and Autumn, 372–289 BC)	Mencius inherited and developed Confucian thoughts and virtues. The Policy of Benevolence was further developed as a core belief of his political thought. But, a few dominant powers were committed to enriching the country and strengthening the military through violent means. The Policy of Benevolence was considered as too idealistic which had not been adopted and implemented.	

* Zi Lu asked what constituted the junzi (superior man). Confucius said, "The cultivation of himself in reverential carefulness." "And is this all?" said Zi Lu. "He cultivates himself so as to give rest to others," was the reply. "And is this all?" again asked Zi Lu. Confucius said, "He cultivates himself so as to give rest to all the people. He cultivates himself so as to give rest to all the people—even Yao and Shun were still solicitous about this" (Analects, 14.42).

† "A youth, when at home, should be filial, and, abroad, respectful to his elders. He should be earnest and truthful. He should overflow in love to all, and cultivate the friendship of the good" (Analects, 1.6).

‡ "What does the Shu Jing say of filial piety?—'You are filial; you discharge your brotherly duties. These qualities are displayed in government.' This then also constitutes the exercise of government. Why must there be that—making one be in the government?" (Analects, 2.21).

§ Zi Xia said, "There are learning extensively, and having a firm and sincere aim; inquiring with earnestness, and reflecting with self-application—virtue is in such a course" (Analects, 19.6).

SERVICE	LEARNING	SERVICE-LEARNING
The ultimate goal of cultivating personal virtue is to reassure the people to serve the public.[*] In the Chinese culture context, the meaning of service is to exercise oneself to serve the others. One should be filial piety at home, respectful and obedient in the community, and serve the public with care.[†] The ideas of service can be expressed in life and society in terms of filial piety and brotherliness. It can be one form of governance and equivalent to contributing to government.[‡]	"Learning is the indispensable combination of absorbing new knowledge and rethinking and digesting the learned knowledge. Exploring and thinking without learning will lead to exhaustion and fatigue" (Yang, 1991, 26). "Learning broadly, sticking with one's own aspirations, eagerly inquiring and thinking deeply about current social problems are the elements of benevolence" (Yang, 1987, 200).[§] The joy of the learning is reviewing the learned content repeatedly and regularly, which is about reflection. "Is it not pleasant to learn with a constant perseverance and application?" (*Analects*, 1.1) You can learn from the peers' advantages and improve yourself based on reviewing the disadvantages of others (Ma, Ma & Wu, 2007). The former leaners learned for self-improvement in virtue. The recent learner learns for serving others.[‖]	Encourage dedication, honorable virtue, and the importance of civic awareness and social responsibility: Confucius advocated that "education served for political and social purposes. Then, he linked education closely with politics (social affairs) closely for rectifying the order and benefiting the people (Application of knowledge)" (Yang, 1991, 34).
People are born with love and benevolence. The feeling of shame and dislike is the principle of righteousness. The feeling of modesty and complaisance is the principle of propriety. The feeling of approving and disapproving is the principle of knowledge. (*Mengzi, Gong Sun Chou I*)[#] Serving others with the similar attitude of serving loved one can benefit society.[**] Four principles refer to benevolence, righteousness, propriety and wisdom. If the people know these four principles and put it into practice, it can help create a stable society.[††]	The meaning of education and learning is to strive for exploring the inherent conscience. "Benevolence is man's mind, and righteousness is man's path. How lamentable is it to neglect the path and not pursue it, to lose this mind and not know to seek it again! When men's fowls and dogs are lost, they know to seek for them again, but they lose their mind, and do not know to seek for it. The great end of learning is nothing else but to seek for the lost mind" (*Mengzi, Gaozi I*).	Encourage dedication and honorable virtue: Service and learning are related to love and benevolence.

‖ "In ancient times, men learned with to the aim of self-improvement. Nowadays, men learn with an aim to help others" (Analects, 14.24).

\# "People are born loving the good side of the others. Serving others is an indicator of benevolence. The feeling of commiseration belongs to all men; so does that of shame and dislike; and that of reverence and respect; and that of approving and disapproving (Mengzi, Gaozi I)" (Liu & Li, 2010, 10).

** "Treat with the reverence due to age the elders in your own family, so that the elders in the families of others shall be similarly treated; treat with the kindness due to youth the young in your own family, so that the young in the families of others shall be similarly treated"(Mengzi, Liang Hui Wang I)

†† "Since all men have these four principles in themselves, let them know to give them all their development and completion, and the issue will be like that of fire which has begun to burn, or that of a spring which has begun to find vent. Let them have their complete development, and they will suffice to love and protect all within the four seas. Let them be denied that development, and they will not suffice for a man to serve his parents with (Mengzi, Gong Sun Chou I)" (Yang, 1991, 64–65).

Source: The translations for this table comes from Chinese Text Project, http://ctext.org.

Table 2. Background, Evolution Reasons, Service and Learning in Dong Zhong-shu (Han, 179–104 BC) and Fu Xuan (Wei and Jin, 217–278) of China

DYNASTY	BACKGROUND	EVOLUTIONARY REASON
Dong Zhong-shu (Han, 179–104 BC)	Dong was an advancing thinker of Confucianism in the Western Han Dynasty. He was a professor who regarded a Confucianism as the official ideology of the Chinese imperial state during Han. Confucian ethics were summarized as *san gang wu chang* (three cardinal guides and five constant virtues)* and Confucianism as the official doctrine and philosophy. Confucianism provided a theoretical statecraft basis for the future feudal rulers.	Daoism advocated for quietism and non-activity (i.e., governing by doing nothing that is against nature) which did not fulfil the changing political needs of the rulers. Han Wudi was ambitious and felt great conflict with Daoism. The thought and ideology of Confucius stressed on the Unity of Spring and Autumn periods, virtues about benevolence and justice, relationship and guiding rules. The ideas of Confucius matched with Wudi's ambition and brought changes to the non-activity situation.
Fu Xuan (Wei and Jin, 217–278)	Fu is a famous politician, scholar and writer in the Wei and Jin Dynasty. He wrote *Fu Zi*, which contains important philosophy and education ideologies. Fu addressed the issue of education and provided insight, especially on the role of education, educational content, methods and teachers' development. His education thought was influential in Chinese educational history.	Fu inherited the education ideology proposed by the previous generation of Confucian philosophers. In Western Jin, Confucian ethics were disdained and the social customs were indecent, loose and secluded. Fu advocated education, especially Confucianism ideology, in a pragmatic manner. Fu developed Confucian education with outstanding statecraft statements and quotes based on new social conditions. Yet, Fu's education theories were hard to implement in a complex and contradictory society and implement in the chaotic period. Confucianism was abandoned after Fu's death.

* Three cardinal guides refer to the emperor guiding the ministers, the father guiding the son and the husband guiding the wife; Five constant virtues refer to benevolence, justice, propriety, wisdom, integrity.

To summarize, there are three layers of the service-learning definition embodied in Confucianism and Chinese education goals: (1) be innovative and practical in practice-based learning (2) encourage dedication and honorable virtues; and (3) set an example of civic awareness and social responsibility.

Service-Learning and Practical and Innovative Education

Service-learning stands for learning in practice. It is a practice-based pedagogy that allows students to systematically reflect on and conclude their experience, as well as fully understand the theoretical and innovative perspectives of their experience. This pedagogy is analogous to Confucianism, which promotes applying what you learn.

In the Analects of Confucius, Kongzi questions, "is it not great to practice (*xi*) what you have learned?" Many scholars in recent decades have interpreted *xi* as *shijian* (practice), which highlights Confucius's philosophy of education—one should study in order to do; theories should be relevant to reality (Zhu, 2002). Another great Confucian philosopher, Xunzi, further developed and stressed Confucius' focus on engaging in practice and experiencing reality: "What is the way of

SERVICE	LEARNING	SERVICE-LEARNING
The law of benevolence is to love people instead of oneself. If you do not love yourself without loving others, it cannot be benevolence. (Luxuriant Gems of the Spring and Autumn-Standards of Humaneness and Righteousness)" (Yan, 1993, 90).	"To advocate that gentlemen should be self-improved and learn consciously. Jade will not have pattern without carving. Gentlemen will not have virtue without learning. Please ask if you don't know, please learn if you are not able to do. (Luxuriant Gems of the Spring and Autumn-Presenting Gifts to Superiors)" (Yan, 1993, p.100).	Encourage dedication, honorable virtue, and importance of practicing learning starting with self, then others, then society: Encourage to love not only yourself, but also others; and to not only have self-learning and improvement, but also learn from others.
"Benevolence is to consider others in one's own place. Do not do unto others what we would not want done unto us. Do unto others and the world what we want done to ourselves. We care and love our parents and the filial piety should be extended to others' and even the world, which also influences others to love and care their parents. People of the world would have no worries of hunger, coldness and bad thoughts" (*Ren Lun, Fu Zi I*).	It is important to shape humanity through education. (*Cong Shu Ji Cheng, Fu Zi III*). Also, nurturing talent is important in education, which can make a direct impact on the level of knowledge transfer. In addition, emphasizing moral education to the public can make them rich and satisfied. Fu believed that school education (social phenomenon that can make impact on society) and social education (means to develop a good social ethical practice) should be developed.	Encourage dedication, honorable virtue, and importance of civic awareness and social responsibility. Service and learning are not only associated with benevolence, but also associated with the community and how we can create moral society and ethical practice.

Source: The translations for this table comes from Chinese Text Project, http://ctext.org.

learning? What I hear I forget, what I see I remember, what I do I understand. True learning comes with doing" (as cited in Wang, 1988). Confucian philosophy of education has detailed categories of learning processes, which are realized in a step-by-step manner. In this philosophy, learning begins with keen intuition and observation, which is then followed by systematic knowledge and theories. The highest function in education is practice and doing. Such emphasis on practice is affirmed and supported by scholars in recent years. In the early Qing Dynasty, educator and philosopher Yan Yuan criticized the norms of sit-and-read study which he believed failed to go beyond theory. Yan was a firm believer in *shixue* (practical-learning) philosophy—to study through practice and test existing knowledge and morality through experience and action. This pedagogy, however, has weaknesses as well. Since practical learning prefers experience over study, students may engage in "blind" practice without fully understanding the meaning of such practice. Service-learning, on the contrary, emphasizes the relationship between practice and formal academic study and stresses knowledge as the basis of all practice. Service-learning encourages systematic and in-depth practice supported by specialization.

Like service-learning, Confucianism does not neglect the role of practice in education. In the Song Dynasty, Master Zhu Xi (1992) declared that prerequisite of action is our knowledge. To Zhu,

Table 3. Background, Evolution reasons, Service and Learning in Kong Ying-da (Sui and Tang, 574–648) and Zhu Xi (Song, 1130–1200) of China

DYNASTY	BACKGROUND	EVOLUTIONARY REASON
Kong Ying-da (Sui and Tang, 574–648)	Kong was a famous educator and Confucianist in the Sui and Tang Dynasty. Tang Dynasty rulers advocated Confucianism policy. Kong was appointed the chief editor of *Wu Jing* (Five Classics) to reconcile and unify different versions and annotations of Confucian beliefs, which became the canonical and orthodox interpretation of Confucianism.	Kong was fully engaged in academic research and *jing xue* education. He was dedicated to the culture and education industry throughout his entire life for the Sui and Tang Dynasties. He was highly appreciated by Tang Tai Zong because of his appreciation for and dedication to political unity. There were various complicated versions, annotations and understandings of Confucianism. A unified interpretation of Confucianism was available.
Zhu Xi (Song, 1130–1200)	Zhu was a leading Confucian scholar in the Song Dynasty. His thoughts on education had enduring and essential influence on the development of the Yuan, Ming and Qing Dynasties.	Zhu was able to theorize and popularize Confucianism rules and virtues. He deemed the three cardinal guides and five constant virtues was the highest ethical standards of society—eternal and immortal. The doctrine played a significant role and was influenced in strengthening the power of the Emperor. It later became the orthodox theory, creating far-reaching and enormous impacts on rulers.

*"One should study extensively, enquire accurately, reflect carefully and discriminate clearly in order to know, understand and learn the knowledge and theories thoroughly. At the same time, one should put the knowledge and theories into practice earnestly in order to re-examine the reality. Learning and practicing are highly intertwined and mutually re-enforcing" (Fan & Yi, 1982, 78, 98)

without the guidance of knowledge, action is done blindly. Action is only correct and reasonable when an individual has understood knowledge and related it to action. Similarly, without application, theoretical morality has no practical value. To maximize learning outcomes, practice and theory must be intertwined and well-integrated. In the Ming Dynasty, this theory of education-advocating knowledge and action as one was further examined and developed. Philosopher and educator Wang Yangming (1992) proposes that knowing the actuality is action and practicing the scrutiny is knowing. Wang explained the natures of and relationship between knowledge and action as interdependent and mutually inclusive. Endorsed by Confucianism, service-learning can promote the integration of practice and theory with traditional Chinese beliefs and modern education reform, thus developing in such a way that fits within the context of China.

After identifying core values and the guiding ideology of education reform, leaders in Chinese education face the challenge of creating effective and reasonable change. In recent years, classroom teaching in higher education, which focuses on a single disciplinary approach, has shown its limitations. Research on educational practices demonstrates that one-dimensional pedagogy cannot foster multidimensional skills. The teaching model of one-way learning could indeed stimulate students' cognitive development as well as their understanding of theoretical knowledge. Nevertheless, application of classroom knowledge is impossible without practice. Chinese scholar Chen Youqing (2005) once stated that activity is where skills are developed. Specific types of activities correspond

SERVICE	LEARNING	SERVICE-LEARNING
To serve the family, neighbor, and the community in order to be a good person.	Teachers teach the principles and encourage students think, rethink, elaborate, and practice. Therefore, students develop the ability to learn deeply and critically. Learning is a process to promote righteousness. The direction of goodness should be chosen at the beginning of learning, so that students could become a good person. People can learn to get rid of ignorance and grow in wisdom. (Sun & Li, 1997, 451, 466, 537)	Encourage dedication and honorable virtues: Serve with love and benevolence, learn to promote righteousness and goodness.
The purpose of university education is to nurture contributive and productive talents for the country, so that they can serve the country. The role of schools is to transfer knowledge and nurture talents. People should be sensitive and care about everything in their families, country, and world. They are well prepared to contribute and serve the country at any time (*Zhu Wen Gong Wen Ji Song Li Bai Dong Xu*).[*]	Sages advocated to cultivate a culture of *Ming Ren Lun* (understanding human relations). All human nature is kindhearted and docile. With hindsight, one should have learned and followed the prophets before one could return to the original human nature. Therefore, *xue* (learning) is defined as "explore[ing] what you do not know and do not understand."[†]	Encourage dedication and honorable virtues; practice learning in life and importance of caring from family to country: Emphasize human relations and that it is important to serve and learn throughout life's journey.

† "Learning is via the modeling from the sages. Humanity is all good and the sense of awareness is different. If one has later awareness of being good, one should learn and model from the prophets. Thus, one will become kindness as the original human nature" (Wang & Hu, 2007, 208).

Source: The translations for this table comes from Chinese Text Project, http://ctext.org.

to the development of a specific ability. Therefore, students' performance in an activity can accurately reflect their corresponding abilities. For instance, students who understand theoretical knowledge and participate in the classroom have only demonstrated their ability to learn theories. Their ability to implement these theories can only be demonstrated through practice and interaction with reality. How can one design relevant practices? Relate practices to the curriculum? Assess students' performance? Establish the roles and responsibilities of involved parties? Universities and colleges in China have grappled with these questions in pursuit of educational reform; however, their pursuit has lacked guidance. As a result, concrete instructions can help Chinese universities and colleges implement service-learning projects successfully. Fortunately, service-learning is dynamic and practical; it can be developed to fit a variety of models, formats, and even cultures.

Service-Learning and Chinese Moral Education

Service-learning advocates the spirit of service and dedication, social justice, and welfare for the disadvantaged. It has traces of the Confucian Five Relationships—*ren* (benevolence), *yi* (justice), *li* (propriety), *zhi* (wisdom), and *xin* (integrity)—which form the core of Chinese ethics, social values, and personal conducts. *Benevolence* means to care for one another in society. *Justice* is social justice that surpasses individual benefits and serves the common good. *Propriety* emphasizes mutual

Table 4. Background, Evolution reasons, Service and Learning in Wang Yang-ming (Ming and Qing, 1472–1528) and Cai Yuan-pei (Modern Times, 1868–1940) of China

DYNASTY	BACKGROUND	EVOLUTIONARY REASON
Wang Yang-ming (Ming and Qing, 1472–1528)	Wang was a famous educator and philosopher in the Song and Ming Dynasty. He was committed to educating apprentices and construction of knowledge. Wang's philosophy has had a great impact on future generations.	Wang was a subjective idealist, who stressed on minds, spirits and perceptions. He developed a doctrine based on Lu Jiu Yuan's Philosophy of the Mind to fight against the *Cheng-zhu xue pai* (Cheng-Zhu school). He proposed that knowledge and action are integrated and originate from the same and knowing and doing are connected.
Cai Yuan-pei (Modern Times, 1868–1940)	Cai was a famous contemporary Chinese educator who proposed *five ways of life* (moral, intellectual, physical, social and aesthetic), education reform in higher education. He made significant contributions for China's education development.	A new generation of intellectuals has been studying abroad. They were influenced by the thoughts of Western scientific spirit. They advocated for innovative educational reform and thoughts after had a thorough observation of the vulgar Chinese society.

* "As a student, the first thing is to study. Study, from a narrow sense, is to increase one's knowledge and skills, to prepare oneself as a useful talent for the society; from a broader perspective, is to examine and advance academic knowledge and theory, so as to make the most valuable contribution to the society, the country, and to mankind" (Cai Yuan Pei Quan Ji VI) (Wang, 2007, 4, 36).

respect, adhering to social order, and upholding social norms. *Wisdom* is what an individual needs to understand others and the society and to resolve conflicts and problems. *Integrity* is the trustworthiness and honesty that individuals need when they deal with the rest of society. At Lingnan University in Hong Kong, these five virtues are seen as the core values of service-learning; the university has even integrated them into its service-learning motto: "benevolence—continue love and care; justice—promote equality; propriety—treasure relationships; wisdom—always practical; integrity—trustworthiness and honesty" (Snell et al., 2015, 22). The motto, which embodies traditional Chinese virtues, is a spiritual guide and moral reference for students participating in service-learning.

If all people abide by these moral standards, humankind will reach the ideal world depicted in Confucianism—*datongshijie* (World of Great Unity). According to "Liyun" in the *Book of Rites* (also known as *Liji*), the World of Great Unity should have "security for the aged till their death, employment for the able adults, upbringing for the young, care for the widowed, orphans, childless elderlies, disabled and diseased." In other words, people should make appropriate arrangements for all people, regardless of age, sex, etc., and should build a harmonious society in which people are kind to each other. Master *Mengzi* (Mencius) also shared the same view: "honor the senior as if they were our parents, care for the young as if they were our children." He advocates fraternity, in which a person should put themselves in another's shoes, respect the elderly, and nurture the young.

Service-learning promotes selfless dedication, which is also elaborated in "Liyun" in the *Book*

SERVICE	LEARNING	SERVICE-LEARNING
Initiated by a pure heart: to serve your father is filial piety; to serve your lord is loyalty; to make friends and rule people is trust and benevolence respectively (*Chuan Xi Lu Shang*). To *serve* is the verb of *service.* Loyalty, trust and benevolence are the virtues of turning this service heart into action.	Advocated for "the unification of knowing and doing." "Knowing is a purpose of doing; doing is a work of knowing. Knowing is the start of doing; doing is the outcome of knowing" (*Wang Wen Cheng Gong Quan Ji. Chuan Xi Lu Shang*). Wang emphasizes *practice*—to learn from doing and implementation. He said, "Asking, thinking, distinguishing, and doing are all for learning; there is no learning without doing."	Encourage dedication and honorable virtues; practice learning in life and importance of caring from family to country. Experiential education is suggested. For example, to learn *xiao* (filial piety), one should serve and look after his parents, and practice filial piety himself. Then he can say he is learning that. How can one learn filial piety simply by saying without doing? To learn filial piety, one should nourish his parents, in order to learn filial piety by practicing it (Gu, 1988, 192).
"The purpose of university education is to cultivate, in every student, an ability to serve the society" (*Zhong guo Cai Yuan Pei yan jiu hui*, 1997).*	The nature of university is to research advanced knowledge. Unlike a vocational school, a university should advocate to its students that the purpose of study is not for a government position or for wealth but for the pursuit of knowledge. Students should be determinant firmly that academic research is their bounden duty (*Cai Yuan Pei Quan Ji III*) (Tian & Xiao, 2005, 478).	Encourage dedication and honorable virtues; practice learning and research in life for pursuit of knowledge and self-learning. "Only self-study will create learning interest rather than fear. By engaging in self-study, learning progresses much faster than by simply listening to lectures" (*Cai Yuan Pei Quan Ji VIII*) (Wang, 2007, 4, 36).

Source: The translations for this table comes from Chinese Text Project, http://ctext.org.

of Rites: "Wealth would neither be wasted nor hidden for personal use. Talents would neither be ignored nor used for personal gains." This is the selfless spirit in the World of Great Unity, "make the most of everything and put a person's talents to good use." Similarly, service-learning also seeks for mutual support and love, common progress, and a harmonious society, also known as Mencius' utopia.

Despite the fact that being respected in society is a value expressed in Chinese culture and education, the PRC has placed little importance on moral education in its previous developments and reforms. After its foundation in 1949, the PRC was in desperate need of technocrats to boost the nation's industrial and economic development. At the end of the twentieth century, China faced both challenges and opportunities brought upon by marketization and globalization. Its higher education has been influenced by waves of industrialization. University education has placed emphasis on practicality and instrumentality while simultaneously neglecting moral education. However, in recent years, the Chinese government has noticed that a lack of cultural and moral education creates catastrophic repercussions in terms of long-term development, stability, and harmony. In effect, the Central People's Government of the People's Republic of China and the State Council of the People's Republic of China released the *Decisions on Deepening Education Reform and Promoting Quality Education* in 1999 in hopes of enhancing and creating quality education in mainland China.

Although many universities and colleges launched quality education and moral education as an active response to the government's decision, the programs are generally criticized as rigid, formulaic, and irrelevant. An effective reform is, therefore, imperative. The current state of China and characteristics of the nation's youth make moral education a top priority in societal development and reform. Since the one-child policy was implemented in China, younger generations have received the proper care and attention needed during their childhood; yet, in conjunction, younger generations also bear immense pressure from their parents and schools to perform well and succeed in society. Consequently, this pressure tends to lead students to focus solely on their studies, neglecting other experiences that would aid them to develop necessary social skills. Often, younger generations lack communication skills and concepts like cooperation and sharing and are unable to develop caring personalities or strong competitive attitudes (Zhang, 2012). Yet, the youth also tend to be highly active, passionate, hard-working, and thoughtful and perform well academically. It is expected that once these youth are taught moral values and views of life, they will be capable of becoming the pillars of Chinese society. In education, moral attitudes and skills are vital and indispensable for society's future progression and success. Students should understand that "while knowledge and skills change one's life; personality and habits change one's fate."

Fostering Civic Awareness and Social Responsibility in China

In the *12th Five-Year Plan in National Education Development*, the MOE (2012) asserts that China must renew ideas of education and persist in reforms and innovations. Moral education and capability come first. Quality education should be fully implemented. Successors of socialist development are educated with a comprehensive curriculum. Many universities and colleges have, in recent years, introduced the Western concept of liberal education, further promoting whole-person development and connecting China with the rest of the world. Liberal education aims at educating all-around talents with thoughts, dreams, wisdom, virtues, and culture (Zhao, 2008). It seeks to enhance students' humanistic concerns and moral behavior. Service-learning is highly connected with liberal education, for it promotes dedication to society and those in the global context. Universities and colleges in China can integrate instrumental service-learning into abstract and theoretical liberal education so they can complement each other and optimize learning outcomes. When service-learning becomes systematic and institutional in higher education, students learn through real-life experiences and put theories learned in the classroom into practice. They experience how good virtues bring positive changes and influence to society, others, and even themselves. Last but not least, students are not only the receivers of moral education but also learn to develop and grow with others in a harmonic and co-existent environment. In the future, they will also become the promoters and practitioners of dedication and nobility, and create the World of Great Unity in the new era.

Service-learning advocates the concepts of attention to society, international civic awareness, and social responsibility—echoing the ideals of Confucianism, modern socialist development, and civic education in Chinese higher education. Civic engagement has a strong basis and plenty of opportunity for development in Chinese education. In ancient China, literati studied for the sake of people and their entire nation. They wished to bring better lives to people and serve their country. Since the Spring and Autumn periods and the Warring States, the principles of "investigation, knowing, rectification, cultivation, family harmony, governance and world peace" (Mencius, n.d.) have been honored by many intellectuals. According to these principles, a person acquires knowledge through investigation of the world. Knowledge is seen as a tool to decrease wrong action and make a person sincere. Additionally, people are supposed to manage their families and support the nation, as well as bring peace to all in the society. According to these principles, learning is the basis of service and effective service is the goal of education.

As the future leaders of China, youth must see their families, country, and the world as their concerns. They must strive to make a difference by using their progressive ideas and beliefs. "Zizhang" of the Analects of Confucius states, "excellence in officialdom leads to scholarship, excellence in scholarship leads to officialdom." This quote explains the complementary relationship between service and learning. *Officialdom* here can be broadly defined as jobs in different sectors. A person should not be limited by his/her identity, age, or background, especially when it comes to paying attention to society and improving people's livelihood. As a member of society, every person has the responsibility as well as the capability to make a difference, be it within a community, a country, or the world.

In modern Chinese society, youth, after many years of formal education and the acquisition of certain professional skills, are able to set the precedent for serving the society and promoting social development. Therefore, before graduation, students should explore the world as much as possible. They should understand the society they live in and learn to develop and create a better future. In a rapidly developing country, Chinese youth need to face a variety of emerging social problems and global challenges (e.g., global warming and financial crises). They also need to tackle regional or China-specific issues (e.g., aging population, widening economic inequality, and lack of housing). Service-learning forces students to explore and test out solutions, so that they, through experience, can improve society. At university/college, they are trained to be keen observers of social problems. By engaging in service, their solutions can be tested, broadening their horizons and enhancing their experiences. In doing so, students are equipped with skills and well-defined goals after graduation. Service-learning can, therefore, follow China's historical development, while, at the same time, meeting new societal demands.

Service-learning can be implemented in diverse learning formats, which enables teachers to address students' needs and fully enhance students' abilities. By incorporating diverse learning formats into the classroom, Chinese education is following a trend of globalization. Through service-learning, traditional Chinese culture and Confucianism, which are tied to service-learning, can spread to other parts of the world. Service-learning seeks to learn from the world, and service-learning in China can let the world learn more about Chinese culture. Confucianism, however, does not contain a clear set of instructions, such as how to conduct systematic reflection—the method to apply theory—or how to develop new theories and solutions. Hence, Confucianism can serve as the spiritual basis that supports service-learning, while service-learning can act as an effective tool that extends Confucianism to address world needs and progress humankind. By implementing service-learning in such a way that benefits China as well as the world, service-learning in China becomes a sustainable pedagogy and methodology.

Since the mid-twentieth century, the Chinese government has promoted and implemented related policies with the goal of training high-quality and well-rounded citizens. The government encourages schools to attach importance to students' developing practical skills, morality, and social responsibility. Universities and colleges actively responded to the government by initiating a variety of field education experiences for university students as well as volunteer activities. These activities have led students into their communities to understand the needs of society and contribute to community development. Students have developed a sense of others' needs and their responsibility towards the society. These activities are no different from service-learning in terms of its outcomes. The ideas of service-learning, in effect, have long been a part of Chinese education and curriculum.

As a result of the similarities between the ideologies of service-learning and volunteering, it is easy to confuse the two different approaches to civic engagement. Some scholars believe there is no need to promote service-learning if universities and colleges already have launched volunteerism. Such a view overlooks the limitations to volunteerism and the additional benefits that service-learning offers. Volunteering projects in Chinese higher education have exposed the shortcomings and limitations of volunteering, which include vague and/or boring content, lack of motivation among students, weak links between services and students' specializations, and an absence of effective assessment. Volunteering, however, is only one part of service-learning. Service-learning also includes training, reflection, assessments, observation of a community, academic learning, and applications of theory in service. In the next section, there is an analysis of the current status, features, and limitations of Chinese volunteerism. This is followed by discussions of how to improve and solve challenges experienced in service-learning.

Service-Learning and Volunteerism in Chinese Higher Education

Current Status of Volunteerism among Chinese Undergraduates

Beginning with the trend of *xue Lifung* (learning from Lifung) in the 1960s, volunteerism developed rapidly in China. The number of participants in volunteering increased steadily over time. Comprising the majority of volunteers, university students possess rich, specialized knowledge, higher awareness, and a philanthropic inclination. The Chinese government and the MOE have emphasized the importance of instilling moral education and social responsibility in undergraduates. Chinese universities and colleges responded in kind by launching social services and volunteering projects, moving toward the institutionalization of volunteerism in higher education.

Large-scale participation and impact are characterizing features of volunteerism in Chinese higher education. Every year in China, millions of university students spend the summer break in volunteer teams to take part in the *Sanxiaxiang* (Three Downs to the Countryside) activity, which first began in 1996. The volunteers go to rural areas and launch cultural, technological, and hygienic services. They also contribute significantly to national ecological and environmental protection projects, such as the Mother Rivers Protection (Yellow River, Yangtze River, and other main rivers). In addition, thousands of volunteers participate in the services for abandoned children and volunteered at the 2007 Shanghai Special Olympics and the 2008 Beijing Summer

Olympics. This volunteer involvement helps to alleviate social problems and bring more harmony to the society. In addition to national projects, Chinese universities and colleges are also active on the local level. Students can give back to their country with their skills and services, which are also needed in national development. This not only satisfies social needs, but also enables young adults to understand the China-specific situation and learn to pay attention to the society. This, in turn, shapes students' values and life views. Without a doubt, volunteerism stimulates social development in China and allows undergraduates to gain valuable experience. Nonetheless, there is still room for improvement.

Good Coordination Motivates Students

Volunteerism in Chinese higher education is usually a response to governmental policies and actions. The top-down approach from the senior administration to the junior level has its advantages for promoting volunteerism: for example, sufficient resources for organizing activities, flexible personnel assignment, and good coordination. The scale of service, number of participants, and target audience are also important factors. Urgent social problems (e.g. post-disaster relief and recovery) can be solved effectively and swiftly. It also meets the demands for services at large-scale events (e.g. preparations and ushering in the Olympic Games). However, in this hierarchical model, a sense of enforcement is embedded in such unified administration because participants are, to a certain extent, ordered or influenced by their seniors. "Forced volunteering" is the result of this arrangement (Lan & Xu, 2011). If students are passively participating and merely aiming at finishing a task, they are not motivated. Thus, charity events cannot maximize their effects on helping the society and training the students. Moreover, many undergraduates participate in one-off, short-term volunteering activities that lack clear learning objectives. With these large-scale events, it might be just a matter of formality; because of their short-term constraints, the projects cannot deepen their substance and develop sustainably. Unified planning and pre-set service content often make a project rigid and mechanic, leaving no space for students to innovate (Liu & Sun, 2011).

To make the best out of existing volunteerism, projects should be designed with an undergraduate mentality in mind. First, content and format must be more diverse, so that students have a choice. Second, the link between one activity and another should be strengthened—e.g., a project can be expanded in the same domain. This benefits students' continuous learning as well as the establishment of long-term and mutual relationships with community partners. Third, organizers should include students in each stage of a project. From design to assessment, student roles should stimulate their recognition and sense of belonging to the project. Their creative thinking will also be boosted. To reach the aforementioned goals, the passive must transform into the active and the unified must diversify. Traditional volunteerism in Chinese higher education was designed to be top–down, whereas service-learning, as a modern and progressive pedagogy, advocates proactivity from the bottom up. Flexibility in service-learning allows creative and varied content in a project. Students' needs and curricula are also taken into account. Finally, students' innovation and proactivity are boosted. They become independent and devote themselves to social services.

Strengthening the Connections between Volunteering and Curriculum

Volunteerism in higher education generally emphasizes service rather than learning. While service aims at contributing to the society and helping those in need, the service itself is not very challenging or relevant to the studies of undergraduates. Although the disadvantaged are provided with a service and social problems are addressed, students do not have the opportunity to put their knowledge into practice. The talents of undergraduates have been wasted due to simple, unified service content even as, after the reform and opening-up policies, students have become more independent-minded and self-conscious after many years of education. Social services that lack connections with their specializations are not engaging enough for students, resulting in short-term volunteering projects (Shen & Wu, 2011). Therefore, volunteerism is often mistaken as an "extracurricular activity," simply learning from Lifung and "doing good" (Han, 2003). Research has shown that 90% of freshmen are passionate about taking part in volunteering activities, but less than 10% of them actually participate in them on a long-term basis (Zhang, Lu, & Jiang, 2010). Shouldn't we question this decline in involvement?

Service-learning, as a new model that combines service and learning, will bring qualitative changes to the role of university students in volunteer activities. As both the service providers and beneficiaries, students develop themselves through experiential learning. This can also set up the correct service example for the students, so that they will not see service as merely "giving" but rather a mutually beneficial endeavor. Students should see the service targets as their friends and companions. They should learn from the targets modestly and proactively while maintaining friendly and equal relationships.

Linking service-learning with academia and volunteering activities is highly instrumental and flexible. For different majors, universities can arrange relevant service practicums. For different classes, universities can adjust the practicums according to students' backgrounds and knowledge, or even launch progressive projects. For example, after selecting a topic, the difficulty of content should increase based on the level of the class. Teaching students according to their aptitude follows the cognitive development of youth, allowing them to progress in a step-by-step manner. They are also more motivated to practice what they have learned in the provided platform and become more proactive.

Emphasis on the Outcomes of Service to Improve Reflection and Assessment

Strengthening the link between academics and service is an externally and objectively beneficial factor. Individual student development, however, is an internally motivated and subjective outcome. Good objective conditions need subjective factors to function. In other words, if the service project and related courses are designed well, lecturers, universities, and community service will cooperate closely. If participating students do not think, observe, and reflect during activities, though, their learning outcomes and development will be very limited. Rather unfortunately, current volunteering activities in Chinese universities put more emphasis on the service projects themselves. They aim for students to finish the service. Once the task is done, the project is considered complete. In this way, service becomes a meaningless task. Even if there is some informal sharing, the experience lacks standard and systematic reflection and conclusion. This restricts students from proactively thinking and learning. Another topic worth discussing is how to evaluate the impact of volunteerism on students. Accurately assessing students' performance and reflection of services can help lecturers understand students' circumstances and responses, upon which service activity improves. It seeks to achieve a win-win situation for both community agencies and students' improvement. Even if there are some universities demanding confirmation from service agencies of whether the students have finished projects or completed certain hours, most of them have not designed a special proposal for volunteering activities. It is thus difficult to investigate the actual impact of services on students and students' performance.

Service-learning emphasizes the importance of reflection, which helps students analyze and learn from their experiences. Research has shown that reflection in social services can deepen students' understanding of social issues. Students can think critically about their experience, analyze the pros and cons of the project, propose a solution, and acquire new knowledge. Organizing systematic and standardized reflection and assessment can stimulate thinking by providing guidance and helping students internalize their personal experiences and cognition in service. It will also help teachers observe students' performance, from which they can then tailor a service experience to optimize student development. Reflection can have many kinds of formats (e.g. reflective journal, report-back celebration, group discussion, reflective presentation, etc.). Many universities that launched service-learning have already established good assessment systems. For instance, Lingnan University in Hong Kong has adopted survey comparisons, focus groups, reflective essays, and so on to assess students' performance. Service-learning programs at Lingnan University takes into account the impact of service-learning on students and the communities and strives for continuous improvement.

How Can Service-Learning Improve Volunteerism in Chinese Higher Education?

There is room for improvement in the design, content, and execution of volunteerism in Chinese higher education. Service-learning can serve as a means to improve volunteerism in Chinese higher education and tackle the roots of problems in field education. Service-learning, volunteerism, field education, and internships are classified as experiential education—differing from traditional education, where students have little to no hands-on experience in order to understand procedures and theories. Experiential education encourages students to participate in and contribute to society. However, there are fundamental differences between the various types of experiential education introduced by Furco (2003) (see Figure 1).

Service-learning is a new pedagogy, which has a firm theoretical basis, yet also aims to incorporate sense of practicality. It benefits both communities and students, placing the same emphasis on community goals as it does learning goals. Volunteerism and internships, however, differ from service-learning in many aspects, particularly in their approach, benefits, and focus. Volunteerism stresses selfless dedication and aims at helping and serving disadvantaged persons or communities. These activities are usually organized to strengthen moral education and require little to no academic knowledge transfer. Internships, on the other hand, emphasize field education and are used to train students to acquire professional skills through practicing in the field.

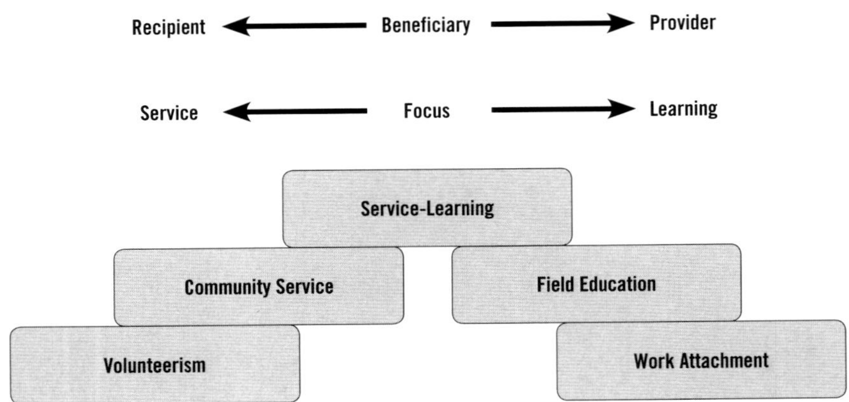

Figure 1. The relationship between service-learning and other voluntary/practical social activities (adapted from Furco, 2003).

Indeed, internships are highly relevant to the curricula undertaken by the students, but they do not stimulate long-term dedication or cultivate the spirit of engaging in service to the community. Service-learning, on the contrary, combines the advantages of both volunteerism and internships—integrating moral education and professional training. When raising civic awareness and social responsibility, it promotes applications and understanding of what students have learned. Social services are therefore no longer just an extra project outside the classroom. Service-learning mediates the competitive relationship between moral education and professional training, and instead builds a complementary and mutually reinforcing partnership.

In organizational management, volunteerism and/or internships are mainly arranged and organized by a department (e.g., Student Affairs Office, Dean's Office, student groups, etc.). A unified management ensures that projects are carried out as planned. With this management in place, implementation and expected results are generally satisfactory. However, when service recipients, students, and/or course teachers play passive roles in the process, it can result in a lack of communication and motivation, as well as failure to meet community needs. Service-learning, on the contrary, places emphasis on active, mutually beneficial relationships among students, course teachers, and communities. At the beginning of a project, a teacher and students meet with community partners to discuss the problems faced by the community, the needs of the community, the community's preferred way of cooperation, any specific preparation or training needed for students, and so on. Then, once community needs are identified, the project design phase begins. In the preparation stage of this phase, proposed implementation is adjusted to meet the demands of the current situation. In effect, all parties must exhibit adaptability and creativity in order to create a plan based on any new circumstances. Better organization skills, communication, and application of knowledge can benefit the community. Therefore, students are the service providers as well as the receivers, whereas teachers and community institutions become co-educators. Both within their own professional domains enhance students' development.

Table 5. The Service-Learning Models of Ningbo Institute of Technology at Zhejiang University and Shantou University

UNIVERSITY	UNIVERSITY SUPPORT	COURSE DESIGN	ASSESSMENT	SOURCE OF FUNDING	CORE VALUES	FEATURES
Ningbo Institute of Technology at Zhejiang University	Lecturers from different departments, associated government bodies	Highly relevant to the curriculum, credit-bearing service-learning projects (e.g., "Walking News" service-learning integrated with Journalism curriculum)	Project assessment and reflection through annual report, annual news prize, etc.	University, associated government bodies	Promote service spirit, strengthen the sense of social responsibility in students; enhance students' learning; proactively learn new ideas, reform education and innovate	Community-based service-learning (format: field education in accordance with disciplines)
Shantou University	All departments; Shantou University Medical College National Medical Aid for the Poor Project	Integrate classroom teaching, experiential teaching, service-learning, and village services; 50 credit-bearing courses on "Public Welfare" are created in different departments	Students' sharing and reflections with data analysis and conclusions	Li Ka Shing Foundation	Liberal arts education, holistic development/ whole person development, equal weight on theory and practice; encourage students to help the disadvantaged, meet the community needs, launch an organized service project	International and local community-based service-learning projects; research-based service-learning (highly relevant to one's discipline)

Source: The translations for this table comes from Chinese Text Project, http://ctext.org.

Service-learning, therefore, could in many ways improve the quality and expand the impact of volunteer activities and field education organized by Chinese universities. Its adaptable structure and process allows universities to build upon existing volunteering activities and projects, and develop the best model of service-learning practice, based on their own particular features and interests. Some universities in the Chinese mainland have already recognized the progressiveness and adaptability of service-learning. These universities have managed to establish service-learning projects in their communities—putting the Western concept and pedagogy into practice within the Eastern context.

The Emergence of Service-Learning in Chinese Higher Education

Although still in its initial stage in China, service-learning has brought significant and advantageous impacts to Chinese universities and surrounding communities. As a result, many universities have started to launch their own service-learning projects, including Ningbo Institute of Technology, Zhejiang University, and Shantou University. Feedback gathered from various stakeholders confirms that positive outcomes have been seen at both the institutional and community level (see Table 5).

The first Development Forum of Professional Volunteers Service was organized by Shantou University in 2012. Participants of the Forum included seventeen mainland universities, four universities from Hong Kong and Taiwan, and five community organizations. It aimed to promote the learning and exchange of service-learning ideas, methods, and practices among all parties involved. Shantou University also became the first university in China to make service-learning a graduation requirement in 2010. Since the Forum, communication among involved parities remains high, yet little has been done to move beyond the discussion stage and into the implementation stage of projects.

Lingnan University established its Office of Service-Learning (OSL) in 2006. As the first university to develop service-learning in the Asia-Pacific, Lingnan University has become the face of service-learning in the region. The university has been successful in promoting and actively expanding service-learning to mainland China with support from the United Board for Christian Higher Education in Asia. Since 2006, Lingnan University has cooperated with six Chinese higher institutions to support thirteen service-learning pilot schemes (see Appendix 1 for project introduction). The universities involved in this partnership include: Sun Yat-Sen University (SYSU), Guangxi Medical University, South China Normal University, South China University of Technology, Beijing Normal University–Hong Kong, Baptist University, United International College, and Zhuhai City Polytechnic. After the first round of service-learning pilot project schemes, all partner universities showed enthusiasm and interest in further developing service-learning projects. Many universities, for instance, are planning to integrate service-learning in liberal education or disciplinary courses, and/or set up independent courses and/or OSLs. The 4th Asia-Pacific Regional Conference on Service-Learning, held by Lingnan University and SYSU in China in 2013, helped increase awareness of the service-learning pedagogy as well as its benefits among Chinese universities, social enterprises, and the business sector in China. More than twenty universities from China participated in the conference and some of them have fully integrated service-learning into various disciplines. China Youth University for Political Sciences has well-designed service-learning courses in legal studies, history, children's rights, social work, etc. Teachers from this university have even translated the book *Service-Learning: A Movement's Pioneers Reflect on Its Origins, Practice, and Future*, written by Stanton, Giles & Cruz (1999), in order to promote service-learning in China. This university strongly believes service-learning is an effective means for practicing character education and more publications in Chinese have been produced. Various forums were held by the China Youth University for Political Sciences in order to promote more institutions using service-learning as a means of character education in China.

In conclusion, volunteerism, field education, quality education, and liberal education all aim to nurture whole-person development and build civic awareness in university students. With this in mind, university graduates become socially responsible citizens and moral professionals who contribute to and enhance Chinese civilization. Service-learning in university settings acts as a catalyst, fostering civic-minded students and developing a noble and talented workforce. In addition, service-learning is a comprehensive, flexible, and instrumental pedagogy. For that reason, it can be well integrated into the volunteerism that currently exists in Chinese higher education. Most importantly, this integration will enhance the system of educating future citizens, who, in turn, will shape Chinese society for the years to come.

REFERENCES

Central People's Government of the People's Republic of China. (2001). *The program for improving civic morality.* (Central Compilation & Translation Bureau, Trans.). Beijing: Central Compilation & Translation Bureau.

Central People's Government of the People's Republic of China & State Council of State Council of the People's Republic of China. (2004). *Zhong gong zhong yang guo wu yuan guan yu jin yi bu jia qiang ge ga jin da zue sheng si xiang zheng zhi jiao yu de yi jian* [Opinion on further strengthening and improving ideological and political education]. Beijing: Central People's Government of the People's Republic of China & State Council of State Council of the People's Republic of China.

Chen, Y. Q. (2005). Liang zhong huo dong zai liang lei su zhi fa zhan zhong de zuo yong ji qi guan xi [The roles of two types of activities and their relationships with two kinds of quality-oriented development]. *Journal of Huazhong Normal University* 44(4): 127-131.

Furco, A. (2003). Service-learning: A balanced approach to experimental education. In *Introduction to service-learning toolkit,* 2nd ed., 11-14. Providence: Campus Compact.

Gu, S. S. (1988). *Zhong guo gu dai jiao yu jia yu lu lei bian* [Ancient Chinese educator Quote series Shanghai Education Press]. Beijing: Guangming Daily Publishing House.

Gu, X. B., & Xu, Y. S. (2009). Gao xian shi jian xue gai ge de yan jiu yu shi jian [Research and implementation of reforms of practical teaching in China's higher education]. *Journal of Yancheng Teachers University* 29(6): 112-114.

Han, J. (2003). Dang dai da xue sheng can yu zhi yuan fu wu de zhang ai yan jiu [The bars to participating volunteering activities among undergraduates]. *Journal of Shandong Youth Administrative Cadres College* 2(102): 33-34.

Han, Y. (1958). *Shi shuo* [On teaching]. In *Han chang li ji* [Han's collection]. Beijing: The Commercial Press.

Hu, J. T. (2007). *Hold high the great banner of socialism with Chinese characteristics and strive for new victories in building a moderately prosperous society in all respects—Report to the Seventeenth National Congress of the Communist Party of China.* Beijing: Xinhua News Agency. http://www.china.org.cn/english/congress/229611.htm.

Lau, D. C. (1979). *The Analects of Confucius.* London: Penguin Classics.

Lan, C. F., & Xu, W. M. (2011). *Fu wu—xue xi zai gao deng jiao yu zhong de li lun yu shi jian* [Service-Learning: Theory and practice in higher education]. Hangzhou: Zhejiang University Press.

Liu, X. F., & Li, N. (2010). Discussion on the self-learning thought on Mencius. *Cheng ren jiao yu* [Adult education] 5(280): 10-11.

Liu, X., & Sun, X. T. (2011). Gao xiao qing nian zhi yuan zhe huo dong de ren shi ji si kao [Understanding volunteerism in higher education]. *Shanxi Education (Pedagogy)* 10:47-48.

Lun Yu [The Analects]. (2003). Shanghai: Shanghai Lexicographical Publishing House.

Ma, X. C., Ma, L. L., & Wu, H. M. (2007). Kong Zi jiao yu si xiang tan xi [Confucius's Educational Thought]. *Weifang Higher Vocational Education* 3(4), 37-39.

Ma, Y., & Liu, Z. L. (2001). Chuan Xuan jiao yu guan ping xi [Chuan Xuan education review]. *Journal of Anhui Institute of Education* 19(5): 92-94.

Markham, I. S., & Lohr, C. (2009). *World religion Leaders.* 3rd ed. Oxford: Wiley-Blackwell.

Mencius. (n.d.). *Gaozi I.* (Legge, J., Trans.). Chinese Text Project. http://ctext.org/mengzi/gaozi-i.

Ministry of Education (MOE) of the People's Republic of China. (2007). *Jiao yu bu cai zheng bu guan yu shi shi gao deng xue jiao ben ke jiao xue zhi liang yu jiao xue gai ge gong cheng de yi jian* [Opinion on implementing reforms of the undergraduate program quality and teaching].

———. (2010). *Guo jia zhong chang qi jiao yu gai ge he fa zhan gui hua gang yao (2010–2020 nian)* [Outline of China's national plan for medium and long-term education reform and development (2010–2020)].

———. (2011). *2011 nian quan guo jiao yu she ye fa zhan tong ji gong bao* [National education development statistical bulletin of 2011].

———. (2012). *Guo jia jiao yu shi ye fa zhan di shi erg e wu nian gua hua* [Twelfth five-year plan in national education development].

Shen, L. J., & Wu J. W. (2011). Ti sheng gao xiao qing nian zhi yuan zhe huo dong zhi liang de ji dian si kao [A few thoughts on improving the quality of volunteerism in higher education]. *Journal of Yichun University* 33(5): 146–148.

Snell, R., et al. (2015). *Annual report of Office of Service-Learning at Lingnan University*. Hong Kong: Lingnan University.

Stanton, T. K., Giles, D. E., Jr., & Cruz, N. I. (1999). *Service-learning: A movement's pioneers reflect on its origins, practice and future*. San Francisco, CA: Jossey-Bass.

Tian, Z. P., & Xiao, L. (2005). *Zhong guo jiao yu jing dian jie du* [Reading about Chinese Classics Education]. Shanghai: Shanghai Education Publishing House.

Tyler, R. W. (1994). *Ke cheng yu jiao xue de ji ben yuan li* [Basic principles of curriculum and instruction]. (Shi, L. F., Trans.). Beijing: People's Education Press.

Wang, B. (2013). A few thoughts on moral education in Chinese higher education. *Journal of Mudanjiang University*, 5: 128–129.

Wang, D. J., & Hu, Z. P. (2007). *Jia yu jiao yuen li* [Theory of Education]. Fujian: Fujian Education Press.

Wang, S. R. (1992). *Chuan xi lu* [Instructions for practical living]. Shanghai: Shanghai gu ji Press.

Wang, X. (1988). *Xunzi ji jie* [Xunxi collection of commentaries]. Beijing: Zhonghua Book Company.

Wang, Y. S. (2007). *Cai Yuan-pei da xue jiao yu si xing lun gang* [Cai Yuan-pei's Thought Outline about University]. Beijing: Guangming Daily Publishing House.

Yang, B. J. (1987). *Annotations of the Analects* [Lun yu yi zhi]. Hong Kong: Zhonghua Book Company.

Yang, R. C. (1991). *Xian Qin jia yu si xiang shi* [Education ideology history in the Xian Qin Dynasty]. 2nd ed. Guangdong Education Press.

Yang, S. Z. (2001). *'Shi yu' ren 'fei zhi' qi—zai tan ren wen jiao yu de ji chu di wei* ["Education," not "machine-making"—another discussion on the utmost importance of humanistic education]. Wuhan: Higher Education Research.

———. (2008, December 19). Wo mem de da xue shi fou zai shui qiu shi qu ling hun de zhuo yue [Is our university in the pursuit of excellence lost soul]. *China Education Daily.*

Zhang, J., Lu, Z. L., & Jiang L. Y. (2010). Hou ao yun shi dai da xue sheng zhi yuan fu wu diao yan fen xi [Analysis of undergraduate volunteerism in the post-Olympic era]. *Forestry Education in China*, 28(3), 26.

Zhang, M. (2012). Research and Comment on One-child Policy in China. *Journal of Chifeng University (Natural Sciences)*, 28(1).

Zhao, L. B. (2008). Ren wen fa zhan yu tong shi jiao yu wen ti chu tan [A tentative study on humanistic development and general education]. Doctoral dissertation, Fudan University, Fudan, China. http://

kxrc.cnki.net/kcms/detail/detail.aspx?filename=2009018567.nh&dbcode=CDFD&dbname=CDFD2009.

Zhong Guo Cai Yuanpei yan jiu hui [China research association for Cai Yuanpei]. (1997). *Cai Yuan Pei Quan Ji IV* [The complete works of Cai Yuanpei, volume 4]. Shejiang: Zhejiang Education Press.

Zhu, X. (1992). *Si shu zhang ju ji zhu* [Interpretations of the four books]. Jinan: Qilu Press.

Zhu, Y. Q. (2002). Xue er shi xi zhim, bu yi shuo hu—e lun kongzi jiao yu si xiang. [It is great to practice what you learned—a short discussion of Confucius' philosophy of education]. *Journal of Ningbo University* 24(4): 45–47.

PART 2

Disciplinary Perspectives

On the Connection and Dynamic Interplay between Service-Learning and Liberal Arts Education

XU Xin-zhong and YU Li-ren

The Definition of Liberal Arts Education

Liberal arts education (*Boya jiaoyu*) is a teaching mode that has profoundly impacted the United States and other Western countries. Jonathan Becker (2005, 25) defines liberal arts education as "a system of higher education designed to foster in students the desire and capacity to learn, think critically, and communicate proficiently and to prepare them to function as engaged citizens." Tu Weiming (1996), a professor at Harvard University, who conducted a study on liberal arts education in the United States, Mainland China, Hong Kong, and Taiwan, concludes that liberal arts has a distinctly different meaning in different regions. It is called liberal arts education in the United States, *Suzhi jiaoyu* (quality education) in China, *Boya* (liberal arts) education in Hong Kong, *Tongshi jiaoyu* (general education) in Taiwan, and character education in Singapore. While different in approaches, these various terms do share a similar notion that universities should place as much value on general education, humanities, and personal development as they do on disciplinary knowledge and teaching.

Service-Learning Today and Liberal Arts

Service-learning in the United States derives from the traditional concept of experiential learning, a teaching mode that has historically been incorporated into many classroom settings. However, it was not until the 1970s that service-learning was integrated into educational curricula. The term *service-learning* was coined in 1967 by two educators, Robert Simon and William Ramsay, as a means to fulfill community needs by integrating intentional learning with task-based learning.

In Mainland China, service-learning is currently in the beginning stage of gaining recognition by education scholars as a form of liberal arts education. On the contrary, service-learning in the United States has already been developed, experimented with, and well-integrated into students' daily lives. In the educational field within the United States, there have been numerous studies on service-learning. In 1990, American scholar Jane Kendall compiled 147 definitions of service-learning and found that it is commonly defined as an experiential learning mode where students engage in a practicum focused on integrating service and study (as cited in Eyler & Giles, 1999). Service-learning and liberal arts education are thus no different in their aims: to develop qualified students who possess knowledge (such as academic theories and subject-related knowledge), and skills (such as versatility and problem solving) (Li & Li, 2013).

Service-learning has been widely accepted as an experiential learning mode in higher education across the United States, Taiwan, Hong Kong, and other regions and, recently, it has been introduced to university curriculum in Mainland China along with liberal arts education development. Lingnan (University) College at Sun Yat-sen University (SYSU) serves as a prime example. With the motto "Education for Service," the College has promoted liberal arts education and service-learning based on experiences from both local and overseas environments as well as university research on how service and learning can work together and facilitate one another.

Liberal Arts Education and Service-Learning at Lingnan (University) College at Sun Yat-sen University

Lingnan (University) College, affiliated with SYSU, is a school of Economics and Management. The College is closely related to Lingnan University in Hong Kong, which was founded over 120 years ago. Echoing the motto "Education for Service," Lingnan University emphasizes the importance and effectiveness of both service-learning and liberal arts education. Since its establishment in 1989, Lingnan (University) College has sought to establish itself as a leading institution of Economics and Management in both the Hong Kong and global contexts. The 2012 academic year represents twenty-five years since the College started service-learning and liberal arts education.

After the Undergraduate Program Reform in 2012, Lingnan (University) College shifted its focus to balancing liberal arts education and teaching education. With respect to liberal arts education, the College has promoted various activities, such as the Lingnan Series Seminars on Liberal Arts. Moreover, students are encouraged to participate in service-learning projects, some of which are student initiated. Additional examples are the "Xiguan Little House Community Service-Learning Project," "Lingnan Volunteer Association Project," and "Guangdong Rural Economic Service and Research Project." These projects have demonstrated the integration of service-learning and liberal arts education.

Lingnan Series Seminars on Liberal Arts is one of the first quality education programs with a practicum element at SYSU. In accordance with the idea digging the study, learning the culture, the seminars highlight student participation in programming and managing events, including the events' topic selection and guest coordination. The seminars are widely supported by the Lingnan Foundation, the University, and the College, and have gained a profound reputation as featured events at the university level. The aims of the seminars are to cultivate rational, positive, and cultured university students who develop a global perspective and actively engage with literature, history, philosophy, and the arts. SYSU hopes graduates will become righteous, open, responsible, knowledgeable, and refined after their participation in the Lingnan Series Seminars on Liberal Arts. The seminars have been held for more than twenty series, thus becoming one of the branding features of the SYSU.

Lingnan Volunteer Association is a student society devoted to community volunteer services. Founded in 2004, the Lingnan Volunteer Association has provided underprivileged community members with tailor-made services. The university students in the Lingnan Volunteer Association are encouraged to be serving to learn and learning to serve. Over the past ten years, Lingnan Volunteer Association has organized 132 volunteer services with over 6,500 participants and served more than 68,000 people. These activities have included volunteer teaching at the schools for migrant children, personal safety alarm hotline services for the singleton elderly, and an English-speaking training program for children of migrant workers, which recruits the majority of exchange students at Lingnan (University) College. Run by the student-led association, these projects represent the real meaning of service-learning and liberal arts education. The services provided reach diverse community populations—the elderly, children, university students, etc.—and stretch from working within urban areas to remote villages. These projects, as part of meaningful extracurricular programs, successfully promote civic awareness and social responsibility.

In August of 2013, 338 undergraduate students, together with eighteen teachers, went to three rural areas across Guangdong Wuchuan in Zhenjiang, Lianzhou in Qingyuan, and Zijin in Heyuan to engage in the six-day Guangdong Rural Economic Service and Research Project. Two analyses of the collected data were published: *Guangdong Rural Economic Development Report* and *Guangdong Mass Affluent Report*. This project enhanced students' local and global awareness, taught students about local lifestyles and social issues, and encouraged students to explore their self-understanding, which, in turn, facilitated their personal growth. Furthermore, materials extracted from student research serve as useful tools to analyze economic and financial development in rural areas as well as local business opportunities in Guangdong, where small businesses are essential in serving the needs and interests of local residents. Students involved in this particular project, therefore, directly contributed to the betterment of the community in which they learned and served.

The case above shows that students in the Lingnan (University) College had a meaningful and mutually beneficial service-learning experience to which they were able to apply knowledge learned in liberal arts education in their service to the community. Additionally, the academic ability of the students improved over the course of the service project. Students also demonstrated growth in terms of their commitment to and care for the community. This, in turn, proves that service-learning and liberal arts education share a similar goal and vision, which enables them to naturally complement one another.

Promoting the Dynamic Interplay between Service-Learning and Liberal Arts Education

It can be concluded that, in the case of Lingnan (University) College, two key components are found to help facilitate the development of and dynamic interplay between service-learning and liberal arts education.

First, both student-led service-learning activities and various types of service-learning programs must be promoted together with liberal arts education. Students are the primary learners in liberal arts education; they thirst for knowledge and are acute problem-solvers devoted to combating social inequalities. With moderate guidance, students are also more likely to participate in service-learning programs related to liberal arts education. Research in the community can be tied to a student's major. Even more, students are given the opportunity to express their creativity by giving innovative solutions to societal problems. As a result, student-led service-learning activities are closely related to liberal arts education, which focuses on whole-person development and nurturing well-rounded global citizens. Lingnan University and Lingnan (University) College are responsible for establishing long-term collaboration with the local community and other higher educational institutions so as to retain sufficient resources for further development of service-learning. It is also important to take students' schedules into consideration. It is typically better to schedule projects during the holiday and semester breaks, in hope that students can take part in the projects during their free time.

Second, to achieve the best outcome of service-learning and liberal arts education learning modes, it is necessary to integrate service-learning into liberal arts education in a logical and intentional manner. While service-learning provides students the ability to practice and strengthen the knowledge learned in the classroom, students may not be motivated to engage in this type of experiential learning or see the benefits of it without being in a liberal arts education setting. Furthermore, service-learning, if mutually independent from liberal arts education, is likely to lapse into nothing but skills training and, in effect, divert from its learning goal. Therefore, at the program's initial stage, universities and colleges should intentionally integrate these two elements with a long-term, logical, and holistic plan. In practice, the contents and rationales of both service-learning and liberal arts education should be closely interrelated as well. For example, the school curriculum should include service-learning courses or the established courses should integrate service-learning into their course plans.

About the Institution

SYSU, founded by Dr. Sun Yat-sen, is a comprehensive multi-disciplinary university with over a 100-year history. It is a key university under the Chinese National Higher Education Project. The university is comprised of "a community of teachers and students," through which "teachers represent the school body" and embrace the idea of "educating with love." The aim of SYSU is to nurture high-quality, interdisciplinary students who possess international perspectives, a sense of social responsibility, and innovative spirits. Graduates are expected to be well-mannered, honest, diligent, positive-minded, innovative, and responsible as they acquire trained career skills. With this vision, the university focuses on life-long learning and development, which is a reflection of the university's core value of "educating with love." The undergraduate programs are in line with "general education, field training, and interdisciplinary innovation." The postgraduate programs are aimed at cultivating innovative, motivated, and productive doctoral candidates in various fields.

Lingnan (University) College at Sun Yat-sen University (The College) is a leading and internationally-recognized business school, upholding the motto promoted by Sen Yat-sen: "Study extensively; Enquire accurately; Reflect carefully; Discriminate clearly; Practise earnestly." Devoted to the internationalization of education and guided by the motto "Education for Service" from Lingnan University, the College provides high-quality economics and management education that draws strength from the liberal arts and tirelessly strives for the advancement of teaching and research of the knowledge of economics and management.

REFERENCES

Becker, J. (2005). Boya jiao yu de nei rong kai fany shi dai [The content of liberal arts Education]. (Yue, Y. Q., & Ying, L. H., Trans.). *Open Times* 2(3): 23–34. http://www.opentimes.cn/bencandy. php?fid=101&aid=1320.

Li, F. C., & Li, L. F. (2013). Meiguo gao xiao gu wu—xue xi: Shen shi yu fan si [Service-learning in American colleges and universities: Investigation and reflection]. *China Academic Journal Electronic Publishing House* 5:43–49.

Tu Wei-ming. (1996). Confucian traditions in East Asian modernity. *Bulletin of the American Academy of Arts and Sciences* 50(2): 12–39.

The Positive Effects of Service-Learning on Overall Quality and Psychological Capital Appreciation of Medical Students

LIANG Yong-feng, LI Yi-ang, and WANG Yu-qing

According to the 2001 United Nations publication *Universal Declaration on Volunteering*, the end of the twentieth century was regarded as the decade of volunteers and civic society, (International Association for Volunteer Effort, 2001) because of an increase in the popularity of volunteer services. In 2001, China also promoted the Volunteer Service Act, classifying voluntary service as a means for fulfilling civic duty. Since this act, however, many youth services, charities, and public services remain fairly basic, simple, and underdeveloped. No evaluation or rating is done to review these services. Too much focus on outcomes has been linked to a decrease in motivation and participation as well as ineffectiveness and unsustainable development of the services being offered (Lan & Xu, 2011). Medical schools are no exception. A call for humanities education for medical professionals surges amidst the common problems facing the medical field today, such as unethical medical practices, declining doctor-patient relationships, collapsing morality, and distorted personal values. It is imperative that improvement is made in the overall quality of medical students. This research, therefore, attempts to verify the feasibility of improving the overall quality and ethics of medical students and demonstrate the positive effects of service-learning on their Psychological Capital Appreciation (PCA).

The Development of Service-Learning and Psychological Capital Appreciation and Their Significance in Improving Medical Students' Overall Quality

Service-learning is a generally accepted, well-developed, and effective learning mode in Western countries. In developed regions, including universities in Hong Kong, it is commonly integrated with community-care education, leadership training, and volunteer services. On the contrary, service-learning research has just begun in China. In the medical context and within this chapter, service-learning is defined as a progressive, step-by-step, and focused medical ethical education that integrates primary medical care services with classroom learning. Breaking away from the traditional classroom teaching, service-learning motivates students to learn medical ethics through active care-giving services, surveys, and professional training. Service-learning is important because it improves medical humanities education and student overall quality. First, it strengthens learning outcomes through innovative approaches that integrate general service with one or more disciplines. Second, with the experiential learning component, service-learning also promotes personal development. Third, it cultivates a sense of responsibility and citizenship, integrating political orientation with civic education (Liang, 2013).

PCA shows that a positive psychological state is gained during personal development, including self-efficacy, optimism, hope, and perseverance, which are defined respectively as: confidence and ability to succeed in the face of adversity, the ability to attribute current and future success to positive causes, persistence and ability to adjust approaches in order to accomplish goals, and the ability to overcome challenges and setbacks in a timely and appropriate manner (Luthans, 2008). Luthans, Avolio, Walumbwa, & Li (2005) claim that society no longer considers the comparative advantages of financial capital, human capital, and social capital, but rather considers the core psychological factor. In other words, Luthans et al. suggest that PCA serves as a significant criterion measuring personal competitiveness. Luthans et al.'s claim is in line with the conclusions of several studies on university students, medical staff, company employees, and rural workers. PCA is found to not only important improve personal competitiveness (Sui, Wang, Yue, & Luthans, 2012; Lu, 2012), but also accurately measure an individual's psychological health. For example, PCA measures negatively associated psychological symptoms, such as anxiety, depression, obsession, antagonism, paranoia, loneliness, decrease in interpersonal networking, and lack of motivation to engage in work and/or study (Zhong, 2007; Zhang, Zhang, & Dong, 2010; Huang, 2011; Li & Zhu, 2011; He & Lu, 2012). As a result, it is highly recommended that a study on antecedents, localization, and the development strategy of PCA is conducted (Ke, Sun & Li, 2009; Chen, Zhao & Liu, 2011). Moreover, it can be concluded that improving the PCA of medical students is important in order to develop their overall quality and core competitiveness. It is thus highly necessary to seek a development strategy for PCA for medical students.

Service-Learning Programs Improve Medical Students' Overall Quality and Psychological Capital Appreciation

The School of Preclinical Medicine at Guangxi Medical University (GXMU) has developed several programs to improve humanities medicine education and students' overall quality. Medical Support for the Poor was one of the Community Service Learning Programs in 2012–2013, which partnered with the National Medical Aid for the Poor project and was funded by Li Ka Shing Foundation at Shantou University, is a prime example of successfully integrating classroom learning, experiential learning, service-learning, and community medical services. This program involves four stages: preparation, practicum, reflection, and evaluation.

Preparation

Teachers and students plan the community medical service-learning program together, outlining the service theme, aim, schedule, venue, and budget. Teachers provide briefing and training sessions on related material, the concept of service-learning, the research plan and practicum, knowledge of common diseases such as hypertension and stroke, interview skills, video editing, safety issues, etc. Training can be in the form of lecture, discussion, role-playing, and/or field practice. As participants, students are also involved in the preparation of identifying community needs, specifying the learning goals and services, rallying support from neighborhood committees and the Party Branch, and attending the training session. This stage is aimed to train students to manage their time efficiently and to adapt to uncertainties. It also provides students an opportunity to learn the importance of self-improvement and their limitations. Additionally, students work with medical professionals, who teach them the primary causes of various health issues, such as lifestyle, heredity, demography, environment, society, economy, psychology, and culture. Students become familiar with how to work with the various parties involved, including recipients of health services and medical departments, in order to promote awareness of health issues. Moreover, students gain research skills to collect data, evaluate materials, and justify assumptions. In general, this program develops students' job values, attitudes, behaviors, and ethics, which are referred to in the general medical education requirement. By participating in this program, students acquire basic medical and health knowledge, as well as communication, critical thinking and research skills. The quality of medical students is further enhanced.

Practicum

The work is divided into different stages of service and assigned to various teams in the practicum. For instance, the charity clinic assistant team, under professional guidance, hands out free medicines, offers physical examinations to the locals and prepares consulting materials for doctors, whereas the promotion team makes posters and banners for lectures and forums on local health issues, such as common diseases, Mediterranean anemia, and sanitary conditions. Students in this program are trained to perceive, collect, and integrate information; understand patients and their relatives through the use of proper communication skills; collaborate with teachers, the community, other departments, and the media; manage medical documents; understand clinical practice; evaluate and analyze patient problems and guide patients to understand the factors affecting health, such as physical condition, mentality, society, and culture; and develop independent learning skills. The program equips students with essential communication skills and clinical skills in line with general medical education requirement and improves the key factors of PCA, including self-efficacy and perseverance.

Reflection

The reflection stage requires students to critically think about their service experiences. After service, medical students discuss and reflect in groups. These discussions and reflective activities include individual and group sharing, reflective essays, video making, research reports, and community talks. Our experience shows that effective reflection must involve the participation of community partners and representatives of the community who benefited from the service. The reflection stage is essential to service-learning, as it positively affects students' attitudes toward the service and the community. Furthermore, reflection provides students with fundamental medical knowledge as well as critical thinking and research skills. It further promotes the other key factors of PCA, such as optimism and hope, which, in turn, improve the overall quality and PCA of medical students.

Evaluation

The evaluation stage aims to assess the effectiveness and overall quality of the community service-learning program and student performance. By having their performance evaluated, students are provided with a better understanding of their quality of service. Several assessments, including a PCA form, a self-evaluation form, a tutor evaluation form, and a community evaluation form, are included in this research. Research outcomes are further accessed in the presentation, broachers, CDs, and poster boards.

The Outcome of Service-Learning on Improving the Overall Quality and Psychological Capital Appreciation of the Medical Students

This research integrates both qualitative and quantitative methods for more effective results and outcomes. It further analyzes the service-learning program discussed above.

In the quantitative analysis, 198 participants were selected from a seven-year clinical program. Participants ranged from year one to year three. Before, all participants' PCA test results were relatively the same. Forty-nine students were grouped into the controlled group, while the other 149 were placed in the experimental group. Participants in the experimental group were required to participate in service-learning at least once. Students were required to attend two rounds of testing after the service as well—one at the end of the service and another two months following, which served as the continuous assessment. The test given was the Positive Psychological Quotient, which was designed by Zhang, Zhang, & Dong(2010) and contains four factors: self-efficacy, perseverance, optimism, and hope. Test results were found to be reliable and valid. The coefficient of internal consistency is over 0.9. The collected data were recorded in EpiDada3.1 and further given a t-test in the statistics software SPSS19.0.

The data indicate the following:

1. The difference in terms of the PCA index, such as self-efficacy, between participants in service-learning and those in the experimental group is significant ($p < 0.05$), meaning that students who engaged in service-learning have higher PCA and PCA-related factors than those who did not engage in service-learning (see Table 1).
2. The higher the expectations of and devotion to service-learning, the greater the improvement on PCA and self-efficacy ($p < 0.05$) (see Table 2).
3. The time of service significantly affects the PCA growth ($p < 0.05$). The more participation or service times, the greater the improvement in each factor. This proves service-learning is effective in improving PCA and its related factors (see Table 3).

Table 1. PCA Comparison between Participants and Others (*t*-test)

| | M ± SD | | | |
	PARTICIPANTS (*n* = 149)	OTHERS (*n* = 49)	*t*	*p*
PCA	3.60 ± 0.50	3.36 ± 0.43	3.020	0.003
Self-efficacy	3.55 ± 0.57	3.30 ± 0.57	2.600	0.010
Perseverance	3.44 ± 0.61	3.22 ± 0.48	2.510	0.014
Hope	3.74 ± 0.63	3.48 ± 0.58	2.479	0.014
Optimism	3.74 ± 0.59	3.47 ± 0.52	2.830	0.005

Table 2. Test on Student Attitudes towards Service-Learning and PCA Factors (*t*-test)

| | M ± SD | | | |
	LOW AND AVERAGE EXPECTATION (*n* = 98)	HIGH EXPECTATION (*n* = 100)	*t*	*p*
PCA	3.39 ± 0.46	3.70 ± 0.49	4.561	0.000
Self-efficacy	3.30 ± 0.61	3.66 ± 0.49	4.518	0.000
Perseverance	3.47 ± 0.49	3.47 ± 0.66	2.174	0.031
Hope	3.50 ± 0.59	3.85 ± 0.60	4.076	0.000
Optimism	3.48 ± 0.56	3.85 ± 0.55	4.618	0.000

Table 3. The Influence of Service Times on PCA

| | M ± SD | | | | |
	ONE TIME (*n* = 31)	TWICE (*n* = 75)	MORE THAN FOUR TIMES (*n* = 41)	*f*	*p*
PCA	3.55 ± 0.41	3.52 ± 0.558	3.78 ± 0.45	3.356	0.038
Self-Efficacy	3.57 ± 0.52	3.47 ± 0.64	3.67 ± 0.46	1.642	0.197
Perseverance	3.34 ± 0.52	3.36 ± 0.65	3.64 ± 0.58	3.187	0.044
Hope	3.68 ± 0.53	3.66 ± 0.67	3.92 ± 0.60	2.462	0.089
Optimism	3.67 ± 0.53	3.67 ± 0.63	3.92 ± 0.52	2.666	0.073

Interviews, student self-evaluation, and open-ended questionnaires were used for qualitative analysis. Service-learning was found to greatly improve public health awareness. The caring services were supported by the neighborhood committee and residents, who wish to continue the program. The School of Preclinical Medicine at GXMU has developed a long-term cooperation with three communities and their respected community hospitals and established a medical service-learning base. Other partners and community hospitals are willing to work with the school continuously as well. Meanwhile, students learned to be responsible and mission-minded. They gained a thought-provoking lesson on medical ethics in volunteer services. The questionnaire evaluating the service-learning in the three communities demonstrates that the participants learned extracurricular and basic medical knowledge, as well as information about doctor-patient relationships. Students improved their adaptability, cooperation ability, presentation skills, and flexibility. They also gained awareness to the importance of medical staff, seeing the need to be responsible in this sacred job. Most students felt that the medical resources in the community were insufficient, including equipment, goods, materials, and medical staff. This program gave students an insight into community medical need. Additionally, students learned team building as well as clinical and communication skills. After the program, a researcher framed this program as "A New Model on Medical Ethics Education through Service-Learning at Guangxi Medicine University" for the Guangxi Universities' Student Summer Social Practicum Competition 2013. This program received the reward for "Best Service Achievement" in the competition for its effective promotion and renovation of youth volunteer services.

Conclusion

It can be concluded that, in practice, support from senior officials is an essential part of a successful program as well as identifying the community who will be served and recruiting experienced mentors and teachers.

From the evidence provided above, it is apparent that the service-learning program "Medical Support for the Poor" is an innovative way to teach humanities in medical education. Furthermore, it is an effective way to promote ethical thought and decision-making among the medical students. This program has served as a model for the National Medical Reform, which aims to "establish greater and more diverse services, finer programs, and better systems" as well as establish "the Quality Medical Staff Scheme." Community service-learning is a mutually beneficial program for both the community receiving the service and the student participants. The students are given the opportunity to greatly improve their Positive Psychological Quotient and self-efficacy, in particular. This program also promotes university students' social responsibility, job commitment, and youth volunteer service. Moreover, not only does the program promote students' overall quality, but it also helps to develop and contribute to a better community.

About the Institution

Guangxi Medical University (GXMU), located in the green city of Nanning, the capital of Guangxi Zhuang Autonomous Region, was founded on December 21, 1934. It is one of the twenty-two oldest medical institutions in China. It is also one of the thirty higher educational institutions in China that offers qualified clinical medicine (English-taught) to international students with the approval of Ministry of Education. As a key university in Guangxi, it is the center of medical education, research, clinical medicine, and preventive medicine. The university consists of twenty-four schools (including eight affiliated teaching hospitals), two teaching departments, and forty research institutes. As a top-level medical institute, GXMU offers undergraduate, postgraduate, and doctoral programs. There are six major disciplines, including medical science, natural science, engineering, literature, management, and law. Students come from twenty-six provinces in China, Hong Kong, Macao, from nineteen other countries, and from a multitude of small regions and municipalities attend GXMU. Today, the university, in conjunction with its students and staff, is striving to be the top regional research-based medical institute that stresses the study of holistic medical approaches.

These approaches are in accordance with the university's tradition of "cultivating talent for local development" and the motto of "Nurturing the Good, Saving the Life."

REFERENCES

Chen, H. Q., Zhao, S. J., & Liu, Z. (2011). Xin li zi ben li lun yan jiu zhan wang [Research and prospect of psychological capital]. *Enterprise Economy* 1:73–75.

He, Z. H., & Lu, Z. H. (2012). Establishing self-check list of college students' employment ability. *Higher Education Forum* 11:123–126.

Huang, W. (2011). *The correlation research between psychological capital and psychological health of college students.* Master's thesis, Guangxi Normal University, Beijing, China.

International Association for Volunteer Effort. (2001). The Universal Declaration on Volunteering. https://www.iave.org/advocacy/the-universal-declaration-on-volunteering/.

Ke, J. L., Sun, J. M., & Li, Y. R. (2009). Psychological capital: Chinese indigenous scale's development and its validity comparison with the Western scale. *Acta Psychologica Sinica* 4(9): 875–888.

Lan, C. F., & Xu, W. M. (2011). *Fu wu—xue xi zai gao deng jiao yu zhong de li lun yu shi jian* [Service-Learning: Theory and practice in higher education]. Hangzhou: Zhejiang University Press.

Li, Y. L., & Zhu, J. H. (2011). Research review of positive psychological capital. *Science and Technology Management Research* 31(8): 210–215.

Liang, Y. F. (2013). Fu wu xue xi yun yong yu ren wen yi xue jiao yu de li lun si kao yu shi jian tan suo [Theoretical thought and implement exploration service-learning in humanistic medicine education]. In Humanistic Management School of Guangxi Medical University, *2012 nian Guangxi ren wen yi xue fa zhan bao gao* [Report of humanistic medicine education development at 2012 Guangxi Medical University], 156–165. Guangxi: Guangxi People's Publishing House.

Lu, Z. H. (2012). *Da xue sheng xin li zi ben yu jiu ye li de xiang guan xing yan jiu* [Correlation between university students' psychological capital and employability]. Master's thesis, Guangxi Normal University, Beijing, China.

Luthans, F. (2008). *Psychological Capital.* (Li, C. P., Trans.). Beijing: China Light Industry Press.

Luthans, F., Avolio, B. J., Walumbwa, F. O., & Li, W. (2005). The psychological capital of Chinese workers: Exploring the relationship with performance. *Management and Organization Review* 1(2): 247–271.

Sui, Y., Wang, H., Yue, Y. N., & Luthans, F. (2012). The effect of transformational leadership on follower performance and satisfaction: The mediating role of psychological capital and the moderating role of procedural justice. *Acta Psychologica Sinica* 44(9): 1217–1230.

Zhang, K., Zhang, S., & Dong, Y. (2010). Positive psychological capital: Measurement and relationship with mental health. *Studies of Psychology and Behavior* 8(1): 58–64.

Zhong, L. (2007). Effects of psychological capital on employees' job performance, organizational commitment, and organizational citizenship behavior. *Acta Psychologica Sinica* 39(2): 328–334.

Philanthropy Courses: A Study of How to Develop Students' Social Responsibility

CAI Ying-hui

The *Outline of China's National Plan for Medium and Long-Term Education Reform and Development (2010–2020)* aims to improve students' social responsibility, encourage them to serve the community, and strengthen ideological and moral education for nonage and university students (MOE, 2010). As a result of this *Outline*, fostering university students' social responsibility has become a primary goal of higher education in China. Colleges and universities, which serve as arenas for nurturing responsible and skilled adults, play an important role of fulfilling the overall aim of the *Outline*. Service-learning, which integrates service and knowledge, can therefore serve as an effective approach to achieve this goal. Through service-learning experiences, students are motivated to care for the community, explore community needs, and use their skills to contribute the community. Moreover, students are given the chance to practice their knowledge and skills learned in the classroom in real-world situations. By participating in this process, students are exposed to emotional conflicts and learn the importance of social responsibility. They are asked to reflect on their experiences during the service-learning project as well as after the project so as to better understand the essence of the course, the subject, and the community.

Service-learning stresses student engagement in accordance with the idea "Serving to learn, Learning to serve," and fosters students' social responsibility and commitment to their community. Service-learning, in terms of its intended outcomes, is very similar to the aim of the *Outline*. As a result, service-learning can be used as an effective method for achieving the desired outcomes of the *Outline*. This article attempts to study the relationship between service-learning and students' social responsibility.

Problems: Lack of Social Responsibility Education for University Students

Currently, social responsibility education at the university level in China has failed to meet the public's expectation. This, in effect, is a result of there being numerous problems in the course curriculum of universities. Firstly, civic education is almost nonexistent in most colleges and universities; rather, there are only courses that focus on political ideology (i.e., Maxims, Mao's and Deng's Thoughts). These courses value political orientation but largely neglect the fundamental aspects of civic education.

Secondly, the courses offered are merely knowledge-oriented and tend to neglect moral education. Social responsibility is a sense of morality, manifested in different stages: recognition, sensation, and action. In fact, even people who fully understand what social responsibility means do not necessarily understand that they are responsible for their community. Habitually littering and spitting in public places, commonly described as unacceptable behaviors, are prime examples. Recognition is the prerequisite of sensation, but recognition does not ensure responsible behavior.

Thirdly, traditional classroom learning environments, where students passively sit in their seats, absorbing knowledge from the teacher, remains a major teaching mode of moral education in China. This teaching method relies primarily on exams to assess students' performance and places little to no emphasis on active learning and students' self-reflection. John Dewey (1990) declared that "[e]ducation is a social process; education is growth; education is not preparation for life but is life itself." In accordance with Dewey, students should learn social responsibility through experiences, which "are the most effective way of learning" (Lan & Xu, 2011, 55).

Fourthly, the service practicum of many colleges and universities does very little to improve students' social responsibility. The service practicum is often seen as an optional component and unorganized extension of classroom teaching. In addition, social service activity tends to be student-led, meaning only a few students partake in the experience and little recognition is given to its importance. As a result, service practicums have become a mere formality in China, therefore failing in their approach and aim (Yuan, 2010).

Reviewing teaching methods in China is essential to improve moral teaching and figure out university teaching outcomes. Additionally, new approaches need to be developed that integrate purpose and content in the areas of course planning, activity organization, program implementation, and valuation. In the United States, service-learning has become a popular method to align purpose and content within the classroom. Since the 1980s, service-learning in the United States has gained a reputation for bridging the gap between teaching aims and methods, as well as linking both the aims and methods to the overall classroom content.

Philanthropy Courses at Shantou University: Social Practicum for Social Responsibility Education

With the goal of creating a quality undergraduate education program, Shantou University has offered philanthropy courses based on the concept of service-learning since June 2010. The courses integrate teaching with services in the community; students learn how to be responsible for jobs and apply classroom learning to service in the community. The courses aim to develop students' social responsibility, civic awareness, and benevolence, and promote philanthropy. After three years, the university has developed a comprehensive philanthropy course curriculum, in accordance with the course development policy. The course involves the following primary stages: course application; approval; teaching staff selection and training; teacher course registration; student course registration; course implementation (including service-learning, training, practicum, report-back presentation, and sharing sessions); course evaluation and report; and sharing of service-learning experiences to various stakeholders.

Main Purpose: To Foster Students' Social Responsibility

The aim of the philanthropy course is to help students understand the society, care for the community, and enhance their social responsibility and commitment to the community. By engaging students in an academic course, students are able to apply and reflect on what they have learned in the classroom for their practicum. This will not only enhance students' skills and knowledge, but also create a successful service-learning showcase for others. Since 2007, Shantou University has implemented a system to develop young leaders. Today, this system is highly advanced (Wang, Ma & Chen, 2011). The philanthropy courses fulfill half of the eighteen goals outlined in the system. These goals for students include: develop a sense of social responsibility and commitment to the community; instill the right values and positive outlook on life; promote values such as tolerance, integrity, responsibility, and care; respect public morality; develop a practical and realistic mind; aspire after truth; foster devoted and trustworthy employees; promote environment awareness and activities; foster leadership and organizing capacity; and improve problem-solving skills through critical thinking. Philanthropy courses prioritize the aim to instill a sense of social responsibility in university students. According to course evaluations, all of the aims above have been met, thus demonstrating the effectiveness of philanthropy courses.

Course Design: To Emphasize Community Needs

The philanthropy courses based on the concept of service-learning aim to develop university students' social responsibility. The university offered sixty-one different philanthropy courses during the 2013 summer term. There were 3,191 registered students, 338 course instructors, and nearly 80 community partners involved in these courses. The services practicum included voluntary teaching, medical exams, public facility maintenance, health promotion in the rural areas, environment protection, community social work, women's development, life coaching, and other activities helping those who are less fortunate. Project titles were as follows: "The Dawn Educational Assistance Program," "Caring Service at Kangfu Village," "Service-Learning on Women and Creativity in Chaoshan," "Caring Project for Children with Cerebral Palsy," "Health Promotion Project in a Rural Area," "Creativity Workshop for Love," "The Color of Life," "The Sunny Classroom for Children of Migrant Workers," "Service and Research in Primary Education in the Mountainous Area in Chaozhou," "Caring Service at Xinhuo Village," "Sanxiaxiang Service," "Our Common Future: Volunteer Services for Environmental Education at Primary School in Shantou," and the "Sunny Project: Service and Research in Criminal Rehab Project in Chaoshan." These services catered to the community in Shaoshan and even extended to the neighboring villages, towns, primary and middle schools, and nursing homes. The philanthropy courses, therefore, serve as an important bridge between institutions of higher education and the community, promoting a mutually beneficial exchange of ideas, practices, and resources.

Philanthropy courses are problem oriented and interdisciplinary. To better achieve learning outcomes outlined in course syllabi, consideration must be given not only to content, but also the specific needs of the local community. Students and teachers from various fields in the program provide for a diverse learning experience. Students are guided to engage in solving realistic problems that contribute to community development. By encouraging students to use their specific knowledge and skills, teachers are able to aid students in better serving the community. Philanthropy courses differ from traditional teaching in terms of their course outline, since the teaching method used in philanthropy courses promotes students taking an active role in solving realistic problems. The traditional learning method focuses on knowledge structure, whereas the service experiences in philanthropy courses enable students to apply their learning from class to practical situations. Students are also encouraged to care for the community while, at the same time, understanding the importance of quality service and helping to improve the service quality in the community. From the information above, it is evident that philanthropy courses have improved students' civic awareness and social responsibility.

Course Implementation: To Strengthen the Students' Sense of Social Responsibility

Philanthropy courses are required general education courses at Shantou University. Each course is offered on a forty-eight-hour basis for one credit, involving four learning stages: service knowledge training, community survey and planning, practicum, and sharing.

Teachers are required to propose a course outline before the start of the course. The theoretical study is comprised of a lecture and an experience sharing. With the teacher's guidance, students from different majors are grouped together and asked to discuss, based on their specific knowledge, a service plan for a field trip in their community. This stage gives students insight into community issues, problems, and needs. In addition, students undergo training sessions to improve their communication skills, cooperation skills, and creativity, all of which are skills that will be vital during the community survey stage. Through the community survey, students are able to gain self-awareness and an understanding of community needs. As the students engage in the community, they are given the opportunity to learn more about society and the importance of social responsibility.

The main component of philanthropy courses is the service to the community. Philanthropy courses are an example of experiential learning, a practice of Dewey's conception that "education is life itself" and "the society is the school," where study, service in the community, and life are integrated. These types of courses extend beyond the traditional learning mode: students not only engage in classroom learning, but also are involved in service to the community. Students, in effect, play a significant and active role, while teachers provide the inspiration and guidance, fostering students' creativity and social responsibility.

The last part of the program is reflection and sharing. During class, students are asked to share their ideas and express their learning in the service with photos, videos, presentations, reports, and other creative methods. Reflection is an important element throughout the service-learning experience as one of the essential approaches to study. Students need to identify the problems in the community, juxtaposed with knowledge and experience. Then, students can enhance their critical thinking and problem-solving skills through service-learning (Feng, 2007). This reflective method is aimed at helping students uncover the root causes of society's issues. It helps students discover practical solutions to complex problems. Reflection not only improves students' critical thinking and problem-solving skills, but also enhances their self-understanding. In the reflective process, students learn to improve their understanding of subject-related knowledge, community needs, and how to care for others. This, in turn, strengthens their social responsibility and commitment to the community.

Course Evaluation: To Improve Students' Social Responsibility

The course evaluation is aimed at assessing the curriculum's implementation and its overall outcomes. The university has developed a comprehensive evaluation system, consisting of four different aspects: teachers-to-student evaluations, student-to-teacher evaluations, student self-evaluations, and partner satisfaction assessments. These evaluations are conducted at the end of each term. They demonstrate that each aspect has greatly improved over time and philanthropy courses have also achieved their specific goals in the last three years.

There are three components used in the teacher-to-student evaluation: course research (20%), practice process (50%), and course summary (30%). For this evaluation, the average assessment score from teachers to students was over 87. Teachers indicated that students achieved the learning goal of philanthropy course, such as developing a sense of social responsibility and a devotion to their work.

The student self-evaluation, with an average score over 87, showed a similar outcome. The score for "social service awareness and caring for others" was 95.29, followed by 94.42 for "unselfish devotion" and 94.38 for "social order compliancy and public morality." These results show that, after the philanthropy course, students witnessed their self-improvement, especially in terms of understanding society, solicitude for the community, social services skills, social responsibility, critical thinking, and problem-solving skills.

In addition to the course evaluations, Shantou University invited students from philanthropy courses and volunteer services to partake in a survey in March 2012 in order to enhance the quality and design of the philanthropy courses. From the survey, it was determined that philanthropy courses proved to be more effective in promoting students' social responsibility than volunteer services and better than volunteer services in improving overall qualities in students, especially in terms of knowledge learning, ideology and morality, organization and coordination skills, social competence, problem-solving skills and research skills, and adaptability (Cai & Zhou, 2012). "Ideology and morality" refers to social responsibility and devotion to the community.

In short, universities and colleges generally have failed to foster a sense of social responsibility in students and thus needs to explore new paths in theories and practices with respect to addressing this issue. Philanthropy courses offered by Shantou University, however, undoubtedly demonstrate an effective practice and teaching model.

Additional Remarks: About the Institution

Shantou University, located in Shantou City in the Guangdong province, is a comprehensive university under the 211 national education projects approved by the National Congress. This public university, partly funded by the Ministry of Education and the Guangdong province, is the first and the only institute in the world that is funded by a private foundation: Li Ka Shing Foundation.

Thanks to the Li Ka Shing Foundation, the university has borrowed management and experience from well-recognized universities in the west and introduced quality teaching resources from overseas. The university has established its unique characteristics as an international school with refined educational ideals. Today, Shantou University is a modern, international higher education institution advancing in school management, teaching resources, and educating skilled and talented students.

As a pilot independent university under "Comprehensive Education Reform in Guangdong," the university offers advanced undergraduate programs and adaptable curricula. Now it has developed a new model for educating skilled and talented students, characterized by resource integration and whole-person education, graduates are expected to be equipped with cultural understanding, acute discernment, creative minds, social commitment, sportsmanship, and leadership in the face of the ever-changing demands of a sophisticated economy. The program provides better access to a lifelong learning experiences. The university has eight full-time undergraduate departments in arts, science, engineering, law, business, medicine, Changjiang news and media, and Changjiang arts and design, and it has a post-graduate college, a lifelong education college, and four residential colleges.

REFERENCES

Cai, Y. H., & Zhou, Y. H. (2012). Da xue sheng gong yi huo dong yu gong yi ke cheng yu ren xiao huo yu ren xiao guo de shi zheng bi jiao [Compare the effectiveness between students' experience on voluntary service and public service course]. *Education and Examination* 5: 70–73.

Dewey, J. (1990). *Democracy and education* (Wang, C. X., Trans.). Beijing: People's Education Press.

Eyler, J., & Giles, D. E., Jr. (1999). *Where's the learning in service-learning?* San Francisco: Jossey-Bass.

Feng, J. X. (2007). *Meiguo gao xiao gong min jiao yu zhong de fu wu xing xue xi yan jiu* [Research on service-learning as civic education in American higher institutions]. (Master's thesis). Huazhong University of Science and Technology, Hubei, China.

Lan, C. F., & Xu, W. M. (2011). *Fu wu—xue xi zai gao deng jiao yu zhong de li lun yu shi jian* [Service-learning: Theory and practice in higher education]. Hangzhou: Zhejiang University Press.

Ministry of Education of the People's Republic of China (MOE). (2010). *Guo jia zhong chang qi jiao yu gai ge he fa zhan gui hua gang yao (2010–2020 nian)* [Outline of China's national plan for medium and long-term education reform and development (2010–2020)]. http://www.edu.cn/zong_he_870/20100730/t20100730_501910.shtml.

Wang, W., Ma, F., & Chen, X. (2011). On the top-level design of talent cultivation mode and the construction of objective platform. *Educational Research* 2(58): 58–63, 76.

Yuan, J. X. (2010). Da xue sheng she hui shi jian yu ren gong neng de pian shi yu kuang zheng [Educational function deviation and rectification on students' social engagement]. *Modern Education Science* 4: 120–122.

Exemplary Practices

Sun Yat-sen University Lingnan (University) College: Service-Learning Project in the Taxation Management Course

LONG Zhao-hui and JIANG Ping

Taxation is the main method for national finance-revenue. In China, taxation is mandatory, relatively fixed, and classified as free property, meaning that taxation revenue does not need to be returned back to taxpayers. Taxation not only collects financial revenue, but also has the function of adjusting the economy and supervising and managing national financial affairs. Taxation acts as a primary resource for coordinating the varying interests among governmental entities, organizations, and individuals. It is also an important strategy for managing national macroeconomics and plays an important role in business micro financial management. Since the Tax Reform in 1994, there has been tax evasion by the government and a detrimental tax flow. The presence of tax evasion in China has brought many challenges to universities, teaching courses in taxation management. The research of Ming & Ma (2012) shows that tax dodging and tax evasion are common in China among 50% of state-owned enterprises, 60% of township and foreign enterprises, 80% of private enterprises, and 95% of individuals. This tax evasion of taxpayers results in a large amount of negative tax flow in China each year. In fact, the rate of tax flow dropped by 57% in 1995 and approximately 20% in 2015.

Tax evasion severely threatens the economic construction of the Chinese market. It decreases the national financial revenue which, in turn, weakens the ability of the government to provide public services; it is unfavorable for the government in terms of carrying out macro-economic control, such as adjusting revenue allocation; it increases the costs of taxes and the tax levy for enterprises and taxed administrative organizations, respectively; it distorts enterprises' financial message, which ultimately affects the economic decisions made by enterprises; it leads to an unfair tax burden, which does align with the market principle of fair competition. Furthermore, tax evasion may negatively affect the credibility of enterprises in other markets as a result of "mob mentality." For instance, before the breakout of the Sanlu milk powder contamination incident, there was a report in March 2006 about a tax-dodging case involving Anhui Huaibei Sanlu Group Co., Ltd. University courses teaching taxation uphold important missions: to cultivate professionals working in taxation services; raise public awareness of taxation knowledge; and promote the construction of an exemplary tax administration and practice in China.

Sun Yat-sen University Lingnan (University) College is located in Guangdong, China. Guangdong's tax administrative organization follows the tax administrative affair's principle—to finance the nation and enforce public law. In Guangdong, taxation has resulted in beneficial outcomes for the province as well as the nation. Not only does it provide an opportunity for the steady growth of national financial revenue, it also supports economic and social developments in Guangdong. However, large-scale tax fraud cases on exported goods, occurring in Chaoshan in 2000 and later in Guandong, aroused national attention to issues of tax dodging in China. The cases of tax dodging in Guangdong were different than the cases which occurred in Chaoshan. In Guangdong, many foreign enterprises passed international transfer pricing regulations and transferred their profits to outside parties. By doing so, these foreign enterprises engaged in what is known as "pretending a loss," which enabled them to hide their profit and avoid taxation (Long, 2008). Public awareness of these cases dramatically affected Guangdong's reputation, specifically in terms of its taxation education.

China's numerous tax-evasion cases and inadequate practices for collecting and paying taxes directly affect the teaching of taxation at the university level. Furthermore, taxation issues directly impact the mindset, career planning, and growth of Chinese university students, especially those majoring in public finance. Under the current external taxation environment, Sun Yat-sen University (SYSU) believes that the Department of Finance must integrate classroom teaching and practical education as well as professional teaching and moral education when teaching taxation courses at the university (Long, 2012). In effect, SYSU actively proceeded to explore and implement such practices within the university's taxation course. The integration of classroom teaching with practical education, as well as professional teaching with moral education, within the course "Taxation Management" has been successfully executed. In 2008, the course was awarded first place in SYSU Excellent Teaching Achievement. Additionally, in 2009, as a result of its research on the exploration of "double integration," the course was recognized for engaging in SYSU Research on Reaching Reform.

Service-learning originated from the Western education system and was introduced to Southeast Asia in the beginning of the twenty-first century. Lingnan University in Hong Kong upholds the motto, "Education for Service." In order to embody the university's motto, Lingnan University implemented a Service-Learning and Research Scheme in 2004 and established the Office of Service-Learning (OSL) in 2006. Lingnan University, in effect, became the pioneer of service-learning in Eastern societies and the first university to set up an OSL in Hong Kong (Chan, Lee & Ma, 2009). In September 2012, SYSU was invited by the OSL to join a "Faculty Service-Learning Training Workshop." Through this workshop, SYSU gained awareness of the impacts that can result when service-learning is introduced into taxation teaching. Firstly, service-learning aligns with the international method for advancing education. Secondly, it helps to combat taxation problems within the Chinese society. Thirdly, it aids in cultivating professionals in taxation services. Lastly, service-learning helps to reform the way in which taxation is taught in SYSU.

The Planning Stage of the Service-Learning Project in the Taxation Management Course

For many years, China has promoted the saying, "put what you've learned into practice." Today, this saying has become one of the important teaching principles in higher education. The teaching of taxation courses must be integrated with practical education experiences to give university students the chance to use their professional taxation knowledge in order to positively impact the community (Long, 1998). Service-learning provides the opportunity for education to do what it should do. The Taxation Management course's service-learning project at SYSU encourages students majoring in public finance and taxation to use their classroom knowledge to bring about the betterment of the society. Students engage in self-reflection to make connections between the service and their academic knowledge. As a result, students are given the chance to improve their presentation, communication, and critical thinking skills. In 2013, with the support of the OSL, SYSU integrated service-learning into the Taxation Management course. It combined the concepts of "Taxation Management and Tax-Information System," "Tax-Checking," and "Tax-Planning" and allowed students to gain an awareness and understanding of the Guangdong community, as well as use their knowledge of taxation to help those who need to provide tax information to the government.

Developing harmonious taxation is essential to maintain national economic development and social stability. However, since the tax system of China is complicated, many citizens are unaware of the nation's taxation practices. Strengthening the promotion of taxation and the public's awareness of taxation practices are essential to developing quality taxation in China. Although the Taxation Bureau continues to carry out the function of "Taxation Promotion Month," citizen's participation still could be done better.

The reasons for integrating service-learning into the taxation course are to increase citizens' awareness of taxation practices and popularize the National Tax Law through taxation promotion and various tax-payment consultations. From the university's standpoint, the service-learning project helps students deepen their professional knowledge and strengthen their commitment to serve the society. From the students' perspective, the project helps them acknowledge how classroom teaching relates to real-world situations. Service-learning can encourage students to apply their professional knowledge to serve the society in the future. Students are also given the opportunities to cultivate independent thought and enhance their communication skills.

The Preparation Stage of the Service-Learning Project in the Taxation Management Course

Connect with Guangzhou Tax-Payment Organizations and Gain Their Support

From the beginning, the university sought to establish a relationship with the Guangzhou Municipal Office, State Administration of Taxation, and Local Taxation Bureau in order to gain the support of tax organizations. With networks from Lingnan (University) College, students are placed in practicums within the Taxation Bureau to understand its business procedures and the nation's taxation policy and law. Students acquire practical knowledge from the Bureau which is beneficial for their future job in taxation promotion and consultation. Professionals of the Taxation Bureau are also invited to the university to train students about the reporting process of taxes, the procedures of social and health insurance, the interpretations of the latest taxation policy, and questions frequently asked by taxpayers. Students also participate in regular taxation promotion events, which are organized by the Taxation Bureau. All in all, the Taxation Bureau provides students with valuable experiences and knowledge, which ultimately lay the foundation of the project's promotion and consultation work.

Learning Service Knowledge in a Community Service Center

Other than working in the Taxation Bureau, students also get a chance to learn from the community service center. Guangzhou Liwan District Caihong Sub-District Community Service Center has an abundance of community services which have been praised by the main leaders of both Guangdong and Guangzhou. Students participating in the project visit and participate in the activities at the community service center and establish a university–community partnership. Through this partnership, students acquire knowledge about the community needs and further think of how they can address the needs from their project. This partnership acts as a foundational stage to start the project implementation and has become the key factor of success.

The Start of the Service-Learning Project in the Taxation Management Course

To ensure the quality of the service-learning project in the Taxation Management course, a project team, guided by the course instructors and managed by postgraduate assistants and course members, was set up to launch and monitor the progress of the service-learning activities. Service-learning activities include promoting tax law, enhancing public taxation knowledge, making contributions to national taxation work, engaging in tax law consultations, and answering taxpayers' questions.

From January 24 to February 22, 2013, the project team helped five students receive practicum opportunities to work at the Guangzhou Haizhu District Taxation Bureau. Through their practicum experiences at the Tax Customer Service Center, students gained an understanding of tax payment services and methods. These five students later became the spark that initiated the beginning phase of the service-learning project.

By March of 2013, the university began cooperating with the volunteer associations of SYSU. Xiguan House, situated in the North Gate Square of SYSU, was the location for the project's activities. The location of Xiguan House was ideal for the project because it was near the student residences and surrounding community where the students would do public taxation promotion and consultations. Eighty-seven students were divided into twelve groups at the Xiguan House for distributing taxation leaflets, provided by the Taxation Bureau, to local residents. Students provided support to local residents and answered their questions related to taxation. In general, the students were responsible for two tasks: (1) tax law promotion (students distributed taxation leaflets to the taxpayers to promote taxation-related laws and policies and explain any changes made to these laws or polices); and (2) tax payment consultation (students provided support for taxpayers facing difficulties and answered residents' questions about taxation policy, application procedures, etc.). These practices helped increase residents' understanding of taxation related to policy and application procedures and also enabled students to enhance their interpersonal and communication skills.

From July 1 to August 31, 2013, the project team arranged for twenty students to do practicums at the Guangzhou Taxation Bureau. In addition to their service-learning activities, these students were able to learn from the experience of the Taxation Bureau staff members. Students were able to receive helpful tips for handling tax administrative work at the Taxation Bureau, which enhanced their ability to serve the local residents.

The service-learning project in the Taxation Management course was highly supported by the Guangzhou Municipal Office, State Administration of Taxation, and Local Taxation Bureau. These tax organizations provided taxation information for the project and also provided trainings for students about tax law and taxation services. As a result, students were better prepared to perform in the service-learning practicums efficiently and professionally. Furthermore, the partnership with the Guangzhou Liwan District Caihong Sub-District Community Service Center enabled students to have a support system when they faced obstacles or challenges during their service. The tax organizations, in addition to the Guangzhou Liwan District Caihong Sub-District Community Service Center, helped to ensure that the initial stage of the project ran smoothly and successfully.

The Achievements of the Service-Learning Project n the Taxation Management Course

Student Outcomes as a Result of Participating in the Project

In general, students believe that the service-learning project in the Taxation Management course at Sun Yat-sen University Lingnan (University) College is an ideal platform to learn and practice classroom knowledge. During the process of the 2013 project, students communicated with residents to enhance their understanding and answer their questions about taxation. The project helped students increase their professional knowledge and communication skills. Furthermore, the project enabled students to engage in applied learning experiences, in which the community became a classroom learning environment. The practicum in the Taxation Bureau provided students an opportunity to integrate theory and practice. Not only did the practicum enhance students' taxation knowledge, but students were also given the chance to understand the affairs and procedures of tax payment services. During the practicums and services, students were able to discover existing problems in the relationship between collecting and paying taxes. Also, students were made aware of how many residents are misinformed about national taxation policy and law, along with the procedures of the Taxation Bureau. As students became aware of these core problems, they were able to recognize the value and importance of their promotion and consultation work. Students even showed an interest in wanting to create changes in China's taxation policy and law to make the policy, law, and the process of tax payment more transparent.

Students were praised by the residents for their activities and service. Many residents were interested in receiving the taxation leaflet. A man in his sixties expressed that "even though his work does not relate to taxation, [he], as a local resident, still must learn about it." This statement demonstrates residents' eagerness and willingness to learn about taxation and that there is hope in terms of solving the existing disequilibrium between collecting and paying taxes. Through the services provided by students, residents gained knowledge and awareness to taxation policies and practices. Furthermore, as a result of the service-learning project, residents wanted to take action to contribute to the nation and create a more harmonious and effective national taxation system.

Problems during the Project

Although the overall service-learning project in the 2013 Taxation Management course was a success, there were a number of obstacles and challenges that needed to be addressed in different stages of the project. As a result of their lack of prior applied learning experiences, students had a limited understanding of the professional knowledge and practice of taxation in a real-world context. In effect, students faced a multitude of difficulties during the initial stages of the project.

THE SERVING ABILITY OF THE STUDENTS MUST BE ENHANCED

Year three students at Sun Yat-sen University Lingnan (University) College who majored in public finance and taxation were the members of the student project team. While students were knowledgeable about taxation management, they lacked practical experience and didn't know how to apply what they had learned to reality. Moreover, since taxation policies and laws constantly change, students sometimes had difficulty answering the questions raised by taxpayers.

LACK OF AN EFFECTIVE FEEDBACK MECHANISM

Since students were divided into groups during the services, some groups were able to provide clear information and high-quality service. Lack of communication among groups caused additional problems in terms of ensuring consistent service quality.

LOCATION

While the service locations were close to the surrounding community, their locations were not convenient for attracting residents with the greatest need for tax payment information and consultation services. Since the North Gate Square of SYSU is a tourist attraction, many neighboring residents and tourists used this service site instead. While the project was a success, it would have been more beneficial for the community if the services were provided for residents who are in urgent need of having more taxation information and consultation.

MANAGEMENT OF STUDENTS

Since year three students have busy academic schedules, it was difficult to arrange their service times. As a result, unnecessary challenges and scheduling conflicts (e.g. time management) often occurred, which could have been avoided if there was better project coordination among students.

INADEQUATE PROMOTION

Promotion could have been improved. In the initial stage, the project used Xiguan House as a core location for regular services. As this was the only service site used in the initial stage, the project's promotion lagged behind. If promotion at other service sites had started earlier, the project could have been more effective and the promotion as well as services could have reached a larger audience. Additionally, the students' limited serving time and inadequate experience in applied learning settings also made it difficult to develop the project in a larger scale.

Suggestions to Improve the Service-Learning Project in the Taxation Management Course

Enhance the Professional Training for Students

Additional trainings can be given to students to enhance their professional knowledge of taxation and allow them to practice their consultation and communication skills. These trainings can be provided by experienced workers from the Taxation Bureau and/or its student association. By participating in these trainings, students will be able to practice answering the frequently asked questions of residents. For example, residents often ask about the application procedure for tax payment and social insurance and health insurance as well as current taxation policies and laws.

Develop a Feedback Mechanism and Sharing Platform

A system can be used to record unanswered questions and students' service experiences. It can be shared as a diary, so that students can discuss and share their problems and difficulties faced during service-learning practicum. At the same time, course instructors and staff from the Taxation Bureau can be invited to join the sharing platform and provide advice to students on how to overcome the difficulties they faced.

Seek Community Engagement

Selecting an appropriate organization for partnership is essential for ensuring a successful project. If students are given the chance to visit different organizations before the start of the project, they can choose organizations that best fit their needs in terms of location and hours of operation. Even more, it would have been beneficial for students to work with an organization that would have enabled them to also have a booth on the street, so that the students could have interacted with pedestrians.

Enhance the Management of Student Groups

At the moment, a written report summarizing students' practicum and achievements is the main assessment of students' service-learning projects. This type of assessment, however, is very limited and does not take into account students' time management, attendance, and individual ability to provide support for residents. In order to ensure students' engagement in quality service, it is imperative to include this type of feedback in future assessments.

Cooperate with Other Universities

In order to increase the promotion of the activity and the development of the service-learning project, it would be highly beneficial for students to collaborate with other universities. During the 4th Asia-Pacific Regional Conference on Service-Learning, teachers from other universities such as Jinan University showed an interest in this type of service-learning project. Jinan University even went to visit the Xiguan House and interacted with the students from SYSU. This was an opportunity for cooperation. In the future, Sun Yat-sen University Lingnan (University) College will further develop this project to service areas such as Guangzhou and cooperate with other universities to promote the development of this project. By collaborating with other universities, SYSU hopes to play a vital role in helping China become a model for effective taxation management and practice.

"There is still a long way to go for searching the truth, but I will try my best to find the truth and explore it." The Sun Yat-sen University Lingnan (University) College Taxation Management course's service-learning project can serve as a model for an education platform. It is not only an example of an innovative teaching and learning approach, but also demonstrates a sustainable method for integrating theory and practice. Taxation service-learning is not a normal activity, for the project goes beyond the scope of public welfare and provides students the opportunity to also serve the local community, contribute to the betterment of society, engage in a reflective learning process, and gain awareness to the practical use and value of taxation. Even more, students are able to acquire communication and critical thinking skills, which will undoubtedly help them in their professional careers and also enable them to enhance the overall quality of the project itself. In addition to the students, local residents and tourists are also beneficiaries of the project, as students provide information and consultations to them when needed. When it comes to the future, SYSU is optimistic about inheriting the Lingnan sprit to "serve the community" and further develop service-learning projects, which promote awareness of taxation knowledge and access to consultation platforms in China.

About the Institution

SYSU, founded by Dr. Sun Yat-sen, is a comprehensive multi-disciplinary university with over a 100-year history. It is a key university under the Chinese National Higher Education Project. The university is comprised of "a community of teachers and students," through which "teachers represent the school body," and embrace the idea of "educating with love." The aim of SYSU is to nurture high-quality, interdisciplinary students who possess international perspectives, a sense of social responsibility, and an innovative spirit. Graduates are expected to be well-mannered, honest, diligent, positive-minded, innovative, and responsible as they acquire trained career skills. With this vision, the university focuses on life-long learning and development, which is a reflection of the university's core value of "educating with love." The undergraduate programs are in line with "general education, field training, and interdisciplinary innovation." The postgraduate programs are aimed at cultivating innovative, motivated, and productive doctoral candidates in various fields.

Lingnan (University) College at SYSU is a leading and internationally-recognized business school, upholding the motto promoted by Dr. Sen Yat-sen: "Study extensively; Enquire accurately;

Reflect carefully; Discriminate clearly; Practise earnestly." Devoted to the internationalization of education and guided by the motto "Education for Service" from Lingnan University, the College provides high quality economics and management education that draws strength from the liberal arts and tirelessly strives for the advancement of teaching and research of the knowledge of economics and management.

About the Department

Established in 1994, the Department of Public Finance and Taxation in Sun Yat-sen University Lingnan (University) College was one of the first undergraduate programs and master's degree providers in public finance among China's tertiary institutions. It has trained more than 3,000 students at different levels for twenty years. In 2005, the undergraduate program of public finance, offered by the Department, was honored as the Most Selective Program of Guangdong Province.

About the Course

"Taxation Management and Tax Information System" (previously referred to as "Taxation Management" when information was collected for this article) is an important course in the Department of Public Finance. Through the course, students understand the system of taxation management and the framework of the taxation management system, taxation affairs, and tax collection and management, along with basic tax law knowledge. Course instructors use the China Taxation Administration Information System (CTAIS) system to teach the operation of the taxation management software and provide students instructions on tax promotion as well as advice on how to deal with challenges faced by many professionals in the field.

"Taxation Management and Tax Information System" is an elective course. The course instructor places importance on teaching students how to integrate academic knowledge with their taxation promotion and consultation work (the service-learning project). The service-learning project provides an ideal learning environment for students to use the knowledge learned in the classroom to benefit the community. Since the service-learning project allows students to understand the practical use of taxation management, the project itself is an important assessment of the course. By engaging in such a project, students are given the chance to raise public awareness and access to taxation information and at the same time gain professional experience in their related field of study.

REFERENCES

Chan, C. M. Lee, K. M., & Ma, H. K. (2009). Service-learning model at Lingnan University: Development strategies and outcome assessment. *New Horizons in Education* 57(3): 57–73.

Long, Z. H. (1998). A tentative analysis of the contents, significance and approaches in practice education at higher education institutions. *Journal of Sun Yat-sen University* S1:219–222.

———. (2008). *Guang dong wai zi qi ye ying hui yan jiu—fen zi kuang jia shu ju, mo xing yu an li* [Guangdong foreign enterprise breakeven study—analysis framework, data, models and case]. Guangzhou: Guangdong Education Publishing House.

———. (2012). Wo guo gao xiao shui shou lei ke cheng jiao xue mo shi gai ge tan xi [Investigate the reform of national universities' teaching model in taxation course]. In Sun Yat-sen University Teaching Affairs Office, *Jiao xue yan jiu yu shi jian—jiao shi lun wen ji* [Teaching and learning research and practice–teachers proceedings]. Guangzhou: Sun Yat-sen University Press.

Ming, J., & Ma, S. L. (July 18, 2002). Ge shui shui ji kuo da you li gong xin ceng. Fu ren mei li you bu jiao ge shui [The enlargement of personal tax base is beneficial to the salaried people. It is unreasonable for the rich not to pay the personal tax]. *International Finance News.*

Waste Separation and Engaging in Civic Education: Waste Management Project Conducted by South China University of Technology

Lily QI Li-li and ZI Yan-fei

Waste has become a prevalent issue in Chinese society. The story of "garbage siege" is well-known and often discussed in Mainland China. Waste separation has become a main concern in terms of addressing many of China's environmental problems. A well-planned waste separation system, found in more developed countries and areas, has positive impacts on waste management, recycling, and environmental sustainability. A well-managed and well-planned waste separation system in China would help to decrease the cost of waste management and also further promote public awareness of environmental issues (CCIDnet, 2010).

Guangzhou is the only city in China to experiment with a waste separation system. Since 2011, the local government, environmental organizations, and residents of Guangzhou have taken action to promote and engage in waste separation (Long, 2009). Furthermore, a service-learning project concerning the issue of waste management was conducted in Guangzhou's Higher Education Mega Center from December 2012 to July 2013.

Designing the Service-Learning Project: Learning Goals and Service Outcomes

The service-learning project was entitled "The Participation and Learning of Waste Separation in Guangzhou Higher Education Mega Center." It was a project under the civic education umbrella which focuses on environmental sustainability. The goal of this civic education project was to provide students an opportunity to enhance their academic knowledge through an applied learning experience such as service-learning. This type of project was chosen because, in addition to being a forefront issue in China, waste separation fit well with students' interests. The problem of waste separation is an issue that affects each citizen; therefore, little effort was needed to persuade participants of the benefits of engaging in such a project. An activity focused on a topic of environmental civic education such as waste separation was also easy to implement at South China University of Technology, a university that emphasizes civic education and applied learning experiences. Moreover, environmental protection has been woven into the traditional culture of the university. On campus, there is a Fresh Environmental Association, which promotes environmental conservation and even helped to supporting the service-learning project. Off campus, the university also partners with Guangzhou's Higher Education Mega Center, which promotes environmental protection messages to the public. With these supports, the South China University of Technology was a very ideal site to launch a service-learning-related environmental project.

The project was large in scale and impacted a total of 150,000 local residents. Participating students were given the chance to learn basic waste separation knowledge and understand the process of waste separation in the Guangzhou Higher Education Mega Community Center. Since students were working directly with the center, students were able to involve themselves in community waste separation actively. Through this experience, students were able to understand the process, challenges, and value of waste separation. As a result, this service-learning project was effective in achieving the goal of the motto of civic education: "Serving to learn, Learning to serve."

Implementing the Service-Learning Project: Methodology

After designing the framework and content of the project, the implementation stage began. In this stage, it is important to recognize how the implementation of a project can fit into societal needs and the ever-changing circumstances of the community. Moreover, it is also vital to identify the best approach for integrating the element of *services* and *learning*.

Adapting *Learning* Approaches to Reach the Basic Goals of Civic Education

In order to ensure smooth and effective implementation of the project, importance was placed on the selection and training of participating students from the beginning to the end. Student training was comprehensive to meet the project's learning outcomes. Since the problem of waste separation is very common in China, students were eager to apply and participate in the project once they were made aware of the service-learning opportunity. A "learn first and serve later" approach was used for the participant selection process. All interested students were trained in basic waste separation and given information about environmental protection. This training achieved the preliminary goal of learning as well as the *learn first* component in the participant-selection process. In order to select students for the project, those who attended training were then asked to participate in interviews. In the end, twenty students at South China University of Technology from the School of Economics and Commerce and the School of Journalism and Communication were selected to join the project. Those twenty students received professional training about civil society and waste separation from a well-known environmentalist, Mr. Basuo Fengyun, from Guangzhou and a doctoral candidate, Zhang Qiubei, from the Department of Environmental Anthropology at Yale University. These two professionals assisted with each stage of the project, which ensured the quality of the learning outcomes, as well.

Using the Spirit of *Service* to Enhance the Quality of Students' Participation in Civil Education

Service-learning emphasizes not only learning, but serving as well. Serving is not only an action, but also a spirit and attitude. The first step in providing quality service is to understand the needs and assets of the community through a multi-perspective critical-thinking lens. It is important to recognize the value of community and the responsibility citizens have to contribute to the betterment of society. The next step is to explore, as well as engage in and with, the community. Civil education places emphasis on helping others and helping ourselves. It is important for students to recognize that by contributing to society, they are also enhancing their own quality of life. Students must learn to embrace the spirit of service and learn to have open minds when working with individuals who come from different backgrounds. Students must then reflect on their experiences in the community in order to enhance their academic study and also question their own values. By questioning their own values, students will recognize their own roles in and contributions to society. Service is valuable for students because it helps to foster these qualities and skills, which may never be developed solely in the traditional classroom setting.

Students designed the survey on their own and distributed it to students from four universities, residents from four villages, and community members from a small district nearby. Furthermore, students also investigated the universities' canteens to measure the amount of food waste at each respective university. By participating in this research, students gained a deeper understanding of their university's campus and surrounding community. Students also recognized and promoted the message that everyone should take responsibility to separate waste and decrease food waste. After acknowledging this responsibility and adjusting their behavior, students were able to take action in order to encourage environmental protection in the community and get directly involved in environmental efforts.

Using the Notion of *Learn* and *Serve* at the Same Time to Facilitate Student Development

For many years, there has been a conflict between Quality Education and Exam-Oriented Education within the education system of Mainland China. Generally speaking, university students have been primarily impacted by Exam-Oriented Education. As a result, university students often believe learning is solely for the purpose of practical use. By participating in the service-learning project, students were given the opportunity to see the practical use of their academic knowledge. On the contrary, service-learning also provided students the opportunity to see learning as a purpose for serving the community. Through this perspective, students viewed the community as the only environment in which they can learn professional knowledge and develop their own values. Service-learning, in effect, helps students view the process of learning in a more realistic and flexible manner; learning is maximized through service and it is the action of serving that facilitates students' growth.

When implementing the service-learning project, attention was focused on students' understanding of service-learning as well as their ability to reflect on and think about issues through a multi-perspective critical-thinking lens. Throughout the project, students were provided numerous opportunities for reflection; students used group discussions, social media, and many other platforms to reflect on their values, rights, and social responsibilities.

Achievement and Assessment of the Service-Learning Project: Degree of Participation and Satisfaction

The service-learning project started in December 2012 and ended in July 2013. More than 100 people were trained during the eight months of the project. In the end, the twenty participating students produced four research reports on the community, engaged in environmental promotion activities, and created one video; therefore, it can be concluded that the students reached the preliminary goal of the project. More importantly, the participating students broadened their horizons, developed professional skills, and enhanced their academic knowledge. Through their participation in the project, students understood what it meant to be a *citizen* and live in a *civil society*, along with the concepts of *community* and *society*. Students' civic engagement and sense of responsibility were also enhanced. Additional achievements of the service-learning project were evident in the self-assessment, which is discussed below.

Assessing the Level of Participation in the Project

Degree of participation was measured in terms of the number of participants and their involvement in the project. Participating students were required to engage in group learning to the best of their ability in order to achieve team goals. Students had to overcome obstacles, manage their workloads, and take the interests of the community into consideration. By committing themselves to the project, students were able to realize their role in the project and also understand their value in and responsibility to the community. Course instructors and team leaders assessed students based on their performance, motivation achievements, teamwork, and ability to reflect on their service-learning experience during the sharing session.

Assessing the Degree of Satisfaction among Participants

The sense of satisfaction among participants is a subjective measurement and, thus, very difficult to quantify. However, in order to receive students' feedback on the project, a sharing session was held and students were asked to post reviews through social media platforms. Students were asked to reflect on their achievements and identify the pros and cons of their service-learning experience. This feedback allowed the university to gain awareness to students' sense of satisfaction about the project. Students' satisfaction with the project was also assessed by their willingness to address the issue of waste separation after the end of the project Generally speaking, students who had a greater sense of satisfaction during the project indicated a strong commitment to expanding upon their service-learning experience and continuing their service to the community.

The Pros and Cons of the Service-Learning Project

The service-learning project benefited both students and the community; however, certain aspects of the project could have been improved. A major benefit of the project was that it helped to address a leading social issue in China. As a result, the project gained the support of students, the university, local residents, and even people working in the waste management field. While the project progressed smoothly and achieved both learning and serving goals, there is still more room for improvement. The pros and cons of the project are as follows.

A Project Designed to Address Society and Community Issues

The theme—waste separation—and the location—Guangzhou Higher Education Mega Center—of the project combined an important social issue with a specific place in the community. This allowed students to not only participate as community members in the implementation of the project, but also benefit from the service, along with other community members. By both participating in the service and reaping the benefits of the service, students became actively involved in and highly committed to the project.

Implementation Leading to a High Level of Student Participation

The project was implemented under the idea, "Learn and serve at the same time." In effect, it was hoped that the project would develop students' potential, motivation for personal growth, and commitment to service and continuous learning after the end of the project.

Assessing the Project and Seeking Continuous Improvement

The project was evaluated using a comprehensive assessment system, which included the following: a self-assessment, a peer assessment, an assessment completed by community residents, and an evaluation completed by the course instructors. Throughout the project, students received continuous guidance, in terms of helping them to understand their roles and value in the project. Many participating students claimed that they gained awareness of the process of waste separation in the community and the severity of the waste separation issue in China. Many students also made commitments to address the issue of waste separation after the end of the project.

Since the project was implemented for the first time, there are many ways in which it can be improved in the future. For instance, the motivation of students could be enhanced through better training and by adapting the participant-selection process. Moreover, improvement could also be made in terms of group management, division of labor, and supervision of student participants. It is, however, imperative to acknowledge the achievements of this experience, which lay the foundation for creating similar service-learning projects in the future. This service-learning project can, therefore, demonstrate an effective model for integrating theory and practice.

About the Institution

South China University of Technology is one of the major universities in China. It is directly affiliated with the State Ministry of Education. Situated in Guangzhou, the thriving metropolis of South
China, the university covers a total area of 294 hectares and is commonly known as "a place for
nurturing entrepreneurs and engineers in Pearl River Delta." Over the years, South China University
of Technology has developed into a multi-disciplinary university, combining science, engineering, business management, arts, and social sciences, among many other disciplines. Subjects such
as Light Industry Technology and Engineering, Food Science and Technology, Rural Planning,
Materials Science and Engineering, Architecture, Chemistry Engineering, and Technology and
Landscape Architecture were rated among the top ten in the nation.

The school is in good condition and offers a pleasant teaching environment. The great development of students' extracurricular activities in technology, social practice activities, and the school's
bright features are the important factors to enhance the students' quality. The school values the
construction of the teachers' qualifications. The tremendous strength of the teachers leads to a
comprehensive system of professional training, which includes bachelor's, master's, and doctoral
degree holders.

About the Department

The Journalism and Communication Department aims to cultivate talented professionals in fields
such as journalism, editing, broadcasting, etc. Basic courses within the department include the
Foundation of Journalism, Introduction to Communication, and News Interviewing and Writing.
In 2014, there were approximately fifteen course instructors and 169 students in the department.

About the Course

"Philanthropy Communication" is an integrated course which combines Philanthropy and Charity
with Communication. The course belongs to a series of liberal studies courses. Students learn the
basic knowledge and theory of civil society, the development of local and international charities,
and the basic knowledge and theory of communication. Moreover, students' sense of citizenship
can be enhanced through enrolling in this course.

REFERENCES

CCIDnet. (2010). *Po jie "le se wei cheng" zhi kun. "Bian fei wei bao" po zai mei jie* [Overcome the dilemma of
    "garbage siege," urgent to turn the waste into "treasure"]. http://miit.ccidnet.com/zt/2010/10271jwc/.
Long, Y. Q. (November 25, 2009). 6,000 families separate waste, pilot in Donghu street. *Southern Metropolis
    Daily*. http://www.h2o-china.com/news/177348.html.

Oral History of Sian Leprosy Rehabilitation Village: A Service-Learning Project Conducted by South China Normal University

HAN Yi-min

Sian Leprosy Rehabilitation Village (SLRV), a division of Sian Hospital, is located on Sian Island surrounded by *Dongjiang* (East River) between Machong Town and Hongmei Town in Dongguan City in the Guangdong province. Established in 1965, Sian Hospital is the only provincial hospital in the Guangdong province that specializes in the prevention and treatment of leprosy. Over 800 patients, including those rehabilitated, stayed in the hospital during the peak time. Over the decades, with medical technology advancements, leprosy has been under control and treatable, and the number of patients at SLRV has decreased year after year. There are around eighty former leprosy patients in Sian currently, half of whom have been transferred from Daiqin Island in Taishan City since 2011. Their average age is over seventy. Due to their experiences of being stigmatized and isolated for a long time, former leprosy patients choose to continue to live at the SLRV. Some of them have gotten used to living here; some were homeless; some worry about being burdens on their families; some are neither accepted nor even acknowledged by their families. Among the sixty-six leprosy rehabilitation villages in the Guangdong province, SLRV enjoys relatively good living conditions. The hospital has been carrying out measures that protect the living of the elders and cater to their medical needs. But the elders still need a helping hand from the outside when facing problems. In this regard, a dozen church volunteers provide housekeeping and wound handling services to them regularly. Meanwhile, a number of volunteer groups visit the village frequently to give performances and deliver household products to the old villagers.

In 2010, I visited these old villagers as a volunteer through the HOPE workshop in Dongguan (HOPE) of Joy in Action, an NGO. It was my first visit to SLRV. Amid the visits to the village, I learned more about the old villagers. Their impressive experiences were unearthed, mirroring the stories of generations of leprosy patients. The complexity of human nature and history is truly reflected by their relationships with their families and neighbors, their personal inner feelings, the government's prevention measures, their bitter living experiences, and their secluded lives in the village and society. A few of them have become self-taught poets, painters, or novelists. Despite hardship, hard people emerge. Time after time, I wished to record their stories as an oral history, a primary resource for studying the history of medical policy as well as the lives of lepers. The lively stories' telling of the facts about leprosy could possibly eliminate discrimination and stigma. For the elders, reminiscing about the old times made their lives free from tedium. The students who interviewed the old people transformed from passive learners to active recorders. Students' historical thinking and skills were also further trained.

My wish came true when Lingnan University brought up the idea of service-learning and the Office of Teaching Affairs at South China Normal University hugely supported it. Upon receiving approval for my project, I recruited eighteen students who wanted to take the oral history course. During the second semester of the 2012–2013 academic year, we traveled to SLRV every one or two weeks, interviewing seven elders for our oral history project. The task came to the final stage. In the coming two years, we will still have students interview suitable villagers in hopes that a booklet would be published to record their life stories.

Ideas and Implementation of the Oral History Project

What we experienced in the six-month phase one of the oral history project at the SLRV could be a reference for carrying out service-learning in the future.

In my opinion, the object of service-learning is that, through cooperation between schools and NGOs or public institutions, students are granted an opportunity to go into the community and apply knowledge and theories to community service to enhance their learning and actualize the motto of school, "Education for Service." As our course is historical sociology, this case study refers to a significant method of sociology research. Oral history, as the most essential subsidiary of history, is a domain through which students could contribute to the society. Besides understanding the theories in books, those who study historical sociology should prove those theories with cases, so that historical narratives can be lively and rational. The history of each single entity—for example, a village—undoubtedly embraces the components and structure of the history of society. Listening to what narrators recall in their minds offers a more real account of history.

Oral history is one of the best amalgams of history and service-learning. First, history students have to encounter and interview historical witnesses, thus recording history that would otherwise be vanished. Students learn from consolidating the interviews and recording history. This is a new way of learning history. Second, knowledge is created for human's needs. So how does historical knowledge do well for people? For most of the elderly, someone listening and recording their stories means a chance for them to relieve boredom, receive social recognition, and have someone else understand their personal values. Third, oral history is professional work that requires organization and cooperation and consumes much time and effort. Volunteers, generally speaking, have their own jobs and may not be able to talk with old people deeply and effectively due to the limited time and effort they have available. However, college students are able to follow through on what they are interested and devote weekends to oral history persistently throughout a semester. The service-learning project is also an assignment of the course. Collecting and understanding first-hand information are of significance when learning history. Besides getting primary sources, students may discern what is true or not after interviewing various individuals at different times, comparing testimonies, and reviewing the literature. Finally, students are able to transform a verbal form into historical materials that are true and biographical. While conducting oral history interviews, students almost get an entire professional history training. Eventually, they gain a new perspective on the world and learn communication as well as cooperation skills. They develop themselves to be real citizens by taking action. All of these experiences are vital lessons for students when they study at university.

We started to explore opportunities in our familiar domains where our students could serve the society. There are a lot of reasons we chose SLRV. HOPE is a volunteer university student group organized by Dongguan Polytechnic College and Guangdong Medical College. With a clear mission and extraordinary energy, volunteers served former leprosy patients who live in SLRV. After working together more than two years, I befriended some of the core members who were devoted to philanthropy and gained the trust of the villagers. With the hospital support of the students, HOPE was furnished with a long-term campsite and necessary facilities that solved the problems of food and accommodation. One more important advantage of SLRV is that Sian Hospital is the best leprosy hospital in the Guangdong province. Sian Hospital preserves plenty of systematic documents, which is an asset that most leprosy rehabilitation villages do not have. Examining the verbal resources along with the written documents gave a more reliable oral testimony. At the same time, our students were trained in reading and filing documents. The management group of the hospital showed interest in our oral history project and offered assistance to us. We were allowed to conduct research in their filing room, and the hospital provided meals and transportation services to us. This degree of support is rare in service-learning projects, and it should be credited to the huge efforts of HOPE over the years.

Considering the funding and basic conditions at SLRV, we could only choose around twenty students for the project. Those who took the course were recruited via Weibo (a platform in China similar to Twitter). Joining the project was completely voluntary, since nothing else could guarantee their passion and sense of responsibility. Initially, over thirty students applied. After we shed light on the project and told them they would be required to reserve time on weekends to concentrate on it, some of them withdrew. Later, two groups of students set off to rehabilitation villages in Xinsha and Sian to meet the elderly people face-to-face. Students were also asked to write journals about their visits. During this process, some students dropped out the project because of the hard journey, fear, or objections from their families. After two months of promotion, sharing, and visits to the villages, we finally selected eighteen students before the beginning of the semester. It was proven that those who stayed voluntarily not only had long-lasting passion, but also stronger capabilities and greater sense of responsibility. One of them, who hurt his eyes when playing ball and almost became blind, even joined the interviews again in June after two months of treatment and recuperation. His attitude exemplified that of most of the students.

Thus, training is a must for all kinds of organizational work in order to let the participants have a full picture of and adapt to the work they are going to deal with. I had inadequate experience, with neither a clear idea of the training needs nor a system for training. This was indeed the most difficult part of the project. But we still considered the matter of training, and explained the situation to the students during the recruitment. Those who want to join the project can also share their views online. The basic information about SLRV, leprosy, and the oral history project was introduced at the first sharing session, which was rather general. For the visits we would pay, we intentionally joined HOPE so that our students could visit the villagers with the volunteers. The sharing of the HOPE volunteers shed light on the village and the elders as well as leprosy. By cooking, playing games, and sharing together, everyone was driven to understand philanthropy and the unique atmosphere of a philanthropy organization. Besides, we organized two sharing sessions on oral history with the Department of Collection and Arrangement of Guangzhou Provincial Archives, which is the foundation that works on oral history in the Guangdong province. Its main method is to collaborate with Guangdong Television to conduct television interviews. Mr. Zhong Ming and his colleagues from HOPE shared the hardships they had experienced while working on oral history and highlighted the issues the students should pay attention to. The students learned a great deal from the sharing talks. For the information about leprosy, we invited a doctor who has specialized in preventing and treating leprosy for more than twenty years at Xinsha Hospital, located in Panyu city, to hold a seminar. The topic was "The Development of Policy for Preventing and Treating Leprosy after the Establishment of the People's Republic of China." All of these were delivered as implicit training. Meanwhile, exploration on our own still played an important role, since I did not have sufficient knowledge because we were service-learning beginners in oral history and we still had much to learn. We would hope to provide a more systematic training to those who joined a service-learning project next time.

Following the recruitment and trainings, a team was formed. In our opinion, oral history interviews should be conducted between two sides who have a basic understanding of each other. With enough interaction, they can talk about the past spontaneously. Questions would be raised again and again during a series of interviews. The resources would be finally consolidated into historical documents. All these tasks take lots of time and it cannot rest on a single person to finish it. We needed to divide the students into different groups and have a division of labor. The eighteen students divided the interviewees into seven groups according to their dialects. While Cantonese speakers interviewed Cantonese-speaking old people, those who spoke Chaoshan dialect did likewise. The division of labor in the group was made among the students themselves. They also dealt with financial issues, records and information management, etc. One of the students volunteered for the role of main contact person, who coordinated tasks among students, teachers, and the hospital. As the project involved reimbursement, the main contact person was asked to collect receipts each time and make a financial report. Those relevant records were kept in the Guangzhou Provincial Archives and the archives of the hospital. Here was another important thing: to create online chat groups and establish online storage space. There was a boy in the group who was a computer guru. He promptly created a QQ Chat (a kind of social media tool from Tencent) group for the project to facilitate the exchange of ideas and sharing. He also uploaded all the information onto Jinshan Fast Drive, including reference books on oral history and leprosy, videos and photos of the sharing sessions, textbooks, interview clips, interview notes, transcripts and drafts of reports, etc. Since these could be added and updated anytime, it was easy to store and share information.

When the interviews stage arrived, all students gathered to join the first two visits to SLRV, so that some general problems could be spotted and the students could raise the issues that night. Later, due to different schedules, the groups started arranging the schedule of interviews on their own. Each group was able to conduct interviews three times or more. When the transcripts were done, the final draft of the oral historical record was not. Each step was very difficult, starting from preparation of outlines of interviews to conducting the interviews to finalizing the draft. Making the transcriptions and finalizing the drafts in particular took enormous effort and considerable time. Some old people spoke unclearly or mentioned terms that our students were not familiar with. Also, the unpleasant recording devices and environment affected the speed of transcription. Some of them took a whole week to transcribe a single interview, and many of them worked on it overnight. If they found anything wrong, they had to revise again and again. A few groups even produced around 70,000 words for transcripts only. The difficulty of finalizing the drafts was beyond wonder. From the beginning to the end, the students traveled to SLRV around every two weeks, staying two or three days each time. As some may know, these students also had heavy loads of schoolwork. It was not easy to be that responsible and perseverant.

Working on oral history usually takes much more time than expected, so we ended at only the middle stage, without assessment. Upon confirmation of the draft, we have invited teachers from our faculty as well as those from other schools and volunteers who are experienced in serving lepers to conduct the assessment. In my opinion, we have been exploring a mind map of oral history and a rather mature implementation. It may have confused the students when they worked on it; for example, there were problems in interviews, designing interview outlines, presentations, and confirmation of the drafts which raised teachers' and students' awareness of the complexities involved in thinking and consolidating information. We would adjust the way of making oral history and provide more systematic training in our next project.

In this context of the project, students still succeeded in broadening their horizons and enhancing their working abilities, communication skills, and cooperation skills, as well as their ability to self-reflect and conduct oral history. I also found that the students were motivated to join philanthropy events such as campaigns for caring for veterans. Some of them carried out oral history projects in the schools where they were on graduation placement. One student even ran a course on oral history for the school while on graduation placement. Reflecting on their opinions in the assignments of the project, the students mentioned that oral history taught them a lot and expanded their horizons. They were also able to learn more about the reality of society, as well as to have concern for the underprivileged that they have never cared about before. Besides, the ability to conduct oral history will be crucial for when they become teachers. In fact, reality stimulates people to be alert to problems and to be more conscious of making judgments, giving a treasured perspective to the students that they never found in textbooks. What is more, some students established personal connections with the elders, so they quite often went back to the village to meet with them after completing the project. With our students' actions and online sharing, more students understand about leprosy, though we did not particularly promote our work. Undoubtedly, it imperceptibly lessened discrimination and stigma against the sickness.

Reflecting on the Developing of Service-Learning

With the above reflections, we noted that there were different inadequacies and problems to be settled, but in the half-year of this project we earned experience and confidence in carrying out oral history service-learning projects. However, what we need to think through further is whether our project could be regarded as a prototype and whether it offers a good reference for service-learning in Mainland China.

Perhaps this project is not representative enough. The time and effort the students had to spend greatly exceeded that of other projects due to the long distance between Guangzhou and SLRV. It is not realistic to contribute that much time to a single course, especially when the students need to take seven, eight, or even more courses in one semester. It might also affect their studies. But conducting oral history interviews as a way of service-learning is realistically feasible, as students have different interests and could interview various people around them: for example, hawkers near the school, security guards in the school, cleaners and cooks of the canteen, gate guards, professors, their families, or others from all walks of life. All these people could be primary sources for oral histories of modern China. With our endeavor, after over three years, our data collections were rich. First, oral history is a key branch of history, as "[o]ral history offers a challenge to the accepted myths of history, to the authoritarian judgement inherent in its tradition. It provides a means for a radical transformation of the social meaning of history" (Thompson, 1988, 21). Second, when encountering the subtleties of life, the students possibly felt the limitations or attractions of theories. The limitations refer to theorists' focus only on what they specialize and their ignorance of other key areas of knowledge. The attraction lies in theorists' ability to condense details. Third, whenever our students were astounded by what they found in oral history and moved by their encounters with history, I, as a teacher, did have great discoveries in historical research and teaching methods.

With reference to this case study, the feasibility and difficulty of launching service-learning in China's universities are set out as below.

In the wake of the expansion of recruitments of students, the enrollment rate has increased substantially year by year, which means there is a plentiful supply of graduates. For most of the students, who are facing huge competition and employment stress, engaging in a philanthropy activity is rather a hard choice. Immense stress, generated by their hectic schedules, probably occupies their time and minds already. Another option is to offer rather superficial service-learning experiences. But does that meet the objectives of service-learning? It seems not. How can we make our students free from hassle? Presumably, we will not come up with a comprehensive solution and we may just keep trying small-scale projects. But in this era, there are serious social issues when community service is running short and social solidarity compromised. Thus people have a great need, from deep down, for community service. Generally speaking, serving the society and others becomes a common wish among college students. Some people jokingly argue that philanthropy has turned into a new style. It is humor indeed, but it truly shows the ideas of the era. I recently carried out a survey among the students who took courses pertaining to philanthropy. Ninety percent of them were willing to serve the communities as long as they could manage it. Although the number was not accurate, it was found that the students are already aware of philanthropy and reflect on certain problems. The students involved in the oral history project were able to shed light on the issues. The teachers were also in similar dilemmas. While competition pressure and heavy workloads are unavoidable, the new ideas are gradually being recognized by teachers. Perhaps stress and hope can coexist.

Let me put it this way: advocating service-learning in these kinds of conditions could be an opportunity for and important method of education reform. If education institutions, especially schools, would give overall support throughout the process, their contributions would definitely play a key role in developing service-learning as well as enhancing students' philanthropy awareness in the community. First, giving credit and allocating workloads encourage students and teachers in engagement. Not every student would engage themselves in service-learning, but the schools could launch a motivation mechanism. For example, students could reasonably earn credits by taking service-learning courses; teachers who organize service-learning would have it acknowledged and counted among their job duties; both students and teachers are thus motivated. For the sake of the quality of service-learning, schools should not only ask teachers to carry out service-learning projects but also to supervise them efficiently. For instance, the proposals of service-learning should be assessed and endorsed by the schools. The number of students should be adjusted in line with the service targets and service agencies. Second, schools should give financial support to the projects. Third, teachers should network service agencies in the schools' names even without direct liaison contacts. With the endorsement of the schools, students and teachers could contact with the community partners by themselves. That would not add an extra workload for the schools, but their reputation would lay a good foundation for service-learning. "Society is best built with helping each other; Serving others serve ourselves; Service to learn and learn to service" (Chan, Ma & Fong, 2006, 8) are the philosophical bases of service-learning. Actualizing the ideas undoubtedly improves the schools' performances in academics and community service.

Lastly, the service direction and partnership should be long-term and stable in terms of various service-learning courses. Sufficient time and sustained focus on the service and research fortify the mission that service-learning calls for—"Education for Service." If resources are available, further action should be taken, such as forming related societies and producing publications. A base for training talent and serving society could be developed with a feasible direction of service-learning. For our project, with the aim of developing oral history, we will set up a society for oral history and publish internal materials. We will train our students to take active roles in recording history as well as writing and develop their ability to rethink history. We will also provide oral history services to people who need to be empowered by having their voices heard. After taking this opportunity, I am truly grateful for the Office of Service-Learning, Lingnan University, for providing funding and inspiring ideas for service-learning.

About the Institution

Established in 1933 and situated in Guangzhou, the South China Normal University (SCNU) has a history of over eighty years and is one of the 100 national key universities in China in the twenty-first century. Despite its recent transformation into a research-oriented university, the SCNU has been dedicated to primary and secondary teacher education for Guangdong and neighboring provinces. Due to its strong influence over the primary and secondary education system, it is undoubtedly important to promote service-learning in the SCNU.

About the Department

The School of History and Culture is one of the first faculties in the SCNU. In the early days, a great deal of the teachers were prestigious scholars, while most of them studied abroad.

Over the decades, the disciplines of both Chinese History and World History have been recognized as national first-degree doctoral programs and established mobile post-doctoral research stations, facilitating the development of academic research and teaching. Scientific research is applied particularly in the domains of French Studies, Religious Studies, Studies of the Six Dynasties, Economical History in the Tang and Song Dynasties, and the History of Modern Thought and Culture.

About the Course

Opened by the School of History and Culture in recent years, Historical Sociology is a course that aims to train students' thinking in historical theory. It originally meant to analyze the impact of various historical factors on historical development by studying the changes of social structure in historical process. We adopted an oral history service-learning project in this course because of the natures of sociology and history. Sociology not only focuses on macro-analysis but also on-site investigation, whereas History concerns details. As long as on-site investigation and details are vital for studying History, oral history contains elements of both. In this regard, a portion of students are encouraged to collect oral histories for their assignments.

REFERENCES

Chan, C. M. A., Ma, H. K. C., & Fong, M. S. F. (2008). *Service learning and research scheme: The Lingnan model.* Hong Kong: Office of Service-Learning, Lingnan University.

Thompson, P. (1988). *The voice of the past.* 2nd ed. Oxford: Oxford University Press.

The Renewal of Earnest Practice: A Reflection on the Practice of Ethics of Philanthropy and the Preservation of Rural Culture, a Service-Learning Program Conducted by Sun Yat-sen University

WANG Shuo, XIONG Huan, and LIU Haijuan

Can service-learning serve as a teaching method in academically focused post-graduate programs? Can it play a complementary part in various subjects of humanities such as Philosophy as well as History? Sun Yat-sen University (SYSU) made an attempt to answer these questions. In the summer of 2012, the graduate school of SYSU, in partnership with the School of Philanthropy, incorporated the idea of service-learning into the "Post-Graduate Summer Philanthropy Program." Through training provided by Lingnan University in Hong Kong, the participating students and teaching staff realized the academic significance of service-learning and recognized its differences from traditional Chinese volunteer modules such as *xueLifung* (learning from Lifung), *Sanxiaxiang* (Three Downs to the Countryside), and volunteer teaching. With support from the graduate school, the Ethics of Philanthropy and the Preservation of Rural Culture (EPPRC) program became an official service-learning project in 2012.In 2013, we relaunched the program twice, during the winter break and the Qingming Festival, with financial support from the Office of Service-Learning at Lingnan University. Two young tutors from the Department of History and the Department of Philosophy led an expedition in the company of approximately ten students from various disciplines in the Humanities. The team began the journey of exploring the path of service-learning.

Redefining *Duxing* (Practice Earnestly)

"*Boxue, shenwen, shensi, mingbian, duxing*" (Study extensively, enquire accurately, reflect carefully, discriminate clearly, practice earnestly) is the motto of SYSU, written by Sun Yat-sen in 1924. These words originate from the Book of Zhongyong, meant by an aphorism: "*Cheng* [integrity] is human nature." By respecting their innate *zhicheng* (spotless integrity) and by studying extensively, enquiring accurately, reflecting carefully, discriminating clearly, and practicing earnestly, one can perfect oneself and become a *junzi* (a true gentleman), according to the Daxue and Zhongyong (2007, 101). The principles of service-learning encourage new insights into this ancient teaching.

In general, *xue* (study), *wen* (enquire), *si* (reflect) and *bian* (discriminate) are theories of how to learn, whereas practice is the application of knowledge to real circumstances at the completion of the learning process. The first four actions lay a solid foundation for *xing* (practice), to which the formers owe experience and *jianyan* (verification) that solely the latter can provide. Service-learning reminds us that "Earnest Practice" is not only the final exit of the process of education and self-development, its margin can also be expanded to become a cultivation of life appreciation. Thus knowledge lies in earnest practice. Effectively, "knowledge" and "practice" together form an indivisible, mutualistic unity. In *Instructions for Practical Living*, it is proposed: "Our ancestors say learning and practice must be performed separately so as to draw a fine line between the two. On the one hand, one may make an effort to learn and on the other hand may make an effort to practice, only until then can produce successful results." Wang Yangming (1992, 4–5) replies:

> What you just said misinterprets the purpose of our ancient teachings. I have always said to know is the purpose of practice yet to practice the effort of knowledge; knowledge is the seed of practice while practicing the fruit of knowledge. If this is understood properly, knowledge can be put into full practice and practice will have knowledge as counsel. Our ancestors mentioned the two as discrete subjects only because there were confused and impulsive men, who did not think clearly and behaved in a reckless and foolish manner. Knowledge is a prerequisite to practice. Men who are groping aimlessly in their wild thoughts where the actual practice is the least of their concerns. Merely shadows and echoes that they were after. They can perceive true knowledge through practice. These words were uttered at exceptional circumstances to avoid defects. If the true meaning is fully grasped, a single word will suffice. But people today treat knowledge and practice as unrelated things, deep in the delusion that knowledge must precede practice. They will discuss ways to gain full knowledge, and then proceed to put it into practice. I fear that eventually they might end up knowing nothing and having nothing done. This myth is not a minor malady and it did not occur only yesterday. (4–5)

The methodology of service-learning is not an abstract, notional *bolaipin* (foreign import); instead, it echoes with the great tradition of Yangming philosophy as critical thinking that exposes the ingrained habits of separating knowledge and practice, and in particular the disconnection between the two in the modern notion of education.

The Meaning of *Fuwu* (Service)

Within the methodological scope of service-learning, earnest practice is achieved through service. *Service* is a common word frequently used in daily speech, but its implications are rich enough to give us insights into the history of Chinese and Western views and contribute substantially to the understanding of the significance of service-learning.

From a Chinese etymological point of view, *service* is composed of two characters, *fu* and *wu*, which were at the beginning used independently. *Fu* belongs to the radical of *zhou* (a raft) and is an archaic sense of "to follow somebody." DuanYucai (1981) wrote as an annotation in the *Shuo wen jiezhuzhu*: "to be of service to the most pressing interests of men, as though it was a raft to its captain; all things can be considered as though it was a raft at the disposal of its captain" (404).

There is also an entry in II Xicizhuan of the *Book of Changes* that reads: "use oxen to haul heavy loads and ride horses to journey far to benefit everyone" (Zhou, 1991, 258). It recounts the stories of the old kings who let oxen be charged with goods and horses yoked to chariots for the interests of all. From this, it is accurate to say the meaning of *fu*, "to serve" is being at both people's service and their disposal. The definition of *wu* derives from the sense of *jizou* (to hurry) of the character *Cu*, meaning "to make haste to achieve something" (Duan, 1981, 699); "to eagerly strive for the completion of something." This interpretation is also underpinned by a quotation from I Jin Xin of *Mencius*:

> The wise know everything; but they only undertake the most pressing issues; the good loves everyone; but they see fraternity with their fellows as their duty. The knowledge of the Great Kings Yao and Shun was not boundless yet they were able to pay heed to what was important; their benevolence was not extended to everyone because they preferred association with the good. Those who cannot observe the three years' mourning required for parents but being fastidious about the bereavement of distant relatives, as well as those who gulp down food and soup but raised questions about gnawing at meat—these are people who do not know what truly matters. (Yang, 1960, 322)

Therefore, the meaning of *wu* can be broadened to the senses of *caolao* (to toil), *zhuiqiu* (to pursue), *mouqiu* (to strive for), *biding* (to ascertain), etc. Tracing back to its semantic origin, one can see that both *fu* and *wu* imply the endeavor to fulfill an objective or a purpose. However, a nuance between the two must be carefully pointed out, as *fu* is usually associated with an object, which is either passively used or exploited for the realization of something. On the contrary, the subject of *wu* is always mankind, stressing humans' strenuous efforts to accomplish something. A tension of dominance and submission, and activeness and passiveness, exists in English, where the word *service* derives from its Latin root *servitium* or *servus*, which mean "slavery" and "a slave," respectively (Oxford Dictionaries, 2015).

In the later years of Hellenistic civilization, Roman philosopher Cicero (2007) first conceptualized the idea of service, which in his treatises can be sorted into two kinds: individual service and national service. Individual service in principle refers to aid delivered to other individuals, which primarily describes the complimentary service rendered by lawyers who stood in somebody's defense on their own volition, as the law back then forbade attorneys from defending in court for remuneration. Defending someone in court free of charge is a form of individual service and an act of benevolence. National service refers to undertakings that honor the interests of the whole nation and the whole population, which represents the functions of public administration. "These two varieties of service should be of equal importance. Nonetheless, any service that is rendered to protect individuals' rights should be also beneficial, or at least not detrimental, to the whole nation" (202). Cicero remarked particularly that both individual and national service must be in conformity with the principles of justice, since "of all that matters, one must not arouse any suspicion of selfishness when engaging in either public administration or philanthropy" (203), and "aid delivered by means of individual service should be subject to its highest principle, which repudiates the admission of any cases that contradict justice or condone falsehood. Justice is the foundation that safeguards the integrity of honor; there cannot be anything praiseworthy if justice is jeopardized" (201). He advocates serving the compatriots: "if it is agreed that in the busiest days of my tenure I could be still of service to my compatriots, then I must also be able to serve them in my idle time" (20). However, *service*, in occidental languages, can be understood to have two senses that are at opposite poles: at one end, it connotes the passive state of enslavement, while the other end represents an active contribution to the benefit of other people. Since 1580, "military obligation" has become one of the mandatory services whose definition has evolved throughout the years between these two extremes. Glorifying servitude to the extent that it is instilled in people's minds as a wholeheartedly voluntary sacrifice is the *fuwu guan* (perception of service) that many rulers desire to bring about. As Wilheim I, King of Prussia, once famously said: "People must wholeheartedly serve their sovereign with the entirety of their means, honor, and conscience and be in readiness to surrender them all. Every earthly possession belongs to me except the heavenly bliss bestowed by God" (Zheng, 2005, 5). "To serve the monopoly" is a different perception of service from that of "to serve the society." Friedrich Engels pointed out that "the oppressed working class are progressively heeding the call of making good use of their fortune and productivity in the interests of society, instead of the current state of serving a monopoly" (Marx & Engels, 1995). Questions like, "who should serve whom?" and "is it a service rendered out of free will?" become the ethical yardsticks that shape people's perceptions of service, or even the political catechism that inspires enormous moral appeal.

Under the influence of Western thought, *fuwu*, the compound word meaning "service," has left many footsteps on Chinese contemporary intellectual history. "To serve the nation," "to be of service to society," and "to serve the people" were slogans and mottos that had enormous influences on contemporaries. In September 1944, at the memorial service of Zhang Chengde, Chairman Mao made a historic speech which was later revised and published as an article titled "Serving the People." In 1945, during the Seventh National Congress of the Communist Party of China, Chairman Mao precisely put forward "Serving the people resolutely and wholeheartedly" as one of the party's leading doctrines. "Serving the People" has been included in the Constitution of People's Republic of China since 1949.

Since the implementation of Chinese economic reform in 1978, the political significance of "service" began to fade into the shadow of its growing economic significance. This ideological clash had an impact on the ways in which we understand service. Some believe the service industry is a demeaning and servile trade. However, in the wake of the explosive growth of tertiary production as well as the constant expansion of the service sector in terms of volume, the economic value of service has assumed importance. Many services can certainly be bought through monetary means, but this is not so as far as public services are considered. Since the last decade of the twentieth century, the massive rise of volunteerism has added a new element to the broad spectrum of service. Still, since government-funded social welfare has eaten up a substantial proportion of the philanthropy sector, many philanthropists worry that if the whole enterprise is to be narrowed down to a kind of *fuwu ye* (service business) and complacent about its new position as *products for sale*, it will eventually lose its spiritual power to precipitate social change. Considering the aforementioned deliberations, in the course of the long development of Chinese and Western concepts of service, there has always been tension between its mandatory and voluntary characteristics, as well as a conflict between whether it is for personal gain or for the benefit of all. Owing to the promotion of ethical equity, liberty of moral choices, and enlargement of the public sphere, the voluntariness and benevolence of service fuse into one entity in "the third department." The fundamental meaning of service should describe the care and tenderness that one gives to another; and service par excellence should be done out of genuine love, mutual empathy, trust, and a sense of life sharing. This resonates with the basic tenets of education; incorporating educational activities into the concept of service is consistent with the ideal model of pedagogical development.

Generally speaking, service-learning is the combination of meaningful community service and academic learning. The objective of service-learning is to expand its educational domain from campus to society and its content from curriculum to daily life. The subject of teaching shifts from teachers to students. John Dewey (1981) once aptly said: "I believe that all education proceeds by the participation of the individual in the social consciousness of the race" (1). Yet the ivory tower of modern education leads to a learning experience separated from real-life understanding. Abstract knowledge and social consciousness are focused on the cognitive level while the development of social consciousness should be cultivated from personal social involvement. Even worse, moral education is also taught as abstract knowledge; the young generation will be fostered as the egoist. Service-learning, on the other hand, shifts the "ethical core from self-absorption to societal service"(62). Education receivers are transformed into self-educators. Their growth in conformity with their own social skills and abilities to serve foster a greater unity between themselves and life, which becomes the goal of the unification of everything; mental training, cultural nurturing, and knowledge constitute the various aspects of growth (Dewey, 1981). Through service, a special kind of *shijian* (practical) training and *lilun* (theoretical) study, service-learning progressively facilitates the societal development of the human race and reinforces our mutually beneficial moral bonding consciousness as well as our capacities to establish such relationships. In other words, service, as a teaching method, possesses educational functions and purposes. Hence, service-learning is a belief that inherits both the idea of and the practice of service, which champions learning through practice to dissolve and assimilate individuality into a societal framework, and through the construction of service-learning the full and free development of individuals is realized. More importantly, the definition and understanding of the idea (philosophy) of service have become the core factors that affect the smooth operation of a service-learning project.

Although the word *service* might imply homogeny with more abstract terms such as *philanthropy*, *benevolence*, and *volunteerism*, service-learning is not the exact equivalent of service only; some thinkers even believe that service-learning deviates from conventional philanthropy because "the notion of service-learning as essentially different from other similar activities, such as philanthropy, charity, voluntarism, or a single act of kindness which are the one-way socially engaged activities. Service-learning is different because it necessarily entails reciprocity and mutuality which are two-way relationships" (Lukenchuk, 2009, 247). At first glance, this explanation might seem sound; still, it fails under critical analysis to account for other marked differences between service-learning and philanthropy or volunteerism. In light of the fact that both the former and the latter can bring about the stated mutually beneficial and reciprocal relationship, a clear-cut approach to differentiate the two by identifying whether the interaction is uni-directional or bi-directional in nature simply cannot hold water. It goes without saying that service-learning must entail a considerable amount of philanthropic work, yet not all philanthropic work falls under the umbrella of service-learning. Why? To put it concisely, service-learning is philanthropy supplemented with a module of academic study, but this does not lead us to a lucid delineation of their definitions. In fact, their difference comes down to their orientation to different values: the values of philanthropy and volunteerism are best manifested through the establishment of an external, mutually beneficial and reciprocal relationship. But the values of service-learning concern itself beyond merely the building of such relationship; it transforms the connection into an internal process that empowers the "benefactors" as well. Its ultimate goal is to enhance the mutual coexistence of "us" with "the others," the symbiosis where benefits are optimally shared, both externally and internally. Hence, mutualism is one of the fundamental values of service-learning as much as caring for other. Eventually, mutual coexistence becomes the final objective of service-learning, with caring for others and self-fulfillment as one's life-long pursuits. In this sense, service-learning is a kind of philanthropic study, which is bi-directional in nature with the dual objectives of caring for others and self-fulfillment.

An Exploration into *Yanxi* (Learning)

The EPPRC service-learning program put philanthropic services targeting Hakka rural communities into practice, mostly through investigations into the neighborhood's latest ethical and welfare situations, as well as investigations of how their traditions evolve overtime. The rest was handled by students and teaching staff who specialize in Culture and Museum Studies and Chinese Philosophy, through their research conducted on the Hakka walled villages' historical architecture and modern significance. Both initiatives were carried out in order to demonstrate that Hakka rural intangible heritage serves a function of patrimony preservation.

The professional academic research consisted of roughly three parts: theoretical preparation, orderly arrangement of materials, and learning outcomes. The first part required a division of work based on expertise in order to assemble and assimilate academic data for a specific subject in a specific manner. Prior to the actual project, an academic community where information is circulated and disseminated freely was set up to facilitate the researchers' processing of material. To enhance a clearer understanding of the research topic and the relevant efforts made in the past, we set up a series of study group meetings, where participating students selected books on which they shared their thoughts so that they could facilitate the discussions pertinent to each topic. These methods characterized the early stages of the program. In addition, conferences and lectures were delivered (on the location where the program took place) by professors and scholars who specialize in related academic fields, with the intention to consolidate students' knowledge of the core arguments and pique their curiosity about the subject. We also invited expert members of the public to host a series of seminars, such as rural *Fengshui* masters explaining how Fengshui knowledge has taken root, retired rural teachers giving lectures on philanthropy, etc.

Moving on to the following two parts, the material-sorting stage was where the team wrote up their own study journal, filmed interviews, polished up recordings and photos, and sorted all rural written sources into the right categories. At the final stage, students were required to submit reports of their findings as well as academic dissertations. Through this academic project that invested heavily in practicality, students applied their professional knowledge in a realistic context with their personal experiences, which stirred up students' interests in research as well as academic investigations. Basing itself on the improvement of the ability to put knowledge to practice, the program eventually strengthened students' professional integrity and conduct.

With regards to the exploring of philanthropy, the principal goals of the program were to record and pass on the Hakka philanthropic culture as well as to protect the Hakka cultural heritage, both the tangible and intangible. These goals were evident throughout the service-learning activities. During the daily interviews, for instance, the team helped the locals harvest rice grains and peanuts; they helped the elderly sort out books and documents and engaged in conversation with them; they helped retired teachers edit their biographies; they looked for low-cost care centers for the mentally ill and children suffering from cerebral palsy. Regarding the protection of tangible cultural heritage, students repaired and renovated many walled mansions typical of Hakka architecture (through helping the elder residents repaint the walls and interviewing a few old carpenters to learn about the architecture of the Hakka walled village as well as maintenance skills). We made a survey on the living conditions of the local elderly (through interviews with the residents and casual conversations) and kept records of geographical knowledge and theories (through running a sharing session of Fengshui knowledge, held by Fengshui masters). For intangible heritage, we kept records of the Hakka rural customs (during the Chinese New Year Festival, where most of the community performed traditional rites and rituals) to understand and document practices such as Hakka ancestor worship, celebration of newborn sons, and *Anlongzhuanhuo* (laying the Dragon God and moving the incense), etc., which in turn contributed to the preservation of Hakka traditions.

Outcomes and Reflections

Our program was successful thanks to the collective effort made by both teaching staff and students. Regarding tangible outcomes, we gathered a tremendous amount of sifted and well-ordered research material, with the academic dissertations and reports written by students.

Reflection and evaluation is a crucial part of service-learning. To start, evaluation is carried out according to feedback given by all participants. For students who have just been through the service-learning project, the hands-on experience leaves an indelible imprint on their mind. It also equips them with diverse social knowledge and practical skills and opens up new avenues beyond the conventions of academic research. As for the teaching staff, while the service-learning projects are progressing steadily, they must take students' needs into consideration in order to provide all-round theoretical guidance and practical advice. This form of teaching fosters a close connection between teachers and students, which helps nurture friendship as well as forge democratic, equitable, and harmonious relationships. Moreover, according to the feedback collected onsite, our service-learning projects not only served as a catalyst for mutual learning and knowledge enrichment that benefitted both teachers and students, but also, and more importantly, proved themselves to be the best way to help participants establish ties with unfamiliar corners of the world. As far as practical teaching is concerned, volunteerism in all the program locations favors building close relationships between individuals, which in turn encourages students to develop their interest in exploring new theories while pursuing academic research and generate the greater resonance between theory and actual practice. Even though the projects came to a close, the strong bonds of the teacher–student relationship and service–location relationships live on, which augments the prospect of launching further on-location service-learning projects.

Shortcomings and difficulties were encountered in our service-learning projects, mostly with regard to programming, content, and sponsorship as well as the ethical facets of service-learning. Firstly, in terms of programming and content, it was inevitable to notice that there was still room for improvement concerning the time allocated for learning and the content of service itself; there are always unfinished tasks at the end. For instance, on the last day of the program, we still had many scheduled interviews with key interviewees to run and some of our charitable initiatives were not arranged and done properly. These problems pinpoint the fact that in the early development of a service-learning program, there will more or less be some defects in both execution and administration, which also explains why service-learning as an educational means possesses the characteristic of sustainable development. Secondly, service-learning is complex in terms of its content. From our experience of the recent two service-learning programs, we found the theme and subject matters to be broad and full of variety. However, an extensive curriculum did mount a lot of pressure on students: they effectively found it a bit taxing that they had to deal with research material on time every day while more than half the day had already been spent providing social service. Meanwhile, they had to continuously look for new areas and interviewees who might be relevant to the core investigation. All these factors resulted in a tendency toward passivity from an operational point of view. Last, but not least, we also experienced a lack of funding, which is an imminent problem we must tackle in order to secure a sustainable and effective service-learning program whose existence relies on the support of available funds. In the context of this program, the money assigned for student activities is not adequate.

Furthermore, particularly in light of the practical background of service-learning, it is high time that we reflected on the most fundamental problem, which is how to realize the ethical framework of service-learning. In other words, service-learning is a practice that positions service as its value orientation, but what does it boil down to in terms of its relationship with ethics and its ethical composition? Analyzing this question from the viewpoints of Hakka philanthropy and cultural preservation yields a new definition for service-learning: within the bounds of public space, it is an attempt to find out the local values, beliefs, and traditions; particularly while understanding the latter, service-learning aims to explore the local values of people in need and respond to those needs with appropriate benevolent action. A critical review of said actions is to follow in order to fully grasp the ethics reflected by the feedback, depict the ecosystem of local values, and empower its public space. In this light, the ethical structure of a service-learning program must clarify its valuable orientation as well as the value feedback mechanism of service practice.

About the Institution

SYSU, founded by Dr. Sun Yat-sen, is a comprehensive multi-disciplinary university with over a 100-year history. It is a key university under the Chinese National Higher Education Project. The university is comprised of "a community of teachers and students," through which "teachers represent the school body," and embrace the idea of "educating with love." The aim of SYSU is to nurture high-quality, interdisciplinary students who possess international perspectives, a sense of social responsibility, and an innovative spirit. Graduates are expected to be well-mannered, honest, diligent, positive-minded, innovative, and responsible as they acquire trained career skills. With this vision, the university focuses on lifelong learning and development, which is a reflection of the university's core value of educating with love. The undergraduate programs are in line with "general education, field training, and interdisciplinary innovation." The postgraduate programs are aimed at cultivating innovative, motivated, and productive doctoral candidates in various fields.

Being one of the leading universities in the People's Republic of China, SYSU includes the humanities, social sciences, natural sciences, technical sciences, medical sciences, pharmacology, and management sciences.

About the Department

Established in 1924, the Department of Philosophy was one of the earliest departments of SYSU. The department proposes "the bearer and the embodiment of the cultivation of human philosophy" as its goal. Its academic degree framework is comprised of "fundamental philosophy," "philosophy by theme," and "philosophy by domain" as a new curricular system. At the post-graduate level, it applies the "Master–Doctor Continuous Course" system, while stressing a combination of knowledge dissemination and independent thinking to train professional high-achievers. In 2013, the faculty of Ethical Studies created the "Comparative Ethics and Philanthropic Culture" as a doctoral research stream, headed and supervised by Professor Li Ping, to provide China with the very first batch of doctors of philosophy specialized in philanthropic ethics.

Also established in 1924, the Department of History is also one of the earliest departments founded in SYSU. Many eminent founding fathers of Chinese modern historical studies like Chen Yin-ke, Fu Si-nian, GuXie-gang, Cen Zhong-mian, Liang Fang-zhong, and Liu Jie taught in our faculty, laying the building blocks of the solid academic foundation of the department.

The School of Philanthropy of SYSU was founded on April 1, 2011, with official permission issued by SYSU as a first-class nonprofit research institution. The School is based in the Pearl River Delta region where charity is comparatively well-developed. With its position facing Taiwan, Hong Kong, and Macau, the institution concentrates on research on philanthropy. Our vision is to promote innovation in philanthropy through action-oriented research and to build a diverse, just, and sustainable society: Our mission is to study, teach, and take part in policy innovation in order to establish ourselves as a globally influential philanthropic think-tank.

About the Course

"A Case Study of Philanthropic Ethics" is a compulsory doctoral course of the "Comparative Ethics and Philanthropic Culture" program, organized by the faculty of ethics of the Department of Philosophy. The course also welcomes students from other faculties or specializations. Moreover, it is also one of the core courses of the "Master of Philanthropic Studies" program. The program aims at exploring the philosophic basis and fundamental principles of philanthropy through discussions and researchers, with a focus on analyzing its ethical difficulties to reveal its value ecosystem and norms, to elucidate the initiation mechanism of moral actions and the mechanism that governs the formation of social moral order, etc. In 2012, as Lingnan University, Hong Kong, was campaigning for the program, our course lecturer, Wang Shuo, was honored to take part in the workshop of philanthropic studies and later on introduce the new teaching approach to this program, which has since produced many positive outcomes.

REFERENCES

Cicero, M. T. (2007). *Lunshen* [Discussion about divinity]. (Shi, M. M., Trans.). Shanghai: Joint Publishing.

Daxue-Zhongyong. (2007). (Wang, K. X. Trans.) Beijing: Zhonghua Book Company.

Dewey, J. (1981). *Duweijiaoyulunzhuxuan* [Dewey's theory of education]. (Zhao, X. L., & Wang, C. X., Trans.) Shanghai: East China Normal University Press.

Duan, Y. C. (1981). Fu. In *Shuo wen jiezhuzhu.* (Xu, S. Z., & Duan Y. C., Trans.). Shanghai: Shanghai guji Press.

Lukenchuk, A. (2009). Living the ethics of responsibility through university service and service-learning: Phronesis and praxis reconsidered. *Philosophical Studies in Education* 40: 246–257.

Marx, K., & Engels, F. (1995). *Makesi en gesixuanji: di erjuan* [Karl Marx and Friedrich Engels collection, 2nd volume]. Beijing: People's Publishing House.

Oxford Dictionaries. (2015). Service. http://www.oxforddictionaries.com/definition/english/service.

Wang, S. R. (1992). *Chuan xi lu* [Instructions for the practical living (volume 2)]. Shanghai: Shanghai guji Press.

Yang B. J. (1960). *Translation and interpretation of the* Book Mencius. Beijing: Zhong Hua Shu Ju.

Zheng, R. L. (2005). *Lai yin zheying.* Shanghai: Shanghai People's Publishing House.

Zhou, Z. F. (1991). *Translation and interpretation of the* Book of Changes. Beijing: Zhong Hua Shu Ju.

The Independent Service-Learning Course: The Characteristics of Service-Learning at Beijing Normal University–Hong Kong Baptist University United International College

Timothy CHEN Ka-kit and Katy ZHANG Lie-ni

In 2006, Beijing Normal University–Hong Kong Baptist University United International College (UIC) began offering service-learning courses. Since then, UIC has developed a unique service-learning model as a result of years of practice and research. Following the standard curriculum model of an independent course, the service-learning course comprises a syllabus, objectives, teaching hours, assignments, and course evaluations. It is a program consisting of five instructors that has enrolled thousands of students over the course of six years. UIC adapts its model each year to align with the course learning outcomes and research results of the previous year. In this way, UIC has developed an effective service-learning program which can be described as "Learning by doing." This chapter introduces the service-learning model at UIC with examples.

Whole-Person Education and Service-Learning

Whole-Person Education (WPE) aims to promote an integrated and well-rounded person. It is an important education to connect to self, others, and the communities (Miller, 2009). Service-learning is one of the ways to achieve WPE. Students can learn how to build relationships and acquire necessary skills to transform not only themselves but also the community.

Service-learning is a teaching method that connects students to their community. It integrates knowledge with practice by encouraging students to understand the meaning of their study. Glenn (2007) has a description of service-learning that includes *service* and *learning*. For example, students pick up garbage on a riverbank (service) and examine the water samples under a microscope (learning). The service-learning for students studying life science is writing a report based on the water samples they collected and analyzed and then presenting the scientific report to a local environment protection agency. Through this experience, students review how they relate to others, their communities, and the world, thus furthering their understanding of these relationships in their personal views of marginalized groups and what causes the social issues.

Moreover, students are challenged to grapple with various opinions and values and discover what is truly important to them. Apart from knowledge, students are able to learn necessary skills as well, such as the skills to communicate with disadvantaged children, the ability to do face-to-face interviews and questionnaires, and the capability to organize an event. This knowledge and these skills help to enhance WPE.

At UIC, WPE is an educational ideal to provide students with a personal development framework that integrates their learning in class with life experiences and practice outside of the classroom. WPE highlights students' development in intelligence, morality, stamina, aesthetics, community awareness, and community spirit. There are eight WPE experiential learning modules at UIC, and one of the most essential modules is service-learning. It is generally known as "volunteer services." It promotes necessary social and volunteer knowledge as well as relevant skills and values aimed at nurturing aspiring responsible citizens. As a result of engaging the community and service, students have broadened their views and put what they have learned in the classroom into practical use in order to address community needs.

The Characteristics of Service-Learning at UIC

Characteristic One: Course Curriculum

Service-learning is an independent course following the standard curriculum model at UIC. It has strict requirements for its syllabus, objectives, teaching hours, assignments, and course evaluations. If students enrolled in the course wish to add or drop a class, take the course evaluation, or appeal their final grades, students must follow the requirements and guidelines of the registration system. The course grade is approved by the Academic Quality Committee before it is released in the registry system for students to view. Any student who has not registered or passed the course is required to make up or retake it in a following term. The students are required to take five credits of WPE courses, with each course worth one credit.

The volunteer service development center was founded in May 2006 and since then has offered service-learning courses. Service-learning courses are offered as required courses under WPE for second-year students. There are 400 students registered each year in these service-learning courses. Not until September 2009 had the university approved service-learning courses under WPE as free electives for year-two students. There are around 380 students enrolled in these types of courses every term.

Service-learning at UIC is subcategorized into four classes concerning different community problems and social issues: children (the disabled, orphans, youth in the community); the elderly (community services center, the elderly under *wubo* [five guarantees of food, clothing, housing, medical care, burial expenses covered by the government] in the nursing houses or day care centers); migrant workers (their legal rights in occupational injuries, children of migrant workers, personal development of new migrants), and other projects (AIDS prevention, support for the poor who cannot afford education, the energy saving program on campus, transportation guidelines for the tourist spots in the mountains, part-time job Internet forum set-up, maintenance of school chairs and desks, hostel cleanliness and management). Students can select a preferred community out of the four classes, and based on their subject interests plan for the services. Each term, there are different plans for community service.

Characteristic Two: Course Preparation

Based on community needs, service-learning courses at UIC are in collaboration with relevant partners in the community, integrating the program into partner projects and providing services to both partner institutions and community members directly being served.

Facilitators run a meeting with partners before the commencement of the course to discuss relevant issues. The facilitator briefs partners on the concept of service-learning, while the partners in turn introduce their institutions' backgrounds and possible collaboration projects as well as any requirements in terms of possible projects. Both parties discuss their individual needs, requirements, and expected outcomes to achieve an applicable and mutually beneficial project. For example, UIC has worked with a rehabilitation center for the disabled since 2008. Having worked together for several years, both parties have signed collaboration agreements on study projects and established a facilitator group that specializes in program design, execution, and evaluation. Before 2012, UIC mainly worked on a rehabilitation project for children with cerebral palsy, in which the program cooperated with the rehabilitation center for the disabled in Zhuhai. In the 2012 spring meeting, the center asked if UIC had psychology students and social work students who would like to participate in service-learning and were interested in setting up a caring group for the parents of the children with cerebral palsy. By the fall of 2013, UIC was already running three parent groups, all of which were well supported by the partners, who hoped that UIC would extend the service to the parents of children suffering from mental health problems, autism, and hearing impairments.

Moreover, UIC has run a comprehensive evaluation on their program with the partners after each term in order to ensure quality service-learning experiences for both the partners and students. UIC also keeps close contact with the partners in order to discuss and prepare for future collaboration. The partnership between UIC and their partner institutions demonstrates that the success and possibilities of a long-term service-learning program depends on how well the service integrates with the community need.

Characteristic Three: Course Arrangement

The course is a twelve-week program with three learning hours a week, which includes theory study in addition to service. There is a three- to five-day in-class study week after the course starts, mainly on theories, such as the development of volunteer services in China, the characteristics of service recipients, the living conditions of service recipients, the existing problems in the community, the solutions to community problems, and appropriate service attitudes and skills. These theories all relate to knowledge, skills, and attitudes necessary for service.

For example, at the first lesson for students serving children with cerebral palsy, these students will learn about the causes of the disease and the mental and physical development of children with cerebral palsy. In the next class, students will learn about the development of these children in a face-to-face discussion; additionally, special education teachers from the partner institution (the association of the disabled) will brief the students on relevant communication skills and any precautionary matters. The group tasks will be given after this class, including topics on:

- conducive education (as what the partner defines);
- a summary of communication skills needed for the children with cerebral palsy, which can be based on their development and personalities in terms of developmental psychology;
- a study on their personalities, mental state and psychological needs, in the view of psychology and sociology; and
- research on three NGOs in a relevant field.

The third class is for students to share their findings. For example, students in charge of the second topic presented a PowerPoint on the normal development of the children at different stages, the characteristics of children with cerebral palsy at early stages, and the personalities of children with cerebral palsy. They ended with a summary of how to communicate with these children:

- repeat one motion in rehabilitation training
- keep facing the child and maintain eye contact to avoid distractions;
- use other means of communication such as body movement, drawing, and toys to overcome any cross-language barriers;
- encourage the children to do their best to finish their jobs to promote confidence and growth; and
- use flexible means of communication such as expressing empathy, guiding at their convenience, and imitating natural responses.

Theory learned in this way is not as accurate as that in the medical school, but students learned them on their own and from their partners. According to the cone of experience proposed by the audio-visual educationist Dale (1969), out of the content of communication, verbal symbols, or those via language, are normally only 10–20% remembered; contrived experiences, on the other hand, are 70% remembered (see Figure 1). Therefore, students master knowledge better in a learning mode with contrived experiences, where they engage in the learning process and act as participants. Furthermore, by doing, students are then able to improve their ability to analyze, design, create, and evaluate.

In the weeks four through ten, students do services in the community. Students are assigned to groups and before service asked to design an applicable service plan though discussion with the partner institutions. The leaders and relevant staff (schools invite social facilitators) assist students in their service. The course teacher and partner institution supervisor hold a sharing session with students to reflect on lessons learned and personal development.

In the eleventh week, a group reflection is held to evaluate the service-learning process. The stages of service-learning generally include a needs assessment, service plan design, service practicum, summary, and evaluation. The reflection can either be demonstrated through group

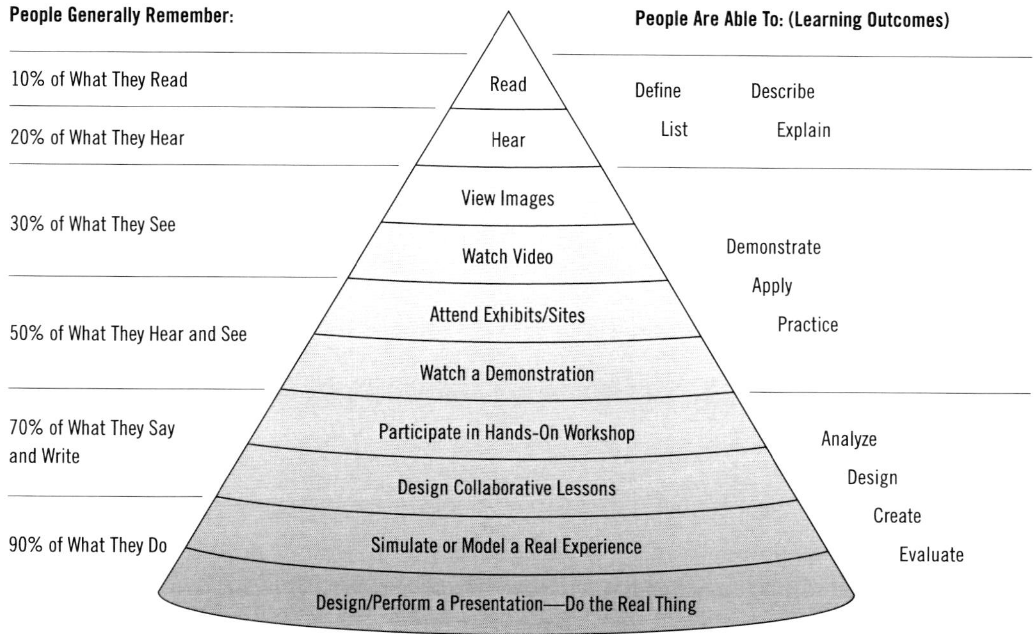

Figure 1. Edgar Dale's Cone of Experience (adapted from Dale, 1969).

discussion or a short play. This reflection session is aimed at helping students understand their social value and the impact of their service-learning experience.

The twelfth week focuses on a group speech report. Each group has ten minutes to introduce its project and demonstrate its ability to reflect on its learning and development as a result of service-learning. Other groups are given the chance to reflect on the presentation as well, during a three-minute Q and A session, where both students and teachers may pose questions.

Characteristic Four: Course Evaluation

UIC service-learning adopts an outcome-based assessment. There are three main parts in the evaluation, including (1) participation and performance in the class and the services; (2) reflection essays; and (3) group work. Each part includes sub-categories with five grades: excellent, good, satisfactory, marginal, and failing. There are clear instructions for marking. The rehabilitation project for kids with cerebral palsy can serve as an example. A detailed marking guideline must be provided to the partner institution prior to service so that the partner is able to supervise and monitor students' performance during their service time (see template in Table 1).

After the form is completed, the institution's supervisor submits it to the course teacher, who informs the students of the evaluation outcome. In the end, the service-learning performance is graded on a scale of *A*, *B*, *C*, *D*, or *F*. The first four grades signify the completion of a one-credit course under WPE, whereas an *F* indicates that the student must retake the course for credit.

Table 1. The Template Evaluation Form for Participation and Service Performance: Children's Service-Learning Program at UIC

CRITERIA	EXCELLENT 4	GOOD 3	SATISFACTORY 2	MARGINAL 1	FAIL 0
Engages in the service during community service	Fulfills all the 5 points below	Fulfills any 4 points below	Fulfills any 3 points below	Fulfills any 2 points below	Fulfills any 1 point or none below
	• Makes proper preparations before the service • Makes a sincere effort to serve the service recipients • Is patient through most of the service time • Respects and cares for the service recipients throughout the service time • Reflects on oneself and is willing to share with others in order to plan ahead for the next service				
Student Name	Excellent 4 Good 3 Satisfactory 2 Marginal 1	Tutor Comment:			

After completion of the course, students assess the teacher's performance through an evaluation system. Moreover, the course tutor holds a reflection meeting with the partner institutions on the service and propose ideas for future collaboration.

The Difficulties of and Solutions for Promoting Service-Learning at UIC

We have come across numerous difficulties in the promotion of service-learning as an independent course; there are two primary reasons for such difficulties.

One of the difficulties pertains to the service arrangement. Service hours are generally available during the weekend and occasionally at night, depending on the needs of the community. If the service is done on the weekend, students may believe that the service takes up too much of their free time, while other students have classes on the weekend. Yet if service is done at night, student safety is a major concern. Regardless, course schedules and venues at UIC are extremely tight, so part of the service-learning course may have time conflicts with other courses. Since the university is located far from the community, it may also cause issues for those who have class after the service. With this tight schedule, students are likely not able to rest between classes. Furthermore, occasionally, a partner institution may temporarily change initial plans, so the service has to be rescheduled. This can create many challenges for students, as another date may conflict with other obligations and plans.

The other difficulty deals with the insufficient study of theories. Service-learning at UIC is community oriented and is not connected to any disciplines. Therefore, as for theory study, students are only given an introduction to relevant social issues, and not provided with in-depth knowledge for further understanding. In effect, students are likely to misunderstand service-learning as volunteer service in the secondary schools, and thus focus solely on the number of service hours but not the quality of service or the reflection on the learning process.

Regarding the problem of the service arrangement, program coordinators met with the registry at the university and partner institutions to suggest that, for example, when arranging courses, the registry should avoid assigning classes before and after service-learning courses, giving students appropriate time for travel and rest. It was also suggested that when meeting with the partner institutions at the beginning of the term, program coordinators should confirm the service period and ask the partner to inform them well in advance if a change in time is needed. This will provide program coordinators appropriate time to inform students and allow them to make new arrangements.

As for the insufficient theory study, and in light of the operation mode of the Office of Service-Learning (OSL) at Lingnan University, Hong Kong, a report has been submitted to the Teaching Management Committee of the university after a service-learning promotion workshop at Sun Yat-sen University in 2012. The report demonstrates student achievement as a result of the integration of service-learning and the University's disciplines. It is hoped that, in addition to the report, a meeting with the general education and humanities departments will also help to encourage the adoption of service-learning as a university-wide teaching mode. As a supporting institution, the OSL at Lingnan University, Hong Kong would like to assist the course instructors to identify appropriate community partners and arrange proper workshops.

The Way Forward for Service-Learning Implementation

A multitude of social issues have developed in China as a result of urbanization. In order to resolve these issues, the government and the social forces must work together. Volunteer services undoubtedly contribute to solutions that combat social issues. The emergence of programs such as "Serving to learn, Learning to serve" reminds teachers of the need to be knowledgeable about the latest educational trends, and to update their teaching methods in order to guide and inspire students to explore. Teachers must facilitate students' putting their knowledge into practice and thus better equip them to face future challenges; even more, teachers must be devoted to building a caring and loving community and developing a service-oriented learning environment.

About the Institution

UIC, located in Zhuhai, Guangdong, is co-founded by Beijing Normal University and the Hong Kong Baptist University, with the special approval by the Ministry of Education. UIC promotes the liberal arts as well as four-dimensional and international education, in line with WPE.

About the Department

The Whole-Person Education Office was founded in July 2006 as the pillar of WPE. Distinct from other disciplines offered at UIC, the new WPE program, developed by Whole-Person Education Office, fosters student development through various experiential learning courses. This helps students fully master knowledge and skills and better apply the knowledge to their lives, fulfilling their life goals.

About the Course

The Service-Learning Course is an experiential learning course in WPE, offered during the second year of undergraduate study. It has four sub-classes, each concerning different community issues and populations, such as children, the elderly, migrant workers, etc.

REFERENCES

Dale, E. (1969). *Audiovisual methods in teaching.* New York: Dryden Press.

Glenn, S. J. (2007). *Discover service-learning—what is service-learning?* http://files.dnr.state.mn.us/education_safety/education/minnaqua/leadersguide/appendix_1/7_3_service_learning.pdf.

Miller, J. P. (2009). *Sheng ming jiao yu—quan ren ke cheng li lun yu shi wu [The holistic curriculum].* (Zhang, S. M., Yang, X. G., Liu, G. L., Zhang, L. Z., Wang, H. L., Chen, X. Q., Qiu, A. L., Jiang, Q. W., Trans). Taipei: Psychological Publishing.

Travel with Sanban Primary School Kids, a Service-Learning Project Conducted by Zhuhai City Polytechnic

LIN Hao-gui, HUANG Ying, and HUO Qiao-hong

Vocational colleges have carried out service-learning projects so students can strengthen their willpower and morality as well as acquire knowledge and skills during practical activities. Service-learning helps students gain deeper understanding of what they learn from class and develops their core vocational skills, work ethic, team spirit, and sense of the value of serving the community. Moreover, it assists with creating a harmonious and humanistic campus environment and community for nurturing decent citizens.

The Background of the Service-Learning Project

Zhuhai City Polytechnic (ZHCPT) is a full-time higher vocational college sponsored by the Zhu Hai Municipality Government. Since establishment, the school mottos have been "Integrity and Professionalism," "Joy of Learning," and "Excellence." The college goal is to develop positive, service-oriented, well-qualified, and practical talents. Teachers put great effort into teaching students how to distinguish right from wrong, keep promises, be civic-minded, take care of and respect parents and the elderly, and rouse their passion for study and self-improvement. The college passed the Higher Vocational Education Work Assessment conducted by the Ministry of Education in 2011 and took the chance to improve the running level and quality of the college. The school has started a comprehensive reform of its School of Tourism management in the aspects of enterprise cooperation, curriculum, Zhu Hai–Macau cooperation, and student affairs. In the field of student affairs, the School of Tourism Management introduced service-learning, a concept from the United States. With reference to the experiences in Hong Kong and Taiwan, the school has started running a service-learning project.

During the process of promoting the service-learning project, the dean of the School of Tourism Management visited Hsiuping University of Science and Technology (HUST). In a meeting with the person in charge of the HUST service-learning project, the dean discussed the feasibility of starting a service-learning in a higher vocational college. Soon after, the Office of

Service-Learning Development (OSLD) was set up and the associate dean, who is in charge of student affairs, became the head of the office. All of the school counselors and class teachers became OSLD members and assisted in the service-learning project for the school. Since the beginning, they visited South China Normal University and Lingnan University to participate in a service-learning conference and workshop. They learned methods of promoting service-learning from other schools' experiences. They were highly motivated to join the "Service-Learning Pilot Schemes in Universities and Colleges in Mainland China" initiative and received guidelines from Lingnan University to do so.

Project Progress Summary

Learning from the experiences of other universities in Hong Kong and Taiwan, the OSLD provided a trial service-learning elective course based on the features of the Department of Tourist Management, the Department of Hotel Management, the Department of Convention & Exhibition Plot and Management, and the student body's characteristic of frequent volunteerism both on and off campus. The OSLD initially contacted the neighboring community and organizations to understand their needs, and then successfully carried out the "Travel with Sanban Primary School Kids" project.

The service-learning elective course was combined with the project. To achieve the desired effects in their lectures and projects, the OSLD teachers prepared adequately for the task of planning, training, servicing, reflections and evaluation.

First, at the stage of planning, to better maintain students' passion for service and spread the service concept, the trial elective course was limited to students on the volunteer team, after students' usual performance in community volunteer service had already been considered. School leaders and the OSLD members assembled and formed a preparation team to discuss and set the course outline, content, and teaching method. The OSLD teachers contacted related community agencies multiple times to confirm cooperation with Sanban Primary School, where students did field visits and research.

After having several rounds of communication with and field trips to the Sanban Primary School, it was found that more than 70% of primary school students' parents are migrant workers from surrounding areas. Migrant workers' families share some common characteristics. First, these families have a weak economic foundation. Parents often have little education in their backgrounds and most of them are from farming villages. They work at factories and corporations in Zhuhai to make their livings. Since the parents are not highly educated, they have difficulties helping with their children's schoolwork and satisfying their needs. Second, these families tend to have problems blending in with city life because of the dual-sector model of the city and village. The family life is affected by long years of working away from home and the high mobility.

These two characteristics of migrant families lead to a lot of the parents needing to work overtime, even on Saturdays and Sundays. They have little time to spend with their children, let alone travel with them. Some parents can spare a little time for their children, but they still cannot satisfy their children's wishes to travel, as they are not familiar with the history and famous attractions of Zhuhai. Children are strongly drawn to extracurricular activities in the city. Therefore, teachers in the service-learning course guided students to combine the content from the course with the specialties of their own departments and design a project that would fulfill the needs of Sanban Primary School students, called "Travel with Sanban Primary School Kids." They planned to bring the primary school students to famous attractions such as Zhuhai Fishing Girl, agriculture wonders, and museums, so that they could broaden their horizons.

Next, in the training phase, the OSLD teachers gradually guided students to understand and establish the concept of service-learning and to master the skills of professional service. In the class, the teacher first played a film, *Pay It Forward*, and asked for students' feedback. Students said that they learned about the joy and the significance of helping others. After that, they watched the Lingnan University service-learning propaganda video and discussed the common types of volunteer work and the differences between volunteer work and service-learning. Then, teachers introduced the development of service-learning and its promotion in higher education. Students at this point had a basic understanding of the concept of service-learning and related content. In the course, students also studied Guangdong tour basics, the business of being a tour guide, travel psychology, etc. Guangdong tour basics familiarized students with the information and the history of the attractions in Guangdong, while the business of being a tour guide teaches students how to meet the demands of different travel groups according to their characteristics and write corresponding guiding speeches. As for travel psychology, it helped students understand the perspectives and mood changes of tourists in order to make better travel arrangements for them. After taking these classes, students mastered basic service skills. A teacher of communication courses was invited specifically to help enhance students' communication skills. Moreover, to build up students' safety awareness, the OSLD teachers talked about minors and college students' health insurance.

For safety reasons, it was required that one student from the service-learning course must take care of one Sanban Primary School student during the trip. Students had been assigned to different duties. Some were tour guides, conducting field trips beforehand, researching the attractions, and preparing guiding speeches. They also designed the tour route and arranged catering. Some were responsible for providing first aid and preparing the Scopolamine patches and cool oil for car sickness, while some were responsible for renting the coaches and keeping contact with the rental company and driver. Moreover, some handled the travel insurance and ensured that everyone could travel at ease, whereas others designed games and led the primary students during the trip. Some took up roles as camerapersons and recorded the trip. The rest were babysitters who took care of the primary school students. During the trip, the teacher observed the service of the students and followed up.

Later, in the reflection stage, the teacher organized a reflection session for students. Each student presented a reflection on his or her performance of duties. They talked about what they gained, such as better communication skills or higher service awareness, as well as their shortcomings. First, they had inadequate knowledge of the attractions and hence could not answer all the questions of the primary school students. Second, they were not familiar with the psychological characteristics of the primary schoolers. During the trip, some students unconsciously treated the children as if they were adults, ignoring their needs. Third, students lacked touring experience, as they did not have enough practice. When they encountered tourists in a real situation, they were easily overwhelmed and did not know what to do, resulting in decreased quality of service.

Students hoped to be able to learn more professional knowledge and get more actual practice in society. Also, students reviewed that when they had previously volunteered for social services, they did not received trainings or debriefing sessions. This time, when the students participated in service-learning, they not only had professional training but also a chance to share their experience with others. They gained a lot from it. As both participant and monitor, the teacher joined the discussion to lead students to reflect from the perspective of social services and help them to achieve self-improvement.

Then, in the evaluation phase, the teacher conducted a survey to understand the trip evaluation according to Sanban Primary School, parents, and primary school student participants. According to the survey results, the Sanban Primary School thought the trip was a win-win. For primary school student participants, travelling was a great opportunity to learn more and see more. For students in the service-learning course, it was a chance to get in touch with primary school children and be able to understand them more. The school also praised the communication skills, problem-solving skills, and organizational skills of the students in service-learning course. This activity had great impact on the primary school. The parents thought that the communication between service-learning students, primary school students, and parents was very smooth, which helped the primary students to understand the history and attractions of Zhuhai and widen their horizons. Parents agreed that the best part of the trip was its organization. The majority of the primary students felt very happy to have participated and that they had met lots of big brothers and sisters. They learned about the attractions of Zhuhai and hoped to have more opportunities to join similar activities.

In addition, before the project was carried out, to ensure that parents were informed and gain their support, student organizers had met with the parents of Sanban Primary School to give a brief introduction of the trip and answer their questions. During the promotion and explanation, parents expressed their consent and signed the trip notice. After that, student organizers also met with the children in person in order to assign one-to-one duty. To ensure trip safety, they actively persuaded all the participants to purchase travel insurance.

Achievements and Problems

Overall, the "Travel with Sanban Primary School Kids" project and the service-learning course was a success and the following goals were achieved.

To Raise Students' Civic Awareness, Enhance Their Sense of Social Responsibility, and Encourage Them to Engage More in Social Services

According to research statistics after the course, students have organized some extra services, like "Sunshine Books Corner," "Southern Tibet Donation," "Tutorials in the Community at 5:30," etc. They have also done social research, participated in caring for sanitation workers activities, given a lecture on tourist-attraction safety, promoted healthy diets in the community, visited the Jingan social welfare centers, etc. The total beneficiaries of different social activities were over 100.

To Improve the Curriculum and Nurture More Talents

Service-learning, which is different from common volunteer service, is combining community service and academic programs to meet the needs of the community and help stimulate students' personal growth. It is a new practice to change courses and implement service-learning. The School of Tourism Management has vigorously reformed the curriculum since 2012, emphasizing the importance of quality service in personnel training programs. As a result of the successful trial service-learning course, all departments in the School of Tourism Management have launched service-learning courses as distributional electives with two credits, which is recommended to other schools within ZHCPT. They will also introduce service-learning into other courses and encourage students to participate in social services, test their knowledge, and raise their social awareness and sense of responsibility.

To Explore New Ways of Teaching and Build a New Curriculum

College teaches students to be decent and have standards of conduct, social responsibility, and skills. Nowadays, students want to learn through practice and are willing to communicate, desires which could not be satisfied by the traditional mode of education. With service-learning enhancing their sense of citizenship and quality, students are able to improve themselves in social service and have sustainable development.

To Promote Service-Learning

It is understood that in recent years, only a few colleges in Mainland China have implemented trial service-learning courses. ZHCPT is the first higher vocational college to launch a service-learning program. The college joined the "Service-Learning Pilot Schemes in Universities and Colleges in Mainland China 2012–2013," held by Lingnan University, and invited professors from there to supervise the service-learning project. A service-learning website was set up and students who participated in service-learning joined the Zhuhai Youth Federation's second representative meeting on behalf of the school. The school has also applied for a research grant on service-learning from the Zhuhai Twelfth Five-Year Plan in Education and Research offered by the government. Many mass-media outlets have reported news about service-learning, like Nanfang Metropolis Daily, Zhuhai Daily, and Jinwan TV, which has aroused wide social awareness of service-learning.

But when reflecting on the whole course, there are still several problems.

Lack of Qualified Teachers

Since it was the first time the teachers in OSLD heard of service- learning, they lacked teaching experience. Although the teachers had a certain understanding of the concept and methods of service-learning after trainings and visits, they still did not have practical experience. Moreover, teaching methods and student characteristics from overseas are very different from that of Mainland China. The teachers could not use their methods without adjustment and faced difficulties as there were no instructions from the school. How to teach? How to attract students' attention? How to integrate theory into community service? These were all problems the teachers had.

Lack of Agencies and Community Involvement and Supervision

Since it was a trial project, the OSLD teachers did not know how to manage the project. They did not have clear communication with Sanban Primary School and provided inadequate supervision for their students. This was a very good learning experience for our team on how to do service-learning.

Feedback from Primary School Students and Parents Were Mainly Collected by Survey

The questions in the feedback survey were rather simple and could not reflect the primary school participants' full evaluation of the project. As for the questionnaire for students who participated in the service-learning, it was mostly open-ended and mainly for qualitative rather than quantitative analysis. Students' performance before and after service-learning was not quantified and analyzed. To improve the assessment methods, it is necessary to design more quantitative surveys for students before and after they join to analyze their performance from multiple angles for future service-learning projects. Students should also be encouraged to write reflective diaries and reports. Moreover, it is hoped to quantify and analyze the work efficiency of the cooperating agencies and the OSLD teachers.

Operation Expenses Were Difficult to Guarantee

As it was the first time launching a service-learning project at ZHCPT, there was no specific financial funding for it. During the process, student participants had to pay a lot of transportation costs, as they had to visit Sanban Primary School multiple times on their own for field trips, research, and holding talks. The OSLD teachers also had to pay in advance for some fees for the trip, like car rental, catering, attraction ticket fees, insurance, etc., because students could not afford to pay such large amounts of money. Hence, getting funds from the Lingnan University's "Service-Learning Pilot Schemes in Universities and Colleges in Mainland China" was important.

The partnership between ZHCPT and Sanban Primary School was unstable. During the process, the college, OSLD teachers, and student participants were actively putting forth effort. The cooperating agency in the community was passively receiving benefits from the service. For example, Sanban Primary School did not need to pay any fees for the "Travel with Sanban Primary School Kids" project. As the project came to an end, the relationship between the schools did not strengthen. The main reason was that there were not enough discussions and interactions with the community partner and their importance in project design, training, and implementation was neglected. It is suggested that in the future projects, communication with community partners should be improved and more frequent in order to know their real needs. The OSLD should also adjust the project according to actual needs and encourage the community partner to be involved in part of the teaching, using their expertise in a different field to help students learn and grow.

Follow-Up Work

A single spark can start a prairie fire. Despite the fact that there are only a few colleges implementing service-learning in the Mainland, it will certainly be further spread and practiced, as it is an advanced idea in higher education. It plays an important role in leading students to well-rounded development. In order to better promote service-learning, improving the following aspects is recommended.

First, the school set up a special office for service-learning, which is responsible for the coordination and promotion of service-learning. The office should be equipped with a full staff and receive special funds. Implementing service-learning in college involves amending personnel training programs in various departments, like Office of Academic Affairs, Department of Student Affairs, Treasury, Schools, etc. It is really difficult to coordinate if only Department of Student Service or one department from the School handles service-learning. It is suggested that a special office should be set up and coordinate all parties involved, like contacting communities, non-profit organizations and enterprises, etc. Staff will assist different departments to launch service-learning projects and distribute funds to help spread service-learning.

Second, the college should train more qualified teachers for service-learning. They need to first study the theory, methods, and promotion of service-learning so that they can guide the students in class. The college can organize visits to other schools in the Mainland that have more experience in service-learning. They can also visit overseas universities and join workshops and promotion schemes for supervision.

Third, the school should establish a stable partnership with the community and institutions. As service-learning emphasizes practice, a platform for practice is key to success. Therefore, when the school is carrying out service-learning projects, it should choose some stable enterprises to work with through cooperation between industries and college or government and college. They can then hold further discussions in order to meet the teaching, practice, and service requirements. For example, the Department of Hotel Management can work with high-star hotels and send top students as interns, which can ease the stress on the hotel during the peak season and give students a chance to practice their skills and learn more about the actual work in the hotel front lines. Another example would be Department of Tourism Management organizing volunteer touring in attractions as a practical class for students so they can train as tour guides for actual tourists in the attractions. These can achieve win-win results.

Fourth, the school should push through the curriculum reform and innovate new teaching methods. Service-learning can be developed as one course. Schools can set it as a free elective course, a distributional elective course, or even a compulsory specialized course with corresponding credits. Moreover, service-learning can be seen as a teaching method to be used in any course to increase the quality of teaching. For instance, add in the seven elements of service-learning in practical courses and design related practicums as course assessments to lead students to apply their knowledge in social services. It will not only aid teaching but also turn students' attention to the community.

Fifth, the school should pay attention to safety problems. Safety is the first priority. Service-learning projects should be carried out under safe and secure conditions. This requires teachers, participants, and community partners to establish safety awareness and pay attention to safety measures. They should also be fully prepared and reduce risk by doing risk assessments on activities, conducting safety trainings, and purchasing relevant insurance. When schools and teachers first launch service-learning projects, they should choose places closer to campus to carry out services, such as kindergartens, residential areas or student dormitories, to reduce the risks in the activity. They should design safer activities in the beginning and then explore more step by step. We believe that, as an idea of education, service-learning will be able to spread successfully among universities in the Mainland. Let us work together to witness the successful outcomes!

About the Institution

Zhuhai City Polytechnic (ZHCPT) is a full-time higher educational college funded by the Zhuhai Municipality Government. Its establishment was approved by the People's Government of Guangdong Province in April 2004 and was recorded in the Ministry of Education. The college persists in higher vocational education, complemented by continuing education, lifelong education, and open education. It follows a new school-running mechanism of "the two types of 'Ternary System,'" a strategy to integrate the advantages of government, college, and enterprises or industries, which results in an open-education model with coordination among industry, colleges, and research. ZHCPT has been transformed into a learning-oriented city and, at the same time, become an outstanding vocational training school in Zhuhai. There are eleven departments, which are the Department of Economics and Management, the Department of International Cooperation and Communication, the Department of Electronics and Information Engineering, the Department of Humanities and Social Management, the Department of Tourism Management, the Department of Industrial and Art Design, the Department of Mechanical and Electrical Engineering, the Department of Aerospace and Marine Engineering, the Department of Ideology and Politics Teaching, the Department of Physical Education, and the Department of Adult Education (Zhuhai Radio and TV University). The number of students is more than 16,000. School's mottos are "Integrity and Professionalism," "Joy of Learning," and "Excellence," which focus on nurturing students' standard of conduct, enhancing their sense of responsibility, and emphasizing their capability to improve skills, serve the community, and care for others.

About the Department (School of Tourism Management)

As a secondary college under ZHCPT, the School of Tourism Management was founded in 2012 and that same year was chosen to be the pilot unit for comprehensive reform in the aspects of enterprise cooperation, curriculum, Zhu Hai–Macau cooperation, and student affairs. The School of Tourism Management designed curriculum in "cocktail" style, and actively promotes exchanges and cooperation in tourism education between Hong Kong and Zhuhai, pursuing in-depth and broadened cooperation between schools and enterprises. With reference to the experience of schools in Hong Kong and Taiwan, the service-learning trial project was a success and is used as an example for the rest of the schools in ZHCPT.

About the Course

Service-learning is a distributional elective course in the School of Tourism Management. It aims to enhance students' understanding of the origin, development, and application of service-learning through studying service-learning theory and serving. Through participating in service-learning activities, students can also test their professional knowledge, improve their comprehensive skills, and enhance their sense of social responsibility. This course emphasizes practical services and trains students to learn in practice and practice when learning. It helps students to distinguish right from wrong, understand society, care about others, and have healthy personal growth.

Service-Learning in the General Education Core Curriculum: An Example from Sun Yat-sen University

ZHANG Si-lu and ZHU Jian-gang

Starting in 2009, Sun Yat-sen University (SYSU) began procedurally implementing general education core curriculum program. Then, the newly designed general education core curriculum consisted of four main categories: "Chinese Civilization," "Global Perspectives," "Technology, Economy, and Society," and "Fundamental and Classic Humanities Readings." Students were required to complete all four categories during their freshman and sophomore years. In 2010, the university began its provisional administration measures on SYSU undergraduate public elective course selection, which required full-time undergraduates in art, science, and engineering majors to finish sixteen credits of general education during their undergraduate studies (including twelve credits of general education core courses and four credits of general education general courses). Specific provisions for credits for students from different majors were also specifically stated.

This chapter discusses the service-learning program developed in an SYSU general education core course, "Civic Society and Philanthropy."

"Civic Society and Philanthropy" by Sun Yat-sen University

Professor Zhu Jiangang from the Department of Anthropology was teaching a course named "Civic Society and Development" at the beginning. The idea came from the global development education program initiated by British and International Oxfam. Through this course, students were expected to understand the status of poverty, environmental health, and other global issues. Students could learn how to reflect on their current communities and know how civil society can contribute to change its problems. The course was a public elective starting in 2005 but was then selected as a general education core course at SYSU in 2011 because of the liberal arts education reform there. In 2012, this course was renamed "Civil Society and Philanthropy" because *philanthropy* is easier to understand in the Chinese context and it shares a similar meaning to *development* in global development discourse. During the course, students have three hours of classroom time per week throughout the twelve-week semester. Credits are rewarded after examination.

At the core of this course is the concept of "Learning–Action–Sharing," which refers to students taking action during learning and learning by taking action. Encouraging students to engage in exchanges, sharing, and learning together ultimately enables them to thrive. Service-learning pedagogy was first introduced to the course in 2007, which aimed to enhance students' learning by expanding it from lectures and classroom discussions to actively serving and engaging in the community.

Before the course even begins, a course curriculum team drafts several topics on service-learning for group division for the upcoming semester. Students from the course then opt into the service-learning component based on their personal preference, in addition to picking a specific service-learning group according to their interests. Since participation in the service-learning component is voluntary, students who choose not to participate in it are not criticized or penalized. Marks are awarded to students who have outstanding performance in service-learning at the final assessment.

Service-learning topics for the semester are determined by the currently prevalent social issues, along with the community organizations we are in contact with. Past topics have included cultural preservation, labor, public dissemination, gender and health, environment, urban–rural interaction and community support for agriculture, a public welfare management survey, philanthropy law and policy, and philanthropy creativity. Cultural Preservation Group activities are funded by Hong Kong's Lingnan University; the activities and experiences of the group are discussed in detail in this chapter.

Service-Learning Integrated into Philanthropy Courses

The concept of service-learning has been closely linked with SYSU's course, "Civic Society and Philanthropy." The planner of the course, Zhu Jiagang, believes that service-learning only truly occurs when there is organic contact with the community. In addition, these experiences allow students to consciously apply knowledge of theory in community services and to bring community service experiences to classroom learning. After many years of implementation, we can now conclude that these practices have allowed us to achieve the following.

Course Instructor Improves Students' Service Skills with Theory and Knowledge

Zhu Jiangang is a professor in the Department of Anthropology at SYSU who cares deeply about community and social organization development. Based on his research and teaching experiences, Jiangang has developed a set of systematic and logical teaching materials for Civic Society and Philanthropy. The course consists of five sessions, namely "Social Transformation and Civil Society," "Active Citizenship and Community Building," "Philanthropy Organizations and Cross-border Cooperation," "Philanthropy Policy and Advocacy," and "Philanthropy Culture and Ecology."

Agency Supervisors as Guest Speakers

In concurrence with the course instructor, the agency supervisor provides service-learning opportunities to the students and is invited as a guest speaker for different lectures. While there, he/

she not only introduces relevant topics (such as cultural preservation) but also shares about the agency's development and other personal experiences. There are two reasons for including the guest speakers. First, the experiences of an agency supervisor serves as a case study for both the course instructor and the students. It enables students to understand the agency's services and analyze its development using knowledge gained in the classroom. This ultimately enhances the students' comprehension of the current situation regarding civic society in China. The second reason is to increase resource exchange between the university and the community. Through participating in discussions with university professors and students, the agency supervisor gains insights about this generation of university students' current situation and ways to engage students for the development of the agency's projects.

Throughout one course, the community partner Enning Road Academic Focus Group served as the service agency for the cultural preservation group and participated in classroom teaching activities. In the lecture, "Volunteering and Community Building," Xing Xiaowen, from Enning Road Academic Focus Group, and a tutor, Liu Ye, were invited as guest speakers to share and discuss their efforts in cultural preservation at Enning Road with all the students of Civic Society and Philanthropy. Through the sharing, all students, regardless of their service-learning participation, gained a clearer understanding of the topic discussed. The sharing session also allowed Enning Road Academic Focus Group to gain a better understanding of SYSU's students, to discuss potential challenges of the project with a variety of people, and to inform more people about their experiences in civic society.

Guests Lecturers Deepen Students' Theoretical Understanding

Apart from lectures by the course instructor and agency supervisor, guest lecturers are invited to share their practical experiences in the community. Students' understanding of the lecture material has been deepened from different perspectives. For example, Chan Kin-man from the Chinese University of Hong Kong was invited to talk about citizenship and civic quality and to help students understand individual citizen identity and their individual role in the community.

Combination of Course Assessment and Service-Learning

While the service-learning component is not a compulsory requirement in the Civic Society and Philanthropy course, all students are highly encouraged to participate. The overall course assessment is primarily based on the students' individual final reports, which are completed at the end of semester. All students, whether they participate in service-learning or not, are assessed by their fellow classmates and graded according to the final report. For the students who participate in service-learning, the agency supervisors and tutors are also invited to grade their performance. Grading criteria include attendance in group activities and contribution to group activities. Lastly, the marks from different stakeholders are summed up in order to assign each student a final grade.

Combination of Course and Workshop

In response to students' need for service-learning, four workshops were organized. The first two workshops target both the agency supervisors and the tutors, while the last two workshops target all of the service-learning students. While the workshops cover a wide range of topics, the main purpose is to allow the agency supervisors, tutors, and students to gain a better understanding of different service-learning elements through a series of sharing and reflection activities.

Through the four workshops, the course instructor has an opportunity to engage in a dialogue with the students, which increases his/her understanding of students' needs and the process of service-learning. The course instructor believes this is an effective way of reflection for himself/herself and his/her students as well. These kinds of workshops serve as platforms for students to exchange with not only the teachers, but also their peers. The students can experience personal growth, increase their knowledge about fellow group members, and understand the meaning of service-learning and the community.

Service-Learning: Learning through Practice

Students learn theories and social backgrounds of civic society and philanthropy from the course. If students wish to have deeper understanding of a specific topic, they are highly encouraged to join a study group. The study group is arranged by the course tutor. The readings and discussions provided by these study groups allow students to further explore a specific topic. The cultural preservation group organized three rounds of study groups that examined various topics, including "Learning from the Perspective of Architectural Planning," "Learning from the Perspective of History and Culture," and "Learning from the Perspective of Action and Struggle." Reading materials, mainly academic articles and books, were prepared by both the agency supervisors and the tutor. The materials included *The Politics of Living* by Guo Yuhua and Chen Yuan, *Seeing Like State: How Certain Schemes to Improve the Human Condition Have Failed* by James C. Scott, *Nostalgia for Today: The Past and Present of Cultural Preservation* by Ip Iam-chong, etc. In the meantime, students also enhanced their understanding of cultural preservation through watching documentaries, such as *Our Home at Kangleli* and *Raging Land 2: Breaking New Ground through Thorns and Thistles*.

Through the learning guidance of the agency supervisors and the tutor, students involved in the study groups gained a deeper understanding of cultural preservation topics. Overall, the study groups allow students to explore and discuss questions that are not addressed in the classroom setting, thus deepening their learning and insights. Under the guidance of the agency supervisors and the tutor, the discussions are professional and scholarly.

Students' understanding of specific social topics is further enhanced through visiting various service agencies and projects of the agencies. With the cooperation of the Enning Road Academic Focus Group, students also had a field trip to Guangzhou's Enning Road. The agency supervisor introduced the current situation and the challenges of Enning Road and Enning Road Academic Focus Group projects to the students.

After learning the combined knowledge and theories and going on visits to the community, students begin designing and implementing service practicums in groups. For example, the cultural

Table 1. Pre-Test and Post-Test Questionnaires of Students Who Participated in Service-Learning in the 2013 Spring Semester (1 = lowest, 10 = highest)

DOMAIN	PRE-TEST QUESTIONNAIRE		POST-TEST QUESTIONNAIRE		DISCREPANCY	t-VALUE
	M	SD	M	SD		
Communication Skills	6.93	1.61	6.54	1.79	−0.39	1.32
Organizational Skills	7.07	1.37	6.9	1.57	−0.17	0.71
Social Competence	7.78	1.02	7.49	1.45	−0.29	1.43
Problem-Solving Skills	7.19	1.34	7.08	1.43	−0.11	0.47
Research Skills	5.69	2.04	6.37	1.84	0.68	−2.23*
Positive Attitude	8.05	1.32	7.79	1.52	−0.26	1.2
Overall Satisfaction	8.89	1.18	8.29	1.76	−0.6	2.7

$*p < 0.01$.

preservation group participated in preparing the service-learning activity "Protecting Tiny Red Buildings." For this service practicum, students cleaned the tiny abandoned red buildings on campus and organized activities that raised awareness of the tiny red buildings. Through different forms of activities, including but not limited to actively inviting teachers and students to give seminars, hold discussions, and organize exhibitions, students raised the university teachers and students' concern for the tiny red buildings. The students also had an opportunity to directly engage in a dialogue with the university and express their ideas for cultural preservation.

In this service practicum, students actively explored the resources around them and contemplated the relationship between individuals, the campus, the community, and society at large. Under the guidance of the service agency and the tutors, students have initiated a wide range of service-learning activities, each of which have addressed a different group's topic; the results of these service-learning activities are very encouraging.

Service-Learning Assessment and Prospects

In order to conduct student assessments, the service-learning questionnaires developed by Hong Kong's Lingnan University were adopted. The pre-test questionnaire was conducted three weeks before service-learning and the post-test questionnaire was conducted three weeks after the end of service-learning; both were completed online. One hundred and eight students answered the pre-test questionnaire while eighty-three students answered the post-test questionnaire. The students included in our sampling completed both questionnaires. After selection, we retained 160 questionnaires (80 pre-test questionnaires and 80 post-test questionnaires). Detailed analysis is as follows.

Seven aspects, including communication skills, organizational skills, social competence, problem solving skills, research skills, positive attitudes, and overall satisfaction were evaluated through the pre-test and post-test questionnaire (see Table 1). The results were that students gave themselves lower marks in all aspects except for research skills after participating in service-learning. It is very likely because students nowadays are overconfident in their abilities and general understanding.

They had thought they understood the society very much; however, what they learned about the society came only from reading books or doing simple voluntary services. Thus, they graded themselves better in the pre-test questionnaire.

After the field trips to the community, students had a chance to contact community organizations, talk to people in need, and conduct interviews. Students gradually realized their individual relationships with the society were minimal and their involvement in society was limited. Some of the students began questioning their communication skills, organizational skills, social competence, and problem-solving skills. In this aspect, the current service-learning programs at SYSU still have room for improvement. First, we have to understand that students will be shocked and may even feel doubtful about themselves when they are initially immersed in a community. Instead of merely "releasing" students from the ivory tower of higher education, service-learning also must guide students to proactively enter the community, understand the community, and serve the community. Only when students are seriously serving in the community will they realize the importance of understanding the community's needs and how to better improve themselves. Through this kind of experience, students are able to understand the relationship between an individual and society, as well as the individual's responsibilities to the society. This is what we call "cultivation of civic awareness," and it is the future direction of improvement for the practice of service-learning.

Of course, one cannot ignore the fact that the students' self-evaluation of research skills improved after participating in service-learning. After running the t-test, it was concluded that service-learning significantly impacts students' research skills because they need to search for more information about the community and the service targets. Thus, students' research skills indeed improve through service-learning.

At the end of the course, all students hand in their final reports. After further examination of these reports, we have found that students gain a deeper understanding of service-learning-related topics and enhanced their personal understanding and insights after application. The following statements were mentioned in students' reports:

"The main focus of Enning Road is to decide whether to demolish it or not. People are not satisfied with the amount of compensation. That is why residents fought against the government."

"I thought about the necessity of cultural preservation. In the process of preserving the culture, we do not only have to focus on cultural preservation, but also pay attention to the feelings of the people who live in the community."

"The cultural preservation movement was not only about the simple matter of letting the government to demolish the buildings or not, but also about practical issues such as city planning, architecture protection, funding, and relocation of residents. These problems are closely related. Pull one single piece of hair and you will move the whole body. If someone wants to protect the culture, we have to answer the questions above. Having the mentality of an antique lover is definitely not enough to solve problems. A comprehensive consideration and professional analysis, appropriate deployment of people, organization, and marking techniques are indispensable in the cultural preservation movement as well. This will be a game between the citizens, the developer and the government. Difficult but exciting."

From these statements, we can confirm that practical experiences with the community, classroom learning, and study group discussions have strengthened the students' understanding of and their ability to critically think about cultural preservation.

Along with deepening students' understanding of cultural preservation, the course has also improved the students' abilities through the learning and service practicum. In the course feedback, students mentioned the following:

"In the process of group learning, my observation and problem-solving skills were improved. It allowed me to look at every existing problem from a more professional perspective and find out the solutions through professional learning and reading non-teaching materials."

"During the exchanges of cultural preservation groups, I watched many videos of the cultural preservation movement in other areas. My horizon was widened, and at the same time it helped me think more about the problems of cultural preservation and of the city and the residents. I haven't come up with any solutions for the time being, but it trained my thinking skills."

The course's service-learning component provides students with opportunities to both physically and personally experience the community they are working with. Through these experiences, the students discover the relationship between the society and themselves, which cultivates the students' sense of social responsibility. In the feedback, students mentioned:

"We have to spread the message to the public in time, to unite different forces, to spread our responsibilities, and to build a more harmonious community."

"From knowing nothing about NGOs and cultural preservation, to now involving myself and gradually formed personal views, this is an enlightenment to me. From an outsider to an insider, from the silent majority to an active citizen, it is actually a sublimation of thinking."

Overall, students prefer the service-learning approach to learning. This preference can provisionally be attributed to the fact that service-learning expands students' horizons while also enabling them to further their understanding and gain more experiences.

"In my opinion, joining group activities allows me to gain more than learning in classroom. There are three main reasons. Firstly, the form of learning is more flexible. Secondly, exploration of the topics through the group activities would be deeper. Lastly, I could meet a lot of people 'with stories.'"

From the students' feedback, it can be concluded that students' skills and knowledge improve after taking a course with service-learning. Involvement in application activities leads to a change in students' attitudes toward the society and to the realization of the link between individuals and society, both of which are goals of service-learning.

Conclusion on Service-Learning and Its Way Forward at the University

With the course integrated with a service-learning component in recent semesters, the relationship between the service agencies and SYSU improved and has made for a partnership mode. Under the guidance of the service agencies, students' service-learning is executed in a more professional manner. Contrastingly, feedback from the students revealed that they have some doubts and criticisms. Thus, based on the past experience, we will continue to improve the service-learning projects of the course.

It is necessary to combine professional knowledge with service-learning into academic courses. From the community partners' feedback, it is obvious that service-learning is different from simple volunteer service, such as those similar to community services. The simple volunteer services only require volunteers to complete assigned community service tasks, such as traffic control or maintenance of community security. Service-learning, on the other hand, emphasizes the process of combining learning with practice and vice versa. This process ultimately involves the students consciously applying professional knowledge. Therefore, we will continue exploring the ways in which students can use their professional knowledge to carry out service in addition to methods and platforms in which course planners can effectively combine professions and services.

In order to achieve this application of professional knowledge, we will continue to invite the agency supervisors to share their experiences in class. This allows students to talk to, learn from, and personally connect with community partners. In addition, more specific workshops will be developed according to the needs of the students and the community partners. These workshops, which will potentially include public seminars, writing, project planning and proposal, etc., will aim to improve the students' skills, enable the application of knowledge and abilities to service, and, ultimately, encourage the practice of "meaningful service."

Service-learning is a process of giving back to the community. Service-learning is not only a learning process for the students, but also a giving-back process to the community. Therefore, in addition to caring about students' gains and growth, how much the community benefits from the students' services is of high concern. In addition to sending students to the community, service-learning also intends to transfer the resources of higher education institutions to the community in order to connect the academy with the community. During the process, students have to participate in serving the community with professional perspectives. Students who have enrolled the Civic Society and Philanthropy course have to grasp the general theories and knowledge of civic society and philanthropy; at the same time, they also need to understand the specific contents of related topics through study groups and lectures. Under the guidance of the course instructor, agency supervisors, and the tutor, students have to then apply their knowledge from the classroom to the community-based service practicum.

After the practicum, students are required to write final reports in addition to presenting on their service experiences, findings, and feedback at the "Report-Back Celebration," which encourages dialogue among teachers, agency supervisors, and students. After receiving opinions and hearing about the experiences of all stakeholders, we hope that students will apply the learning outcomes of the studies and services to community development.

SYSU was one of the first universities to develop philanthropy courses with service-learning elements. After six years of organizing and directing the practicum, we accumulated a vast amount of experience, which we plan on promoting to other higher education institutions. At the same time, we also recognize that we can learn from other higher education institutions that are engaged in service-learning because their experiences and programs may differ from ours. Therefore, we have to continue exploring service-learning models that are applicable to our classroom, as well as projects that can be effectively associated with existing courses.

About the Institution

SYSU, founded by Dr. Sun Yat-sen, is a comprehensive multi-disciplinary university with over a 100-year history. It is a key university under the Chinese National Higher Education Project. The university is comprised of "a community of teachers and students," through which "teachers represent the school body," and embrace the idea of "educating with love." The aim of SYSU is to nurture high-quality, interdisciplinary students who possess international perspectives, a sense of social responsibility, and an innovative spirit. Graduates are expected to be well-mannered, honest, diligent, positive-minded, innovative, and responsible as they acquire trained career skills. With this vision, the university focuses on life-long learning and development, which is a reflection of the university's core value of educating with love. The undergraduate programs are in line with "general education, field training and interdisciplinary innovation." The postgraduate programs are aimed at cultivating innovative, motivated, and productive doctoral candidates in various fields.

Being one of the leading universities in the People's Republic of China, SYSU, includes the humanities, social sciences, natural sciences, technical sciences, medical sciences, pharmacology, and management sciences.

About the Department

The academic tradition of the Department of Anthropology of SYSU can be traced back to the National Sun Yat-sen University Institute of Language History Studies. The institute was established in August 1927 by director Fu Sinian. In 1931, it was renamed Institute of Literature and History Studies/Institute of Liberal Studies. In 1981, SYSU became the first university in the country to reopen a department of anthropology. In the same year, the department was granted the right to confer PhDs in anthropology as well as sociology, and so became the first PhD-granting anthropology department in China. The Department of Anthropology became the only educational department that offers three degree levels of education—PhDs, master's, and bachelor's degrees—in the country.

Sun Yat-sen University China Institute of Charity Studies is a Level 1 non-profit study organization approved by SYSU on April 1, 2011. The Institute was built in the Pearl River Delta region, where charity is relatively well-developed and is of concern for adjacent areas in Mainland China, Hong Kong, Macau, and Taiwan, thus making the region a suitable place to study charity. Our vision is to promote innovation in charity and to establish a pluralistic, fair, sustainable, and better society by undertaking action-oriented studies. Our mission is to become a charity think-tank of world influence through studies, teaching, and participation in policy innovation.

About the Course

Civic Society and Philanthropy is a core course of SYSU's general education. Philanthropy is the core concept of this course. Through an analysis of theories of the concept and application cases, the course aims to encourage students to understand civic society and philanthropy. Concretely speaking, the course attempts to allow students to (1) understand citizenship, civic virtue and civil society organizations; (2) reflect on related topics on the domain of philanthropy; (3) learn and develop charitable action-related strategies, mentality and leadership; and (4) learn the relationship between the country, market and civic society and how they form cross-border collaboration.

Pioneer in Various Forms: Discussion of the Service-Learning Model of Lingnan University in Hong Kong

Carol MA Hok-ka, Alfred CHAN Cheung-ming, Fanny MAK Mui-fong, and Alice LIU Cheng

Lingnan University, which is the only liberal arts university in Hong Kong, has a long history in both Chinese and Western learning. Focusing on the comprehensive development approach of Whole-Person Education, Lingnan University is committed to establishing students' civic awareness; cultivating their knowledge, skills, and observation power; allowing them to pursue their goals; and developing their abilities to think, judge, and care about the world as well as take responsibilities in the ever-changing social, cultural, and economic environment. Lingnan's teaching objectives are not only about nurturing scholars, but also fostering future pillars who know how to take from the society and give back to the society. The concept that service-learning advocates, which is a combination of "formal academic studies," "meaningful service," and "reflection," fully embodies the teaching philosophy of liberal arts education and the motto of our university, "Education for Service." Through active participation in social services, students apply what they learn, use knowledge and skills in real life, and deepen their grasp of knowledge to witness their growth and accomplishments. In the process, students build their sense of social responsibility, learn about different social issues, and enhance their whole-person development.

From 2004 to 2005, with support from the Kwan Fong Charitable Foundation, Lingnan University launched a service-learning pilot scheme, which formed the basis for the development of the university-wide service-learning programs. After receiving support from a donor and the university, the Office of Service-Learning (OSL) was officially established in 2006 and, to this day, remains committed to integrating the concept of service-learning into the liberal arts curriculum among institutions in Hong Kong. Over the years, the OSL has successfully launched a series of local and international service-learning programs, each of which provide students with opportunities to apply academic theory to service. In addition, under the guidance of course instructors and community agency representatives, these service-learning projects allow Lingnan students to cultivate active and positive attitudes and practical working skills. We insist on working on the following four missions: (1) manifest Lingnan University's motto "Education for Service"; (2) promote interactive learning and district service activities; (3) provide whole-person development learning environments to students; and (4) enhance learning and teaching efficiency and quality through applications of service-learning. Although the concept of service-learning was initiated in the West, its core ideas are very similar to those of Chinese traditional Confucian culture. In correspondence with the core thinking of Confucianism, Lingnan University has adopted the core values of *ren* (benevolence), *yi* (justice), *li* (propriety), *zhi* (wisdom) and *xin* (integrity) into service-learning. While Lingnan University as a whole focuses on students' whole-person development, various service-learning projects also aim to promote the core values and to make positive impacts on students' development.

Characteristics of Lingnan's Service-Learning Model

Four Service-Learning Models

Lingnan University's service-learning-related courses and activities are directly organized by the OSL and various academic departments. The primary responsibilities of the OSL, besides simply organizing projects, include investigating community's needs, organizing training for students, developing reflection activities, organizing collaboration between professional subjects at the university and community service agencies, and ensuring the quality of the projects and the students' learning outcomes together with the course instructors. Currently, there are four service-learning models at Lingnan University.

DEPARTMENTAL SERVICE-LEARNING COURSES OFFERED BY DEPARTMENTS

This model integrates service-learning into academic courses by encouraging students to apply the theory and contents learned in a course to a service-learning project. Students who participate in service-learning as a part of an academic course not only gain credits, but are also given an opportunity to deepen their understanding of theory and academic knowledge through application. This model is a core part of Lingnan's service-learning and its promotion has successfully reached the entire university. Currently, fifteen out of eighteen academic departments—Faculty of Arts: (1) Department of Cultural Studies, (2) Department of English, (3) Department of History, (4) Department of Visual Studies, (5) Department of Philosophy, (6) Department of Translation, (7) Department of Chinese; Faculty of Social Sciences: (8) Department of Economics, (9) Department of Sociology and Social Policy, (10) Department of Political Sciences, (11) Department of Applied Psychology; Faculty of Business and Administration, (12) Department of Marketing and International Business, (13) Department of Management, (14) Department of Accountancy, and (15) Department of Computing and Decision Sciences—from all faculties at Lingnan (Faculty of Arts, Faculty of Social Sciences, and Faculty of Business) offer academic courses with service-learning components.

SERVICE-LEARNING COURSES CO-TAUGHT BY THE OFFICE
OF SERVICE-LEARNING AND DEPARTMENTS

This model, which emphasizes the multi-disciplinary characteristics of service-learning, allows different course instructors and OSL staff to co-teach credit-bearing service-learning courses. By having OSL staff and an academic instructor co-teach, the courses enhance the students' understanding of community service skills along with their professional knowledge, both of which are combined in their application project. This model eliminates the limitations of service-learning in a course because it allows teachers and students to investigate and address social problems from different perspectives holistically. Higher demand for coordination between different departments and the OSL needs to be considered. "Service Leadership Practicum through Service-Learning" is the first joint service-learning course between OSL and Department of Management. Service leadership involves serving society and/or contributing to the well-being and development of others by taking initiative in collaboration with service recipients and other stakeholders while also meeting the service leaders' personal needs. Through this course, students are able to explain how they have attempted to practice a range of service leadership attributes; evaluate their own effectiveness in practicing service leadership to diagnose and meet the needs of service recipients through service-learning; explain the organizing principles that facilitate and support effective service-learning and service leadership; initiate and deliver services that are perceived to be of value to the host community organization; and develop realistic plans for self-improvement in relation to salient attributes of service-learning and service leadership.

SERVICE-LEARNING COURSES OFFERED BY THE OFFICE OF SERVICE-LEARNING

This model designs independent credit-bearing courses according to service-learning concepts and theories. The courses fully integrate service-learning into teaching, allowing students to understand topics like social structure, policies, and welfare through activities. Through this integration and understanding, the course enhances students' civic awareness, sense of social responsibility, and ability to discover and solve difficult problems in addition to providing local and overseas service-learning opportunities to students.

SERVICE-LEARNING COURSES OFFERED BY OVERSEAS INSTITUTIONS AND APPROVED BY THE DIRECTOR OF OFFICE OF SERVICE-LEARNING AND HEADS FROM DEPARTMENTS

This model provides recognition for students who enroll in courses with service-learning components offered by overseas institutions which are on the list of Lingnan University's exchange partners. If students participate in service-learning related projects and/or courses during their exchange programs, they can gain credits through credit transfer at Lingnan University by getting approval from either their department head or Director of Service-Learning. Recognition and approval of diverse and internationalized service-learning experiences improves students' active participation and strengthens sharing and exchanges of local and overseas service-learning experiences; thus this model also helps achieve the goal of not only learning local community knowledge, but also learning from each other, including course instructors, fellow students, and community partners.

The four service-learning models of Lingnan's service-learning programs emphasize the combination of teaching and learning. Each project abides by standard procedures and principles, such as the systematic planning, preparation, training, application, reflection, and conclusion stages. Combining theoretical knowledge and community service distinguishes this advanced pedagogy from simple volunteerism. Through participating in activities such as training, consultation, reflection, presentation, and exchanges/cooperation with community partners, students gain diversified learning experiences in addition to enhancing their abilities in a variety of learning outcomes. Throughout the service-learning process, the involvement of course instructor is very important, as he/she needs to design the linkage between service-learning and academic learning. With the deliberate design of course instructor, project arrangement, course learning outcomes, and the service targets are interrelated. There are also corresponding assessments to evaluate course effectiveness and student learning outcomes in designated periods of time. From 2006 to 2016, more than 6,000 students, or 600 students per annum on average, participated in credit-bearing service-learning courses at Lingnan University.

Below is a brief introduction of the important elements, standard procedures, and steps in Lingnan's model of service-learning projects, as a reference for institutions interested in developing service-learning for mutual exchange and sharing.

Organization Structure

The organization structure of a service-learning project consists of four stakeholders, namely the course instructor, the program coordinator, the agency supervisor, and the students. Each participating stakeholder has different tasks in the preparation, implementation, and evaluation process, as stated in Table 1.

Implementation of the Service-Learning Project

The implementation includes four main stages: preparation, orientation, practicum and conclusion. These four stages are closely related. Table 2 illustrates process and framework.

Assessment Design

In order to assess the effectiveness of service-learning, as well as learning and teaching plans, all stakeholders are required to complete specific evaluation tasks (see Table 3).

Lingnan University Service-Learning Outcomes

Lingnan's model of service-learning successfully entered its tenth year in 2015–2016. In the previous ten years, we seized every opportunity to develop the Service-Learning and Research Scheme as a whole, expand the social network to strengthen local and overseas partnerships, and design influential service-learning programs for the students, the university, and the community. We yielded fruitful results in these ten years.

Over the years, service-learning has developed rapidly at Lingnan University. Not only are the forms of service-learning programs becoming more diverse and innovative, but the number of participants and interest and support from faculty grows every year. We have been closely tracking the Service-Learning and Research Scheme and its associated outcomes in order to ensure improvement in students' learning outcomes and the effectiveness of service-learning. The learning outcomes mainly include seven main categories: subject-related knowledge, communication

Table 1. Responsibilities and Tasks of Different Stakeholders in a Service-Learning Program

UNIT	CORE TASKS	WORK AND TASKS
Course Instructor	The core role of course instructors is to develop close working relationships with the program coordinator and service agency, make suggestions, organize suitable training workshops, and fulfill student needs in learning. Course instructors are required to create continuous learning opportunities, give students practical advice, and assess students' overall performance.	1. Design courses (both tutorials and lectures) to accommodate service-learning project (please see attached course outline for this mode for reference). 2. Identify and communicate with potential service agency and prepare a list of tasks that specific organizations will require students to undertake. 3. Draft a simple guideline (a guideline for a tutorial, for example) for students interested in service-learning. 4. Integrate service-learning approach into the course outline. 5. Set a participant limit for service-learning project. 6. Inform students about the option to choose service-learning project in the first class and allow them to decide whether to participate. Arrange a second guiding meeting and a visit to at least one of the service agencies, letting them know about their responsible tasks. 7. Confirm the schedule of service practicums and arrange students to form groups (four to five students) to prepare for the service. 8. Supervise students' process of the service. 9. Conduct assessment: reflective assessment essays, group report and presentation. 10. Fill in evaluation questionnaire.
Students	Students' primary task is to provide service for service agencies under the guidance of the agency supervisor and course instructor. Students are required to apply knowledge of their majors, follow service agency's general practice, respect service recipients' privacy and personal data, participate in all assigned training workshops, guiding lessons and reflective meeting, and submit all assessment documents.	1. Participate in training workshop 2. Participate in service practicum 3. Assessment: journals, reflective assessment essays and group report and presentation 4. Evaluation: questionnaire, focus groups with specific topics
Agency Supervisor	Agency supervisors' primary responsibility is to provide suitable service-learning for students. Supervisors provide suitable practicum opportunities and professional guidance according to students' learning needs. They are required to build a close working relationship with program coordinator and course instructor, supervise service-learning quality and assess students' overall performance.	1. Supervise service practicum. 2. Conduct assessment: assessment form. 3. Conduct evaluation: questionnaire survey and in-depth interview.
Program Coordinator	Program coordinators' role includes participation of all three major stakeholders: coordinate course guiding meeting, training workshops, and service-learning classes. Program coordinators are responsible for planning and acting as a liaison, coordinating and assessing the service-learning programs' effectiveness and outcomes. They are required to stay in contact with different partnering units and are responsible for student enrolment, student participation and assessing students' performance. If the number of students participating in service-learning scheme is relatively low (normally speaking, four students form a group, less than twenty students in total), the program coordinator will assume the role of course instructor.	1. Coordinate different units (provide consultation, if necessary). 2. Arrange preparation and consultation meetings.

Table 2. Service-Learning and Research Scheme Implementation Procedures

MAIN STAGES	SPECIFIC PROJECTS	RESPONSIBLE STAKEHOLDERS
Preparation Stage	1. Identify course instructors and service agencies interested in the project.	Course instructors, program coordinators, and agency supervisors
	2. Integrate service-learning into the course, prepare outline for students, and revise pre-test and post-test questionnaires for all participants (optional).	Course instructors and program coordinators
	3. First lecture: debriefing and student enrollment. Students have to decide preliminarily in the first week of the semester and visit at least one service agencies. In the second week of the semester, confirm the final list of students participating in service-learning and the practicum list.	Course instructors, program coordinators and students
	4. All participants are required to fill in pre-test questionnaire (optional).	Course instructors and program coordinators
Orientation Stage	5. Arrange a site visit to the service agency for students, help students familiarize with service agency background and meet with supervisors.	Course instructors and program coordinators
	6. Provide training workshops that allow students to understand suitable techniques. Arrange topic training workshop for students to help them complete practicum tasks.	Course instructors and program coordinators
	7. Organize consultation meetings related to practicum and activity plan for students. Discuss feasibility of activities which are required to comply with course concepts and theories.	Course instructors, program coordinators, and students
Practicum Stage	8. Students undertake community service practicum. Primary mode includes one-on-one tasks (interviews and family visits), group activities (students organize group activities and service target exchanges), community projects (large-scale activities such as exhibition and studies group), and indirect service (helping social enterprises design promotion and development strategies, enabling them to better serve the society).	Course instructors, program coordinators, agency supervisors, and students
Conclusion Stage	9. Hold reflection meeting on service and conduct field assessment (journal).	Course instructors, program coordinators, and students
	10. The end of practicum Assessment (Reflection) meeting	Course instructors, program coordinators and students
	11. Administer post-test questionnaire assessment (survey questionnaire, personal assessment report, and all participating stakeholders' assessment report) and conduct in-depth interview with service agency.	Course instructors, program coordinators, agency supervisors, and students
	12. Conduct student focus groups with specific topics (optional).	Program coordinators and students
	13. Collect practicum group report, individual reflective essays.	Students
	14. Hold in-class presentations by students.	Course instructors, program coordinators, and students
	15. Have a report-back ceremony (optional).	Program coordinators

Table 3. Assessment Tasks of All Units in a Service-Learning Program

RESPONSIBLE STAKEHOLDERS	ASSESSMENT	TASK INTRODUCTION
Students	Pre-test and post-test questionnaire Journals Practicum group reports Reflection essays/self-evaluation reports Groups with specific topic	In order to assess students learning outcomes during the service-learning scheme, students are required to fill in pre-rest and post-test questionnaires. These questionnaires assess students' subject-related knowledge, communication skills, organization skills, problem-solving skills, studies skills, civic awareness, and social competence. Other assessment methods include journals, practicum group reports, reflection essays, and self-evaluations. The purpose of the journals is to understand how students organize their practicums, understand their feelings and thought-process, and their learning situation in the practicum. Practicum group reports assess students' application of knowledge in real life situation and the ability to identify service target's needs and project planning. Reflection essays are the students' complete evaluation for each tasks. They are effective for understanding the students' ability to integrate what they have learned to their service. For Mode 3 students, self-evaluations may assess students' learning experience and performance strengths and weaknesses. At the end of each semester, an optional session with students from different groups units may be arranged in order to encourage sharing about their teaching, guiding and practicum experiences.
Course instructor	Conclusion questionnaire In-depth interview Groups with specific topics	Course instructors grade students' service-learning proposals and reports and suggest ways in which they can improve. For Model 3 students, course instructors assess their service-learning performance by learning attitudes, application abilities, knowledge expansion, and ability to integrate theory and practice, and their mid-term and final assessments. Course instructors are required to fill in conclusion questionnaires at the end of the course to assess students' learning outcomes during service-learning program.
Agency supervisor	Conclusion questionnaire Group with specific topics (optional)	Agency supervisors supervise students and provide practical guidance to students according to their specialties and experiences. Since they coordinate and lead the practicum services in the field, they can therefore assess students' performance in the areas of participation, working attitudes and responsibility. When the practicum ends, agency supervisors are required to fill in a conclusion questionnaire to assess students' learning outcomes. In addition, agency supervisors are required to conduct in-depth interview with students to assess the students' performance in practicum and learning experience, and improvement methods in preparation, coordination and execution.
Program coordinator	Collect opinions Conclusion questionnaire Group with specific topics (optional)	Program coordinators assist the course instructor to assess students' performance during service-learning by evaluating their service-learning proposals, practicum reports, reflective essays, and journals. In addition, they collect opinions and feedbacks from social service agency supervisors and course instructors. Program coordinators are required to fill in conclusion questionnaire to assess preparation, execution, students' learning quality assurance, students' learning efficiency and impacts to the community. In addition, program coordinators also arrange reflection meetings to facilitate students' learning during practicum.

Table 4. Learning Outcomes of Pre-Test and Post-Test Comparison of Students Who Participated in Service-Learning during Academic Years 2006 to 2014 (local credit-bearing service-learning courses)

	NO. OF PARTICIPANTS	PRE-TEST		POST-TEST		IMPROVEMENT RATIO	p-VALUE*
		M	SD	M	SD		
Subject-Related Knowledge	2268	6.29	1.59	7.15	2.40	13.65%	0.00
Communication Skills	2272	6.43	1.33	6.78	1.33	5.47%	0.00
Organization Skills	2272	6.67	1.32	7.14	1.26	7.03%	0.00
Social Competence	2272	6.74	1.35	7.36	1.20	9.20%	0.00
Problem-Solving Skills	2272	6.61	1.28	7.19	1.19	8.84%	0.00
Research Skills	2272	6.06	1.48	6.76	1.44	11.55%	0.00

*$p < 0.05$; when the p-value is smaller than 0.05, a statistical significance is observed in results between pre-test and post-test.

skills, organizational skills, social competence, problem-solving skills, research skills, and civic orientation (Chan, Lee & Ma, 2009). Pre-test and post-test questionnaires indicate positive feedback in all areas in self-evaluation from students who participate in service-learning. The results are encouraging, as shown in Table 4. Since the student learning outcome assessment area "Civic Orientation" was not included until 2011, no relevant results are shown in Table 4.

In the university, the number of student participants in service-learning grew from 284 in 2006 to 1,320 in 2015. By the academic year 2014–2015, Lingnan University had successfully launched thirty-nine courses that have service-learning elements and four large-scale local and overseas service-learning programs. One thousand, three hundred and twenty students have served more than 19,400 people in the community, with more than 46,300 service hours in total (OSL, 2015). Starting in 2016–2017, service-learning will become a graduation requirement at Lingnan University; all students will be required to participate in at least one service-learning course/project before graduation. It is apparent that service-learning has not only become an educational focus, but also a symbol of Lingnan University as a whole. After this advanced pedagogy was established at Lingnan University, other institutions in Hong Kong actively engaged and started launching service-learning programs of their own. As a result, many higher education institutions in Hong Kong have started vigorously promoting service-learning. Lingnan University also organized the first "Asia-Pacific Regional Conference on Service-Learning" in 2007, which led to extensive discussions among higher education institutions in Hong Kong about local development and opportunities in service-learning. The OSL at Lingnan University initiated the Higher Education Service-Learning Network (HESLN) in Hong Kong. Participating institutions include the University of Hong Kong, Chung Chi College from The Chinese University of Hong Kong, Lingnan University, Hong Kong University of Science and Technology, City University of Hong Kong, the Hong Kong Institute of Education, Hong Kong Shue Yan University, Hong Kong Polytechnic University, Hong Kong Baptist University, and Hong Kong College of Technology. HESLN serves as a platform for sharing service-learning experiences and resources in order to facilitate mutual support among institutions and develop partnership schemes. Studies' results include successful establishment of the "Common Outcome Measurement," which standardizes measurement for learning outcomes of students from different institutions participating in service-learning and hopefully serves as an important policy to seek support from the University Grants Committee to implement service-learning.

Lingnan University is not only a member of HESLN, but also one of the members of Service-Learning Asia Network. The network members consist of twenty-three higher education institutions from twelve countries and regions. They are all committed to facilitating regional collaborations and promoting development of service-learning in Asia. Since Lingnan University remains the role model for initiating and promoting service-learning in Asia, the university was elected as the secretary-general of the network. In addition to facilitating sharing and exchanges among higher education institutions in the Asia-Pacific region where service-learning has already been developed, Lingnan University has also actively promoted service-learning ideas to Mainland China in the recent years. In the 2012–2013 year, the university organized and launched a promotion plan for service-learning in China, providing grants and training to six higher education institutions in Mainland China and assisting them in successfully completing service-learning pilot projects schemes. It has received positive feedback, and some universities in China have also started to set up OSLs; for example, Sun Yet-sen University has established the first OSL in the Guangdong region.

With local and international support, Lingnan University is able to create various case studies for sharing and exchange among different stakeholders. Below are three case studies of service-learning project integrated with courses at Lingnan (see Table 5, 6 and 7). They are from the Faculty of Business, the Faculty of Social Sciences, and the Faculty of Arts.

Case One: Value Food and Be Gracious

From Food Waste to Food

According to the HKSAR Environmental Protection Department (2014), 3,600 tons of food waste is produced in Hong Kong every day, which is the weight of 200 double-decker buses! Although the department has plans to recycle food waste into useful resources, only 200 tons can be processed each day, which is far less than the amount produced. Actually, the most effective management method is to reduce the food waste. In 2011, the People Service Center (PSC) launched a "Food Collection Program" for the disposal of leftover food in markets and food chains. Through recycling food and redistributing to those in need, the Food Collection Program reduces waste of food and also helps to relieve the pressure of low-income families.

Helping Others, Helping Yourself

The philosophy of the Food Collection Program service, as Ms. FONG Wing Ling, Carol noted, is to establish a neighbor network of mutual assistance between service recipients through the process of food distribution. According to FONG, "Food Recycling is just the start to interact with residents. Our long-term goal is to develop a network in the community through the recipients so that they can help other people as well as themselves." FONG stresses that services should not be in one-sided. Therefore, the PSC asked the elderly recipients who are capable of being volunteers to help maintain community relations. The elderly further promote the program to other members of the community, so that more people in need can benefit.

Table 5. Case One: Value Food and Be Gracious

COURSE	BUS301 STRATEGIC MANAGEMENT
Course Instructor	Prof. Chen Tingting (Assistant Professor, Department of Management)
Service Agency	People Service Center
Service-Learning Project	Strategic Planning for "Food Collection Program"
Students' Role	Have in-depth research and strategic environment analysis on the program;
	Analyze the research and strategic environment analysis on the program;
	Propose possible strategic suggestions to improve the program and foster its sustainable development; and
	Propose possible strategic plan for agency to operate
Interviewees	Fong Wing-ling (Project Manager, People Service Center)
	Liu Ka-keung (Project Coordinator, People Service Center)

Table 6. Case Two: Youth Investigate Elderly Care Services

COURSE	SOC333 HEALTH, ILLNESS AND BEHAVIOUR
Course Instructor	Prof. Chan Cheung-ming, Alfred (Chair Professor of Social Gerontology, Department of Sociology and Social Policy)
	Dr. Ma Hok-ka, Carol (Adjunct Assistant Professor, Department of Sociology and Social Policy)
Service Agency	Yuen Yuen Institute Social Service Department
Service-Learning Scheme	Questionnaire Interview: "Youth Career Navigation Scheme in Elderly Services" (YCNSE)
Students' Role	Design a survey for evaluate effectiveness and incentives of YCNSE members to join the program
	Conduct survey interviews with YCNSE members in the center
Interviewees	Ma Hok-ka, Carol (Adjunct Assistant Professor, Department of Sociology and Social Policy)
	Yiu Man-hon (Year 3 Undergraduate Student, Faculty of Social Sciences [Contemporary Social Issues and Policy])

Table 7. Case Three: Unite the Deaf and Hearing, and Together We Build a Harmonious Community

COURSE	TRA108 / GEC364 / CLE9008 BILINGUAL CYBER CULTURE
Course Instructor	Prof. Chan Mei-hung (Assistant Professor, Department of Translation)
Service Agency	Hong Kong Association of the Deaf
Service-Learning Scheme	One-on-one tutorial for deaf children
Students' Role	Assist six deaf secondary students of Lutheran School for the Deaf to improve academically in English; organize a cultural or educational activity for the deaf children
Interviewees	Zhang Mochou (Project Officer, Hong Kong Association of the Deaf)
	Lam Oi-wing (Year 1 Undergraduate Student, Faculty of Arts)

Difficulties Are Just Things to Overcome

Even though the PSC just wants to help people, as a small social service organization, it has encountered many difficulties. At the beginning of the program, the PSC lacked resources and felt patronized by the shopkeepers. After initiating many efforts, the PSC finally successfully runs the program in Sham Shui Po. In order to benefit more people, it actively expands services to different districts, such as Tuen Mun. Developing new service areas is not easy, especially when shop owners routinely think that collecting and distributing leftover food will negatively affect their profits. While cooperating with Lingnan students, the PSC built trust with the merchants in Tuen Mun.

FONG recalled that students strengthened the understanding between the PSC and shopkeepers through field work and research surveys, laying a solid foundation for cooperation.

Launching through the Youth

This cooperation not only helped the PSC develop a community recycling network in Tuen Mun markets, but also improved Lingnan students' knowledge of social enterprises and food recycling. One group of students even helped the PSC contact the Lingnan canteen contractor to discuss the future direction of recycling food on campus. It encouraged the PSC for future public campaigns at universities. As the future leaders of society, university students need to be more concerned about the community and do their best to make use of social resources and make the city more sustainable. Let's take action now!

Case Two: Youth Investigate Elderly Care Services

Responsible Youth for Elderly Care

According to government projections, Hong Kong is becoming an aging population—there will be one elderly person over sixty-five years old out of every four persons by 2030 (HKSAR Census and Statistics Department, 2012). In the meantime, 7% of the elderly in Hong Kong are living in care homes for various reasons, which is higher than the global average of 4.4% (Leung, 2013). The elderly medical service industries in Hong Kong face many challenges, especially in the elderly care industry. They are encountering a substantial increase in demand as well as a shortage of health workers. The Yuen Yuen Institute Social Service Department and the Open University of Hong Kong have jointly organized "Youth Career Navigation Scheme in Elderly Services" to motivate young people to take up employment in residential care services for the elderly. The scheme is expected to alleviate the manpower shortage and improve the quality of service. To examine the scheme's effectiveness in attracting young people, Lingnan students assisted the Yuen Yuen Institute to conduct a questionnaire. The surveying process deepened students' understanding of the elderly care sector. YIU Man Hon, Douglas tried to articulate what he learned in class during this service-learning experience, "Besides wages, it is important to provide ancillary and support for health workers to attract young people to enter the elderly care industry. The units should emphasize more on the satisfaction of being caregiver and attract interested parties to participate in."

From the Heart

The healthcare system in Hong Kong divides into three levels of care. Primary care is the first point of contact with the healthcare system for the public. It provides direct access to comprehensive, continuous, coordinated, and people-centered care (HKSAR Department of Health, 2014). Elderly daily care is a kind of primary care that should provide the most basic and common services. Nevertheless, the shortage of health workers leads to questions about their service quality. As a result, the elderly do not have dignified lives in their later years. MA foresaw that the aging of the population would exacerbate the current situation. She brought this topic up in class to encourage students to think about the future direction of the elderly care industry development. She says, "The elderly care industry is an important part of primary care. It is closely linked with my course. If there is a serious lack of qualified health workers in care homes, a great burden rests on the entire healthcare system. We hope the students can understand the operation of the healthcare system through studying elderly care industry. And then they can have a deeper perception on topics such as health, illness, and behavior."

Respect and Cherish

The elderly have contributed greatly to society. The community should give them more support when they retire, so that they spend their later years in suitable and lovely places. Hong Kong faces the issue of an aging population now. But if we can uphold the spirit to "honor the aged of other families as we honor our own," perhaps we can also mitigate the burden on the elderly care service industry together.

Do you have a *treasure* in your family too? If so, please cherish it.

Case Three: Unite the Deaf and the Hearing, Together We Build a Harmonious Community

Sign Language Is also a Language

How many languages do you speak? Is sign language one of them? Would you regard it as a skill or a language? To the deaf, sign language is their mother tongue. It allows them to express themselves and communicate with others. It is no different from oral language. Unfortunately, many deaf people throughout the world suffer discrimination, making it difficult for them to open up their hearts to hearing people. To promote an inclusive society, students studying "Bilingual Cyber Culture" helped Hong Kong Association of the Deaf (HKAD) translate website information, organized tutorial classes, and visited the Hong Kong Science Museum for deaf children.

Feel the Innocence with Heart

Since the students lacked experience, they were concerned about getting along with the deaf children. They prepared some ice-breaking games to build teamwork and were surprised to receive very positive responses from the lively kids and their enthusiastic families. LAM Oi Wing, Irene recalls, "It may be trivial to us, but for the deaf children, these activities helped them get in touch with or even integrate into the society. The effects are greater than we've imagined." Throughout the two months, Lingnan students found that there was no great difference between deaf and hearing children. As long as one is patient and attentive to them, they are just as active as hearing children.

Translate for Target Audience

You may be wondering what the relationship is between this service-learning project and translation. The participating students also had this question. They had no prior knowledge of sign language and did not even understand the articulation between the service and their discipline. However, during their time with the deaf children, they understood the close relationship between languages and identities. Translation is a process of communicating. Besides translating the meanings of texts, interpreters have to pay attention to facial expressions and body language. "Serving to Learn" has always been an important part of service-learning projects. Through this service, students were able to get in touch with their target audience and learned to consider their needs. This is precisely the essence of translation.

Embrace the Deaf: Mutual Understanding

As an alumnus of the Department of Translation, Lingnan University, ZHANG Mo Chou, Iris led collaboration between the association and the university, which showed the spirit of a deaf and hearing communion. Lingnan students exchanged their culture with the deaf students. When asked about the results of this collaboration, Iris had deep feelings. "Compared to translating other languages, sign language interpretation conveys a culture," she stressed. When the Lingnan students spent time with the deaf children, they treated them just as hearing children so that a genuine deaf and hearing relationship was built.

Deaf people are not disabled—they only use unspoken communication. As long as we are willing to "listen" carefully to the deaf and accept each other, we will live in harmony.

Challenges and Opportunities

Although the OSL has made outstanding contributions to the development of service-learning at Lingnan University, in Hong Kong and even in the entire Asia-Pacific region, we are still faced with numerous difficulties and challenges. When service-learning becomes a graduation requirement of Lingnan University in the 2016–2017 academic year, the number and scale of projects and courses will increase, along with the number of local and overseas collaborations. Thus, the OSL continues to conduct self-evaluation, identify difficulties and downfalls, and establish potential solutions. Below are the four prevalent challenges that we are facing or that we predict we will face. We plan to actively respond to each of them and turn them into motivational opportunities.

Challenge One: Service-Learning Requires Active Cooperation and Full Support from Professional Course Instructors

Although the majority of professors have been actively developing and supporting service-learning, small portions still have doubts about the service-learning pedagogy and ways in which service-learning can be integrated into their academic courses. Currently, there are three out of eighteen departments that have yet to integrate service-learning into any of their courses. As for the departments that have already developed service-learning, there is still room for improvement, especially in regards to professors' individual participation.

The OSL is going to address this challenge in three different ways. First, the office will hold regular meetings with the course instructors in order to explain the details of applying the service-learning concept in teaching and enforce the quality assurance policy, including course approval procedures from the department, OSL, and the university's Academic Quality Assurance Committee. More importantly, the OSL will work closely with course instructors in order to develop tailor-made service-learning projects for their different subjects and service-learning departmental coordinators will be appointed by the department in order to share best practices among different teachers within/across departments at Lingnan. In addition, we will establish concrete responsibilities and guidelines for service-learning projects in order to ensure the quality learning outcomes of the courses. We will also provide the professors with a *Service-Learning Course Instructor Handbook* and other reference materials in order to help them develop their service-learning projects. Second, the OSL will increase the number of course instructors in the Service-Learning Program Committee. This will allow them to gain a better understanding of the overall development of service-learning at Lingnan regarding the university's policies. The Program Committee will also ensure the students' learning outcomes through "Quality Assurance Control," by evaluating the projects' effectiveness, quality of teaching, and students' learning outcomes. Third, with the generous support of Lingnan Foundation, course instructors may apply for funding to develop projects or courses related to service-learning.

Challenge Two: Reinforces Project Coordination between Different Stakeholders

The OSL has been taking on the vital role of coordinating various stakeholders' needs, including course instructors, students, service agencies, community partners, etc. As the number and scale of projects grow, the numbers of participants and agencies involvement also increase. We have to make sure the service-learning projects and the coordination of the different stakeholders maintain good quality. For example, the course instructor and students may propose assisting a service agency on its leadership and development program, but the agency may wish to receive direct and material services. Thus, managing stakeholders' expectations is always important to ensure the smoothness of the service-learning projects. Similarly, specific service-learning projects can only be decided after the students finish the course-selection process. This may cause students to be disappointed if the actual project they participate in does not match with their expectations when they first sign up for a course.

In order to address the challenge effectively, the OSL has been putting a lot of effort on communicating with different stakeholders, which helps to ensure they understand their roles and goals. Service-learning program coordinators will not only have in-depth exchanges with different departments to discuss specific situations, the needs of the agency and community, and the goals of participating in service-learning, but they will also facilitate exchanges and discussions among different stakeholders in order to ensure that all parties benefit. We also encourage course instructors to contact the service agencies through their personal networks or to develop service-learning projects with existing partnering agencies. The OSL is now building a platform that will allow all stakeholders who are involved in service-learning to engage in direct exchange and sharing. For example, course instructors, students, and community partners may discuss the needs, objectives, and proposals of their projects through the platform. Interested departments may have direct contact with each other, and thus effectively promote activeness in cooperation.

Challenge Three: The Need to Increase the Number of Program Coordinators and Ensure Stable Funding

Currently, the OSL coordinates all of the service-learning projects at Lingnan University. Though there are departmental service-learning coordinators being appointed in 2015, service-learning is still new to them. In order to ensure quality service-learning courses are implemented smoothly, it is suggested that all departments introduce an effective incentive-based system, in which internal staff members will be rewarded with funding or recognition, for example, to take on additional responsibilities in coordination and include service-learning in the promotion and tenure guidelines.

The majority of funding for Lingnan University's OSL comes from private donations, consultation projects and special grants from the government. The Lingnan Foundation, United Board for Christian Higher Education in Asia, and the Li & Fung Foundation have been generously supporting our work. Many donations, however, will soon be expired and lack of funding will severely affect the normal operations of the OSL. Furthermore, when service-learning becomes a graduation requirement at Lingnan University in the 2016–2017 academic year, the OSL will require more manpower and financial resources. The office will also need to employ more experienced and academically advanced staff members to supervise, administer, and ensure the smooth operation of projects and courses. Therefore, continuous and stable funding from the university is vital to sustain the OSL. Funding will ensure there are adequate staff members are responsible for the existing service-learning projects in different departments, the establishment of new courses, and the overall university service-learning policy management.

Challenge Four: Foster Community Partners to Be "Co-educators"

The existing service-learning projects and courses are primarily arranged by the program coordinators of the OSL and course instructors from various academic departments. Community partners are highly involved in the service aspects but lack in participation regarding student supervision and learning facilitation. As a key player in service-learning, community partners must take up the responsibility of being "co-educators" in order to provide effective guidance to the students during their service practicums and enhance their personal and professional growth.

Currently, quite a few of the community partners are merely aware of the concept of being co-educators. The OSL aims to strengthen training and communication with the community partners. One of the important points is to develop students' practical skills by making use of the agency supervisors' professional knowledge. We hope that they can provide valuable suggestions in the planning, execution, and conclusion stages, and actively participate in student training and supervision.

Future Development of Service-Learning at Lingnan

Service-learning is rapidly yet continually developing at Lingnan University. It is one of the key characteristics of Lingnan's liberal arts education. In order to prepare for the service-learning graduation requirement in the 2016–2017 academic year, we will improve current service-learning projects and courses (i.e., continue to integrate service-learning elements into more academic courses), implement more diverse service-learning models (i.e., the establishment of the OSL and course collaborations with academic subjects, and recognizing credits gained by Lingnan students participated in service-one earning courses of other higher education institutions while in a student exchange program, etc.), and improve evaluation of project effectiveness and student learning outcomes (i.e. make use of the longitudinal study method to track the impact of service-learning on students' abilities and learning outcomes over a long period of time).

Service-learning promotes combining professional knowledge with service experiences; therefore, cooperation between related stakeholders are vital and necessary. In order to enhance this cooperation, the establishment of a comprehensive Service-Learning Quality Assurance Control will become a top priority. This assessment will examine the students' learning environments, the effectiveness of service-learning in enabling professors to achieve teaching goals, and the benefits of service-learning activities for communities. Since the establishment of the office in 2006, there has been a strong focus on the quality and supervision of service-learning programs. In order to assess the quality and development of the service-learning programs at Lingnan University, three committees have been formed. The major roles of these committees include providing guidance and advice as well as monitoring the quality assurance process in the contexts of planning, developing, and reviewing the service-learning programs.

The first committee, the Service-Learning Program Committee, aims to review service-learning programs; assess the programs, forms, and content of courses; evaluate the development processes, academic relevance, and students' learning outcomes; and make further suggestions. The committee will also be responsible for promoting service-learning development in different academic subjects and will approve the launches of new courses with service-learning elements. Members of the committee are the Vice President, the Director of Service-Learning, department heads (or representatives) of all faculties, course instructor representatives, student representatives, and staff members of the OSL.

In addition, we also set up the "Service-Learning Advisory Board," which combines with overseas service-learning experts, department representatives, and community leaders. The board meeting is held one to two times annually to review service-learning courses and projects and to determine if they align with local and international standards and cooperation concerned in relation to local, regional, and international needs. This committee will also offer advice on the development of the OSL at Lingnan University in the context of Hong Kong and facilitate the cooperation between the OSL and different local and international service agencies. The committee will also review and evaluate the quality and overall development of service-learning programs of Lingnan University.

The third committee is the "Faculty–Community Committee." This committee will hold one to two meetings annually with course instructors from different departments, community partners, as well as a representative from the OSL to discuss the concrete planning and implementation of service-learning projects, which will ensure both that community needs are met and that the university's teaching and learning goals are achieved.

About the Institution

Lingnan University is Hong Kong's only liberal arts university. Using "Education for Service" as the motto, the university is committed to providing quality education with emphasis on whole-person education, cultivating students' independent thinking, judgment, caring for others, and overall social responsibility. In the rapidly changing environment of Hong Kong, the region of Asia, and even the whole world, Lingnan University's liberal arts education aims to build students' civic awareness and to cultivate their knowledge, skills, and observation powers. These abilities will ultimately provide students with vision, passion, the ability to serve the community, the knowledge to understand complex problems, intellectual endurance in emotionally taxing situations, and mature judgment after graduation.

About Office of Service-Learning

The OSL was established in November 2006. The donation of five million Hong Kong dollars from executive chairman of Onwel Group of Companies, Leung Kai-hung, Michael, and a donation of the same amount from the University Grant Committee established the first independent service-learning office in Hong Kong. We are committed to promoting experimental learning models, encouraging students to participate in subject-related community services, and fostering the development of social changers.

REFERENCES

Chan, C. M. A, Lee, K. M. W., & Ma, H. K. C. (2009). Service-learning model at Lingnan University: Development strategies and outcome assessment. *New Horizons in Education* 57(3): 57–73.

Government of Hong Kong Special Administrative Region (HKSAR) Census and Statistics Department. (2012). *Hong Kong population projections.* http://www.statistics.gov.hk/pub/B11200150520012XXXXBo100.pdf.

———. Department of Health. (2014). *Ji ceng yi liao zhi nan* [Primary care directory]. http://www.pcdirectory.gov.hk/tc_chi/welcome/welcome.html.

HKSAR Environmental Protection Department. (2014). *Problems & solutions: Food waste recycling partnership scheme.* http://www.epd.gov.hk/epd/english/environmentinhk/waste/prob_solutions/owt_food.html.

Leung, M. F. (April 2013). Xianggang an lao yuan she fu wu xu qiu [Service demand for elderly's homes in Hong Kong]. Paper presented at Development Direction of Elderly's Home Services in Hong Kong Seminar, Hong Kong. http://www.povertyrelief.gov.hk/pdf/speech20130430.pdf.

OSL. (2015). *OSL, Lingnan University annual report 2014–2015: Step by step.* Hong Kong: OSL.

Summary and Discussion of Service-Learning Pilot Schemes in Mainland China

Carol MA Hok-ka, Fanny MAK Mui-fong, and Alice LIU Cheng

Features and Outcomes of the Pilot schemes

The pilot schemes were successfully implemented through the combined efforts of Lingnan University and other participating institutions. Being the first of their kind, the schemes achieved observable results within the pilot year. To better understand the impact of the pilot schemes on teaching, Lingnan University requested that the teachers involved in the schemes (from all six institutions) complete questionnaires both before and after they finished the schemes (See Appendix 2 for the full version of the questionnaire). Teachers were self-assessed on four aspects in the questionnaire: (1) Teaching and Learning: teaching effectiveness on the subject and students' learning outcomes; (2) Community Engagement: teachers' willingness and capability to understand, serve, and collaborate with the community; (3) Personal and Professional Development: teachers' awareness of their own abilities and academic professional knowledge; (4) Understanding of Service-Learning: teachers' knowledge about the concept, principle, practices, and process of service-learning.

A total of nine teachers (at least one representative from each participating institution) completed the questionnaire both before and after the schemes. The results of the paired samples t-test demonstrate that teachers viewed themselves as having significantly improved in terms of community engagement and understanding of service-learning after their participation in the pilot schemes. They also indicated growth in terms of teaching and learning and personal and professional development (see Table 1 and Figure 1). Since the schemes were carried out in a relatively short period of time and the number of participating teachers was relatively small, the survey results cannot be applied universally. Regardless, it is still important to recognize that service-learning brings about positive change and significantly impacts teachers' teaching and learning, community engagement, personal and professional development, and understanding of service-learning. With this in mind, it is essential that there are more in-depth, comprehensive studies investigating the impact that service-learning has on teachers, students, and the community. Figure 1 illustrates the comparison results of the self-assessment of Mainland China's tertiary

Table 1. Self-Assessment of Mainland Tertiary Education Teachers Who Participated in the Service-Learning Pilot Schemes (mark 1 for *strongly disagree*, 10 for *strongly agree*)

	N	PRE-TEST		POST-TEST		DIFFERENCE	*p*-VALUE*
		M	SD	M	SD		
Teaching and Learning	9	8.13	1.75	8.20	1.87	0.07	0.793
Community Participation	9	8.24	2.12	8.76	1.53	0.52	0.022
Personal and Professional Development	9	6.93	2.31	7.48	2.24	0.56	0.056
Understanding of Service-Learning	9	6.06	2.24	8.49	1.02	2.43	0.000

*When *p*-value is smaller than 0.05, there is a significant difference between the results in pre- and post-test.

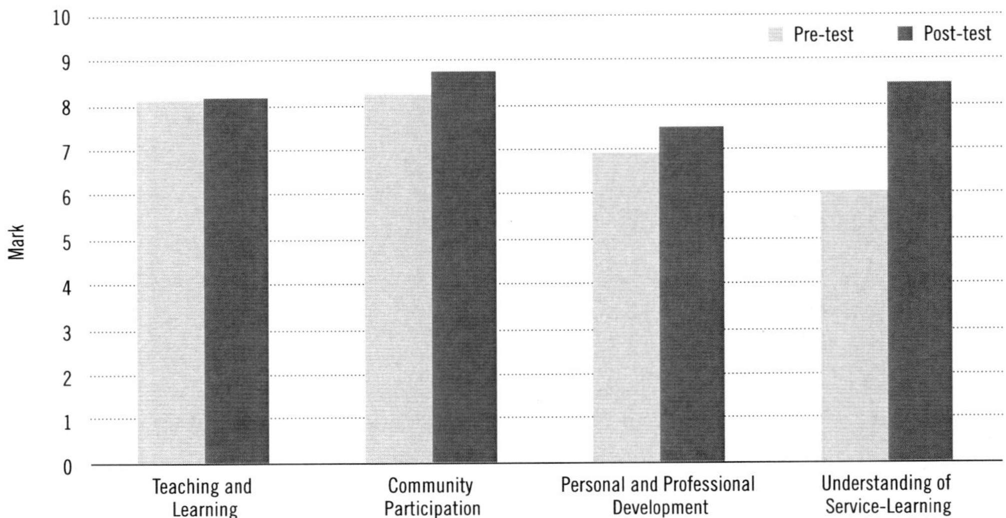

Figure 1. Self-assessment of Mainland China's tertiary education teachers who participated in the service-learning pilot schemes.

education teachers who participated in the service-learning pilot schemes, where 1 marks *strongly disagree* and 10 marks *strongly agree*.

In the pilot, participating institutions designed their own service-learning models by strategically aligning the teaching pedagogy with their institutions' specific teaching missions, course curricula, and education reform plans. Each institution worked with each community to identify particular social needs. After community assets and needs were recognized, institutions sought to work closely with the communities to provide services and use students' subject-related knowledge to benefit the communities. In doing so, students were able not only to reach academic learning goals, but also play active roles in addressing societal needs. This, in turn, created a win-win situation for tertiary education, along with its students and the communities. Since the success of these pilot schemes, most participating tertiary institutions have become proponents as well as promoters of service-learning. In the future, these institutions plan to strengthen their foundations of service-learning, expand their projects' scales, increase diversity, increase their campus-community impact, and build stronger partnerships in their communities and with other tertiary educational institutions, both locally and internationally.

Using Service-Learning to Address Various Social Issues

The pilot schemes strived to address a wide range of social issues, some of which are of national concern (e.g., environmental pollution, tax violations, etc.) and some of which are more focused on combating regional and/or community-specific situations (e.g., discrimination against leprosy patients, eco-environmental education in ethnic minority regions with high ethnic minority populations, etc.). At the initial stage, each service-learning project had a mission of tackling a particular community concern. It was important that each participating institution carefully chose a suitable topic. In order to do so, institutions needed to take into account not only their own course-specific needs, but also the needs of their surrounding communities. At each institution, students underwent training prior to their service experiences. Training topics included but was not limited to the following: background knowledge and discussions about the related community and social needs; how feasible it was to use service-learning to address the identified needs; and specific methods to connect the project with classroom learning and practical services experience. Services only began after students were trained and prepared and showed readiness to carry out the projects and work with the community. During the service period, students were encouraged to observe the community, recognize and understand the root causes of different social issues, and reflect regularly and share what they felt and experienced. Throughout the process, students were given opportunities to modify and improve their project plans in order to better meet both To increase students' knowledge and understanding of social issues, participating institutions placed emphasis on students' active involvement during different stages of the projects. Throughout the process, student participation and self-initiated learning were highly valued. For example, at the early stages of training, students met and established relationships with community partners. This introduction helped students better understand the current situations and circumstances of their service targets. It also gave students the opportunity to gather useful information from the staff of the community partners. After meeting with these community members, students were asked to research information about their chosen service projects through websites, books, visits, etc. By engaging in research, students were prompted to share their findings, ideas, and knowledge with their teammates through discussion. This teaching approach is vastly different from the traditional, one-way teaching and learning method. Service-learning fosters an active student-oriented learning environment. To make the training relevant to real-world circumstances, many institutions not only relied on teachers teaching theoretical knowledge, but also on specialists and leaders of the community who were invited to share their knowledge in seminars. Through this preparation, students were able to gain broad perspectives and engage in comprehensive studies that would better prepare them for their service projects.

These pilot projects contributed to the improvement of the local communities. This is a direct result of participating institutions choosing service projects that relate to their course curricula and the institutions' efforts to familiarize themselves with the community partners and related social issues. Institutions were, therefore, able to direct their students' studies, leading to a better understanding of community issues and needs. This, in turn, also enabled students to appropriately apply subject-related knowledge in their service and contribute to the betterment of the communities. This example shows us the flexibility of using service-learning to alleviate social problems. Service-learning that includes systematic and in-depth project execution, as well as effective student participation in various parts of the project, allows for a meaningful and transformative education experience for students.

Interdisciplinary Projects: Flexible Mixtures of Service-Learning and Professional Courses

What makes service-learning different from volunteer service is that service-learning helps students better understand academic concepts and knowledge through practical experiences. The participating institutions integrated service-learning into a variety of traditional courses such as Historical Sociology, Thoughts and Politics, Whole-Person Education, Philanthropy, and even independent courses with service-learning elements. Areas of specialization spanned the humanities, economics, medicine, etc. A multi-model approach, however, shows how higher education institutions may flexibly integrate service-learning into their own discipline teaching, course curriculum design, campus management style, and university development.

Some institutions also expressed concern that services in the community can only be integrated into certain humanities curricula, but not most of the professional curricula. For instance, teachers and students from the Taxation Management Department of Finance at Sun Yat-sen University (SYSU) analyzed how tax violations economically threaten China, and then presented their findings to residents in the local community. This helped to reduce potential tax violation crimes in the future. Also, at Guangxi Medical University, students of the course "Situations and Policies" worked on the topic of environmental education. Here, students disseminated eco-environmental knowledge to children from ethnic minority backgrounds. Through this project, students improved their knowledge of the environment and passed on such knowledge and environmental values to future generations. These kinds of service-learning projects allow for deeper, more systematic, and more creative student learning than traditional types of volunteer service (e.g., visits to elderly home, cleaning public facilities). Service-learning, in both its conception and practice, does not need to be limited to certain disciplines. Students in many courses and from various academic disciplines can serve and learn from the society and help other people. What is truly most needed, is for students and teachers to think anew, to break away from old frameworks of thought and tailor projects to creatively combine service and theory. Students need to possess rich knowledge and practical skills and, more importantly, they must be daring and adventurous.

It is worth mentioning that the pilot schemes not only engaged undergraduates, but also research postgraduates. Students from the Department of Philosophy at SYSU engaged in service-learning focused on rural culture and conservation through the course "A Case Study of Philanthropic Ethics." Students and teachers reflected that this service-learning experience provided new paradigms for research. Certain students even used this service-learning project for their master's or even doctoral research. This is a prime example of the *research* element in service-learning. Through service in the community, students put knowledge into practice, gather useful research materials, and expand their intellectual and conceptual thinking. This leads to breakthroughs for and long-term development of students. These pilot projects focused on matching services with specific courses already being offered. When the coordination and management of these projects can be further improved, future service-learning projects may take on new models, for example, cross-disciplinary collaboration, joint local-foreign service-learning projects, etc.

Achieving a Win-Win-Win Situation for Students, Institutions, and Community

A highlight of success is creating a win-win-win situation for the students and institutions as well as the community. Whether looking at the students' feedback or the teachers' observations, it is clear that service-learning is effective in promoting students' holistic development. It enhances their subject-related knowledge, social awareness, professional learning, research skills, civic orientation, practical skills, communication skills, team spirit, creativity, organizational skills, time management, problem-solving skills, etc. Unlike traditional volunteer service, service-learning provides various multi-level learning paths for students. Students first learn basic theory through classroom instruction and trainings; then, they practice what they learned while engaging in service. Through reflective thinking, students merge practical experience with theory, furthering their critical thinking skills and expanding upon the knowledge they acquired in the classroom. Finally, students apply and examine their revised knowledge and skills in practice, which creates an experiential learning cycle (Kolb, 1984). Throughout the entire process, teachers and community partners provide guidance to students, facilitating their connection of theory with service and solving practical problems. This encourages student-directed learning, and also a quality education experience and guided learning environment for students.

Education institutions implementing service-learning are transforming the way in which education nurtures talented and professional students. These institutions provide students with multi-dimensional learning modes. This, without a doubt, benefits contemporary students in tertiary education, who demand new and different learning techniques, and desire practical knowledge that they can use beyond the boundaries of their institutions. Certain institutions even make service-learning part of their formal curricula, and students earn credits for their involvement. This mechanism stresses the academic nature of service-learning, and separates service-learning from ordinary extracurricular activities. Students are spared more homework and are more motivated to learn. On a pedagogical level, this kind of learning both inside and outside the classroom fosters interaction between students and teachers. Some participants view service-learning as a method to enhance both student and teachers' development and interaction. Teachers do not simply pass on knowledge to their students, but rather guide them through the knowledge application process. This provides students continuous support and comprehensive guidance. The new, creative minds of students, as well as their youth and passion, may also help teachers develop new modes of teaching. Thus, both learners and teachers benefit from such a process.

The mission of service-learning is to develop whole-person characteristics, which echo the long-held conviction of quality education and the recent reform of general education in China. In spite of the fact that service-learning originated in the West, China's educational development and core values align with service-learning. In order to match with China's educational reform and suit

China's social, economic and political conditions, tertiary education institutions in China need to adjust their methods for implementing their core values. In terms of globalization, service-learning may also serve as a bridge to connect China's education system with the rest of the world. Foreign scholars may come to understand models and characteristics of service-learning in China. Countries can thus share their positive stories as well as the difficulties they encounter in the process of their service-learning development. Through contrasting comparisons, valuable experiences can be consolidated and learned. It is, therefore, important to let China be exposed to the world so that China can learn from the world and the world can learn from China. For example, in June 2013, Lingnan University and SYSU of Guangzhou jointly organized the 4th Asia-Pacific Regional Conference on Service-Learning. Speakers from China demonstrated and discussed their service-learning experiences and shared what they learned from pilot service-learning schemes. This aroused the interest of global delegates at the conference, who were eager to learn about China's service-learning models and actively discussed the possibility of future collaboration.

From the community perspective, service-learning offers direct support to groups from disadvantaged backgrounds. It helps reduce bias or discrimination against marginalized groups and helps those from underprivileged backgrounds gain confidence and recognize their self-value. Through service-learning experiences, university students become more aware of and passionate about combating social issues such as environmental protection, village children left behind by their parents who work in urban cities, AIDS education and prevention, etc. Service-learning also helps track historical changes and secure cultural heritage. Service that involves learning to research in order to conserve Hakka rural culture and conducting oral histories to record historical events and voices of the community are two examples of projects that help document trends and preserve cultural traditions. Moreover, service-learning helps build a direct relationship between university and community, making the former less of a separated ivory tower from the latter. A university serves as the guardian, messenger, and protector of social knowledge; its close link with the community promotes and enhances society's overall culture and economy. It also makes academic research relevant and beneficial to the community, especially in regard to addressing social needs and issues.

In summary, service-learning is vastly different from volunteer service, which tends to focus solely on unilateral benefits. On the contrary, service-learning opens up new opportunities for students, institutions, and communities to benefit altogether. In effect, tertiary institutions must use their limited human, material, and financial resources efficiently. This is in line with China's current education reforms; it also corresponds well with China's tertiary institutions' large sizes and student populations, as well as the idea that one small change can lead to a chain of changes.

Motivations for Teachers and Students to Advance Service-Learning

As a result of the pilot schemes, participating institutions have successfully set a precedent for integrating service-learning in China's tertiary education system. Most of the teachers and students who participated in the schemes were passionate and motivated to engage with and pursue service-learning. After their involvement, some institutions even made specific plans for the development of service-learning at their institutions in the future. Quite a few universities are planning to add service-learning to their major curricula, link service-learning with their general education curricula, create independent courses with service-learning elements, start independent units to coordinate service-learning projects, or allocate specific human and material resources for service-learning development. For example, teachers in the History Department of South China Normal University were so inspired by their service-learning project, "Oral History of Leprosy Rehabilitation Village," that they quickly developed a new course called "Philanthropy and Social Change" to further promote the idea that philanthropy and academia are inseparable. The course is an elective course open to all students of the university. The teachers of the course are also trying to set up a space on campus dedicated to community oral history. They hope to use oral history as a method to train students, empower groups in need, and give those from disadvantaged backgrounds a voice in the community. Additionally, Beijing Normal University–Hong Kong Baptist University United International College uses service-learning to help students and teachers understand and solve social problems. Zhuhai City Polytechnic plans to collaborate with the government and other enterprises to make service-learning more influential and diverse. Guangxi Medical University and SYSU both show interest in continuing and developing current service-learning projects and courses.

Trends of reform in China's current education system and the quick emergence of social enterprises are major mobilizing forces for the development of service-learning in the nation's tertiary institutions. In recent years, general education reform is sweeping through Chinese universities and colleges. Focusing on professional learning, practical skills, and the spirit of service, service-learning provides an effective path for higher education institutions to reach their learning goals and objectives. The concepts of social enterprises and NGOs were first introduced in China during the early twenty-first century. In a short period of time, there has been a rapid expansion in the amount of grassroots non-profit organizations and social enterprises, along with philanthropic risk-management organizations. These organizations aim to serve society through commercial means, which is vital for China's development and stability. On the other hand, most the public has limited knowledge about the social enterprises and NGOs in China. Many social enterprises are facing difficulties or challenges in terms of sustainability. This is a direct result of lack of professional guidance, innovative spirit, or social recognition (Yang & Ma, 2013). Service-learning not only helps tertiary institutions build and maintain long-term partnerships with the community, but also helps support the growth of the social enterprise sector.

Difficulties Encountered and Suggestions for Improving on the Pilot Scheme

Many goals were reached because of the pilot schemes. Nonetheless, there is still room for improvement. Service-learning is only at an inaugural stage within China's higher education system. Participating institutions encountered difficulties and challenges due to lack of systematic and comprehensive student training and project management, for example. Working with community partners and making academic connections were yet further challenges. Effective ways to evaluate outcomes of service-learning projects and students' learning have also not been implemented. Participating institutions drew useful conclusions about and made useful recommendations regarding the limitations of the service-learning projects. Detailed accounts of those suggestions are described in-depth below. Recommendations from the Office of Service-Learning (OSL) at Lingnan University are also attached for reference.

Enhancing Systematic Training during Service-Learning Projects

It is important to offer thorough training before a service-learning project is executed. For the teachers involved in the pilot schemes, it was their first time engaging with service-learning and they were far from familiar with appropriate training methods and practices. For example, they struggled with answering the following questions: What should a comprehensive training entail? How long should a training be? Who should be in charge of different training tasks? At the end of the service-learning projects, some teachers and students realized they were lacking certain kinds of training throughout the service-learning process. For instance, students did not have enough understanding of the actual situations in the communities; they were not equipped to deal with unexpected circumstances; they were not prepared to answer questions from community members; etc. From this experience, it is recommended that future training involve more community representatives or experts from related fields. This would enhance students' ability to effectively carry out service-learning projects. Meanwhile, students should also be encouraged to conduct additional, more in-depth research studies to identify and understand the genuine needs of their communities and/or service targets before the projects are executed. This would make the service more relevant to the needs of the community.

Although some teachers reflected that they were not aware of appropriate training objectives, important key elements were still included in the trainings, such as connections between the service-learning projects and course content, sharing from NGO volunteers, seminars by experts in related fields, etc. These key elements were part of trainings that took place at various stages throughout the service-learning experience. While improvement is certainly needed, these trainings did provide students with professional theoretical knowledge and practical guidance. To further improve the training quality, institutions must mobilize students into active learning roles and create cross-over opportunities or interactions among different projects through visits, student forums, and preparations or discussions among course instructors, community representatives, and service-learning coordinators. This ensures that students learn about the prevalent social issues facing each community prior to their service, thus preparing them for a more active and effective experience.

Improving Management and Execution Skills

Since service-learning is a new development in China, there are limited examples and experiences to reference. Most institutions are still exploring how to best implement service-learning as a teaching and learning practice. With this in mind, it is essential that China improve its overall project management, planning, and execution of service-learning in hopes of expanding the number of higher education institutions integrating the concept into their curricula.

Some invited institutions expressed concern that they were not clear on how to operate a service-learning project. Teachers and students felt confused, since many institutions lacked experience and knowledge in how to start and plan community projects. As a matter of fact, it is understandable that they felt confused, as service-learning was an unfamiliar method and teaching strategy. In order to overcome this concern, it is recommended that teachers, students, and community partners hold sessions to discuss needs and possible projects and/or partnerships. Continual reflection will help to ensure that both the campus and community benefit from the service-learning experience. Teachers of service-learning should make an effort to join relevant trainings on project management, read relevant scholarship, and/or make reference to procedures and plans of others (e.g., institutions, subjects, projects). Detailed execution plans are needed that clearly list out the work and goals of each stakeholder at every stage throughout the process. Timetables and a monitoring system is also crucial as well. By preparing well before the start of a service-learning project, generating appropriate questions, discussing foreseeable issues, and implementing applicable solutions, teachers, students, and community members can work together to ensure success and minimize the chances of encountering problems.

Most teachers and students involved in the pilot schemes were passionate about the service-learning project they conducted and wished to use their professional knowledge to help those from underprivileged groups. In fact, they were so active that they met new service targets and then modified their project plans in order to include those new service targets. While it was positive that teachers and students were highly motivated, the increase in number of service targets led to an array of unexpected problems. It is thus recommended to set clear objectives and schedules at the early stage of the service-learning project. All activities should be conducted around the defined set of objectives so that the projected number of service targets can be met. If new plans or themes emerge during the service-learning process, they should be followed up only after the main project has been completed. If needed, additional service-learning projects can be created. Service-learning seeks to improve community situations and meet individual needs through a step-by-step process. Following this process ensures the quality and sustainability of the project.

Making Teachers and Students More Involved and Active in Service-Learning

Some tertiary institutions suggested that participants needed to be more motivated to engage in service-learning. Preparatory work and service in the community took additional time outside of the classroom and students felt stressed about the unfamiliar learning environment, leading them to feel apathetic about service-learning. To encourage them, it is recommended that institutions help students gain an understanding of service-learning and an appreciation for personal, campus, and community capacity-building. This would help avoid students' misconception that service-learning is just another form of volunteer service that only "helps others." Students also grow and learn during the service-learning experience. Through the practical application of knowledge, students are able to enhance their social competence and gain awareness of ethical issues and concerns. To avoid unnecessary chaos or workloads, the service-learning projects should be organized more sensibly. Students should undergo training to acquire time-management skills and understand the importance of organizational skills. When students are encouraged to view service-learning with a positive attitude, their initial feelings of pressure can be transformed into mobilizing power.

Second, due to a lack of experience, some teachers expressed that it was difficult for them to design a service-learning project and/or attract students. It is only after teachers gain adequate understanding of service-learning and recognize its advantages and long-term significance that they can and will actively engage in service-learning and encourage students to participate. Perhaps teachers could establish better service-learning knowledge through reading relevant scholarship and attending training workshops. Interactions with counterparts who have service-learning experience can also help inspire and initiate interesting, diverse service-learning projects that expand learning opportunities for students. Last, but not least, it is imperative that higher education institutions give sufficient support for service-learning initiatives, including but not limited to offering resources and reward mechanisms for teaching and participating in high-quality service-learning projects or courses.

Improving Community Connections

The community partners in the pilot schemes were mostly chosen by the course instructors themselves, based on their own social observation and networks. It was found that some community partners were not active in getting involved in the preparation, training, or reflection sessions for students. Some did not even assign supervisors to guide students throughout the service-learning period. This means that community partners were passively served, and some even expressed concern about the whole service-learning project. This certainly made it difficult for higher education institutions to build long-term relationships with community partners. To improve in this area, teachers and students need to strengthen their communication with community partners; they also need to uncover and identify the real needs of the community. When students are able to adjust their project with regard to community needs, they can provide valuable support to the community through service-learning. In other words, it is service not for the sake of service only. It is important for students to view the community as co-educators and for teachers to empower community partners to view themselves as co-educators. Higher education institutions have a social responsibility to nurture talented and civically aware professionals. It is also essential that community partners do not view themselves as only service recipients, but rather service providers. Community partners not only provide students with knowledge about the community, but also encourage students to use and practice their professional skills during service activities.

Some teachers reflected that their service-learning projects were rather small in scale and seems to have had limited positive impact. When students serve for only a limited time, when activities are limited in depth and breadth and both teachers and students are exploring possibilities at the start of a service-learning partnership, it is expected for both students and teachers to feel as if they are having a minimal impact. Long-term development and significant impact requires the teachers and students to search for and build their own partnerships in the community. Service-learning projects with high impact also require strong partnerships between community partners and higher education institutions. Promotion also plays a major role in recruiting volunteers, publicizing activities, and even securing additional resources and funds. Furthermore, consistent and active participation in service-learning conferences and forums helps build new networks and spread service-learning models and frameworks.

Enhancing the Connection between Theory and Service

Integrating academic theory with service in the community is a key feature of service-learning. In fact, the linkage between theory and practice is what makes service-learning a groundbreaking pedagogy and learning experience. Some teachers and students expressed a need to strengthen the theoretical element of service-learning, especially with projects where the service and subject-related knowledge are indirectly related. When students are unable to see the connection between service and subject-related knowledge, it is often a result of a lack of appropriate training or failure of the teacher to guide students to go beyond what is seen at the surface level. Students must, therefore, examine and discover the underlying themes and root causes that are connected to the service activities. If students fail to see these connections, training and reflection can easily turn into shallow discussions of social issues, rather than in-depth conversations that promote critical thought and a deeper knowledge of both the academic discipline and civic issues. By integrating service-learning into the existing professional curricula or general education, institutions would enable teachers to not only match course objectives to service-learning goals, but also connect theory and practice. Teachers would, therefore, be able to create course syllabi and teach course content in a way that guides students to see the connections between the service and subject-related knowledge. As a result, students would be able to use and practice what they learn in the classroom when engaging in and with the community.

It is also important to highlight theory throughout the service-learning process. First, students systematically learn theory in order to build a foundation for professional knowledge. Then the preparation for, development of, and reflection on their service-learning project helps them formulate the connection between theory and practice. Effective guidance to students during the process from course instructors and community partners helps students engage in critical and in-depth reflection, and encourages them to apply theoretical knowledge into their everyday life.

Some teachers are still concerned that service-learning can only be integrated into certain disciplines or subjects. This is a drawback when trying to establish service-learning as a universal practice across the curriculum. However, it is important to note that service-learning allows for great flexibility, as it relates to all types of professional training and social issues. In the United States and many parts of Asia, service-learning is already a component and primary objective of higher education. Tulane University, Taipei Medical University, National Taiwan University are some prime examples of higher education institutions that place importance on service-learning. Through university websites, one can find the kinds of service-learning initiatives being offered at these institutions. It is also possible to get such information through corresponding service-learning offices at the universities. Teachers of higher education institutions in China can learn from the models, examples, and practices of foreign universities or institutions. Teachers can learn how to integrate service-learning into different courses, using a variety of flexible approaches to create campus-community impact. When service-learning has developed and expanded at institutions in China, it is hoped that interdisciplinary projects can develop, increase students' critical thought and ability to understand multiple perspectives.

Assessing the Project Development

Most of the participating institutions found both the feedback and assessment mechanisms of the service-learning projects ineffective. Some institutions were relatively loose in terms of their management and supervision of students, leading to numerous teamwork and communication issues. A principle aspect of service-learning is that students choose to engage in it voluntarily. Effective management of students would ensure that they accomplish their goals. For example, students could be encouraged to write and share in work journals; regular sharing or reflective sessions could be held to stimulate interactions among students; course instructors and community representatives could hold meetings and discussions with students and give useful suggestions. A certain degree of assessment makes a service-learning experience more systematic and regulated, and helps maintain teaching quality. Attendance and attitude during service are some examples of items for assessment. Methods of assessment include, but are not limited to, oral classroom presentations, reflective journals, essay writings, pre- and post-test questionnaires, focus groups, and in-depth interviews. All these methods together give a multi-perspective evaluation of students' learning, performance, and growth. They also help teachers modify their teaching at different stages within the course.

The pilot service-learning scheme that SYSU adopted was also a type of service. Teachers conducted a survey on students before and after their participation in service-learning. The survey included six categories: communication skills, organizational skills, social competence, problem-solving skills, research skills, and positive attitudes. The results of the survey were surprising. Apart from a growth in research skills, students showed a decline in other five categories. An explanation for this could be that, before service-learning, students were limited to textbook learning. When they engaged in service-learning, a new and unfamiliar type of learning, and were exposed to real issues and made aware of the problems in the community, it is highly likely that their sense of self and self-confidence decreased.

To better assist students with their learning and development, and help them better cope with problems encountered during service, institutions must ensure that students receive appropriate training prior to their service activities. During these trainings, students should be forewarned of difficulties, so that they are better prepared to psychologically and emotionally overcome obstacles. When students do face problems or failures, course instructors should offer timely support, and help students understand that issues are expected and part of the overall learning experience. Teachers must ensure that they do not personalize problems or brew negative emotions of self-denial. Students should be encouraged to face problems positively and seek solutions from various angles. For instance, students can discuss with team members and get advice from course instructors. Course instructors should also observe how students respond and behave throughout the service-learning experience, paying close attention to any changes in their emotions. When institutions assess the results of service-learning, they may use quantitative means, such as questionnaires and surveys, as well as qualitative approaches, such as focus groups and in-depth interviews. This helps form a comprehensive and deep understanding of students' service-learning experiences, as well as their changes in terms of attitude and ability.

Developing Sustainable Service-Learning

Higher education institutions are generally concerned about the sustainable development of service-learning. Some have expressed that effort and time spent on social services decreases the amount of time teachers can spend on enhancing their teaching and scholarship. The competitive atmosphere of higher education and the pressure administrators, teachers, and students feel to meet requirements and standards is yet another reason why there is resistance to the service-learning movement. Fortunately, however, there are still many who are passionate about social services and willing to devote their time to this kind of work.

In view of this situation, students should have a comprehensive understanding of service-learning. Students must see the long-term benefits of service-learning: preparing them to enter a competitive and ever-changing society and contribute to a better society. Service-learning greatly improves students' whole-person development during university and beyond, in their life experiences after graduation. Secondly, students should be encouraged to form positive self and social awareness as well as a humanist spirit. They should grow first in terms of developing self-love and then developing love for all human beings. Even more, they should explore what the words *competition* and *success* mean. Thirdly, students and teachers of service-learning should be encouraged to combine their academic pursuits with desire to serve society, which should not be limited to traditional, simple volunteer services. There should not only be an increase in the number of long-term, multi-disciplinary, and mutually beneficial service-learning projects, but also deeper discussions and collaborative efforts at the campus–community level that lead to transformative change for students, teachers, and the community. When service-learning projects are first formulated, they must start small. This reduces the pressure and challenges faced during the service-learning process, especially in terms of management, human resources, and capital. The focus should first be placed on increasing both students' and teachers' knowledge of service-learning. Through first-hand experience and participation, students and teachers of service-learning can develop greater social concern increased civic participation, and a stronger sense of social responsibility.

Institutional support, along with material support from bodies of education, helps make service-learning practices sustainable. For example, there should be a relevant reward system for students engaged in service-learning. This reduces the pressure students face with schoolwork and makes service-learning part of a systematic mechanism within the institution. The management of service-learning projects should also be enhanced. This includes establishing specific funding and personnel for service-learning; giving systematic accreditation for service-learning projects in order to ensure high-quality teaching and learning practices; and collaborating with community partners through institutional channels, which help to maintain longer-term partnerships. It is also viable to arrange matching services with specific needs in the community. Additionally, it is recommended to establish corresponding organizations or draft internal publications that increase the knowledge about and positive attitudes towards service-learning on campus and in the community. Secured funding has both a direct and indirect implication on the sustainability of service-learning projects. Apart from institutional funding, it is important to gain support and establish partnerships with the local government, social enterprises, or NGOs, who can engage in, and possibly help fund, service-learning initiatives. Joint social efforts can, therefore, aid in establishing as well as sustaining service-learning projects.

Objective Limitations of the Service-Learning Projects

Service-learning goes beyond the classroom. It involves the collaborative effort of the community, students, and teachers. Through service-learning experiences, it is inevitable to encounter practical problems and limitations. For example, some project locations are far away from a central landmark or not in ideal environments. A long travel time to service requires more time from the students and teachers, along with additional expenses. In addition to project locations, there are other challenges that often occur during service-learning experiences. For instance, time-clashes between service time and students' courses, or working with a community partner who makes last-minute changes that cause unexpected delays.

Teachers and administrators at higher education institutions can take advantage of the flexibility within service-learning and start with the local communities near university campuses. Students can begin by investigating and identifying the social problems in their immediate environment. Once projects gain momentum, more in-depth studies can be conducted, deeper discussions can evolve, and more transformative action can be taken. If the location of the service is far away, students can work in groups, especially if safety is a primary concern. When conditions allow, a service-learning project coordinator or leader should also accompany the students to the service. In order to provide more choice and autonomy for the students, it is advisable to develop a variety of service-learning projects. For example, there can be projects within the boundaries of campus, projects that include an indirect service to a social enterprise, projects during the summer vacation, and research studies that benefit the community or a local agency. Diverse projects give students a chance to engage in service-learning that fits their unique interests, needs, and abilities.

Service-learning has started to increase its prevalence within China's tertiary education sector. As a result of this growth and in terms of short-term strategic development, China should place emphasis on the following: (1) fostering the development of service-learning in various institutions and regions in China; (2) continuing to improve existing service-learning projects and courses; (3) increasing the academic value of service-learning, and (4) creating platforms for the exchange of information.

Cases in this book are mostly drawn from the southern regions of China. There are numerous higher education institutions in this country, including Beijing, Hunan, Shanghai, Ningbo, and many other institutions looking to join the list. What the above examples (from different universities, courses, regions, etc.) demonstrate is that service-learning will most likely expand many more regions and institutions in the near future. The OSL at Lingnan University has been more than willing to assist any institution in setting up effective, feasible, and progressive development plans for service-learning. The OSL will also help provide training and resource materials. Institutions that are less familiar with or hesitant to begin service-learning can gain experience and more information through seminars, forums, academic platforms and research materials. This exchange can help build a better knowledge of service-learning both locally and internationally. It is also hoped that the Service-Learning Asia Network can encourage interaction and sharing among institutions.

Practical actions implemented by this network include regular seminars and forums, building resource sharing platforms and training bases, among many others. While it is important to build a stable national service-learning network in China, it is also vital to strengthen the connection and relationship between the Asia-Pacific region and those institutions in the West. This network building, in effect, improves the educational and service-learning experiences of both the Eastern and Western institutions that have started service-learning and should substantiate their work and courses. While they continue to improve their current projects, they should also encourage more teachers and students to actively participate in service. More disciplinary subjects, diverse courses, and community impact actions are needed. With an increase in the number of service-learning projects, it is crucial that we also enhance existing projects and ensure their campus–community impact. Student learning outcomes, as well as community outcomes, should be assessed to ensure high-quality service-learning projects.

Service-learning is a progressive teaching and learning pedagogy. Unfortunately, however, some teachers and students still have a misunderstanding that service-learning is the same as volunteer service. As a result of this misunderstanding, it is crucial to highlight the close connection between academic knowledge and community engagement at the initial stage of service-learning implementation. Course instructors can make reference to the assessment models of other service-learning courses, while developing their own based on their individual teaching philosophies and academic discipline. This enables course instructors to improve their course designs, create more reasonable and effective course assessments, and help students better acquire subject-related knowledge. Furthermore, course instructors can also make use of service-learning to connect with the community. Service-learning creates an ideal platform for bridging and integrating professional research with community concern. In general, the preliminary achievements of the current projects in each invited institution were very positive and encouraging. Teachers successfully transferred their knowledge in service-learning to their own institutions. For example, the course instructors from South China Normal University introduced the service-learning pedagogy to the university's School of History and Culture. Now, four more teachers have started to adopt the service-learning approach in their academic courses. Furthermore, SYSU also set up an OSL to promote service-learning across the campus. One of the professors from SYSU also received a grant from the Education Bureau to develop a service-learning related syllabus for the primary school curriculum, focused on civic and moral education. Some institutions also intend to expand service-learning in different ways, such as extending and following up on their current pilot schemes and launching new projects in more academic subjects. For example, Santou University has made service-learning a graduation requirement. It is also very encouraging to know that Zhuhai City Polytechnic has set up a team to further promote service-learning. Zhuhai City Polytechnic has not only promoted service-learning in their curriculum, but also plans to organize a service-learning forum for local China institutions and scholars from overseas to exchange ideas. The teachers also successfully applied for and received funding from the government to further promote character education through service-learning.

At the start of the pilot schemes, the concept of service-learning was new to many teachers in mainland China. As a result, the teachers strived to: better understand the concept and different practices of service-learning; learn how to conduct project evaluations and student assessments; research approaches and methods for cooperating with community partners; and study the curriculum design and publications of other institutions. More collaboration is needed between institutions engaging in service-learning and institutions that have no service-learning experience but are interested in adopting the approach. Given that there are many international service-learning associations, such as Talloires Network, International Center for Service-Learning in Teacher Education (ICSLTE) and International Association for Research on Service-Learning and Community Engagement (IARSLCE), it is imperative that these organizations work with other Asian partners to enrich and expand service-learning opportunities. Joint partnership is the only way forward for the service-learning movement as well as for bridging the gap between higher education institutions and the world.

REFERENCES

Kolb, D. (1984). *Experiential learning.* New Jersey: Prentice Hall.

Yang G. F., & Ma, X. X. (2013). The predicaments and opportunities of local social enterprises: Practical observation and theoretical thinking. *Guangzhou Public Administration Review* 00: 129–143.

The Office of Service-Learning at Lingnan University: Overview of Service-Learning Pilot Schemes in Universities and Colleges in Mainland China

UNIVERSITIES/ COLLEGES	PILOT SCHEMES	TEACHER(S) IN CHARGE	FEATURES
Sun Yat-sen University	Service-learning and public welfare ethics and cultural preservation Integrated course: A Case Study of Philanthropic Ethics	WANG Shuo, XIONG Hong	To accompany old people in villages, especially those who live alone, during Lunar New Year To document activities organized by the society for the elderly, and assist in its construction and expansion To document and protect the tangible and intangible cultural heritages in Hakka villages
	Oral history of Enning Road community Integrated course: Theories of Cultural Anthropology	ZHU Jian-gang	To make an oral history on Enning Road based on fieldwork in Enning Road together with the Enning Road Academic Focus Group To assist the Concern Group of Enning Road in hosting screening events, salons and other small activities for the community. To promote public participation and look into sustainable development in the old area with the locals.
	Community tax consultation Integrated course: Taxation Management	LONG Zhao-hui	To answer local residents' questions on taxation To promote tax laws and spread knowledge of taxation
South China University of Technology	University students and green neighborhoods Integrated course: Philanthropy Communication	Lily QI Li-li	To promote "waste sorting" as the theme, a series of green promotion is arranged for residents in neighborhoods. To appreciate students' efforts in tailoring the activities for them, residents in neighborhoods have learnt the importance of waste sorting in environmental protection.
South China Normal University	An oral history of leprosy rehabilitation villages in China Integrated Subject: Historical Sociology.	HAN Yi-min	To serve leprosy patients, volunteers, and rehabilitation villagers, and work together to improve the living conditions in a rural area To record interviews with old villagers and sort out the data
Beijing Normal University–Hong Kong Baptist University United International College	Service for children with cerebral palsy Integrated course: Volunteering in Whole Person Education	ZHANG Lie-ni	To participate in the classes for children with cerebral palsy, assist the teachers in classes and keep the children company during their rehabilitation sessions To organize thematic activity groups for parents of children with cerebral palsy
Zhuhai City Polytechnic	Travel with Sanban Primary School kids Integrated subject: Service-Learning	LIN Hao-gui, LIN Hai-yu, CHEN Qian-yu	To broaden the horizons of children from Sanban Primary School, a day trip to Zhuhai is organized.

Promoting Service-Learning in China: Questionnaire for Teaching Staff

The Office of Service-Learning wishes to know the impacts of this project on teaching staff. Please fill in the questionnaire below. Data collected will remain confidential. Personal identification and specific situations of universities or colleges will not appear in any publication. Should you have any enquiries on this research or questionnaire, please contact the Office of Service-Learning in Lingnan University.

Name:

Affiliated University/ College:	Sun Yat-sen University South China University of Technology BNU–HKBU United International College Beijing Normal University, Zhuhai	South China Normal University Shantou University Guangxi Medical University

Part 1: Teaching and Learning

Please indicate the extent to which these statements are applicable to you. 1 = Strongly Disagree, 10 = Strongly Agree

In the course(s) that I teach:

1. Students can apply what they learnt in classroom in daily life.	1	2	3	4	5	6	7	8	9	10
2. Students understand my lectures and reading material.	1	2	3	4	5	6	7	8	9	10
3. In my opinion, if I devote more time on lectures rather than community service, there will be better learning outcomes.	1	2	3	4	5	6	7	8	9	10
4. What my students learnt is very useful to their future career development.	1	2	3	4	5	6	7	8	9	10
5. My teaching method is effective.	1	2	3	4	5	6	7	8	9	10
6. I have a good relationship with my students.	1	2	3	4	5	6	7	8	9	10

Part 2: Community Engagement

Please indicate the extent to which these statements are applicable to you. 1 = Strongly Disagree, 10 = Strongly Agree

7. I am aware of the community needs around the campus.	1	2	3	4	5	6	7	8	9	10
8. I value the opportunity to cooperate with community partners.	1	2	3	4	5	6	7	8	9	10

9. Teaching staff set the example for students in participating community service.	1	2	3	4	5	6	7	8	9	10
10. I can tell the community my opinion.	1	2	3	4	5	6	7	8	9	10
11. I have close ties with the community.	1	2	3	4	5	6	7	8	9	10
12. I have responsibility to serve my community.	1	2	3	4	5	6	7	8	9	10

Part 3: Personal and Professional Development

Please indicate the extent to which these statements are applicable to you. 1 = Strongly Disagree, 10 = Strongly Agree

13. I understand the strength and weakness of my specialization.	1	2	3	4	5	6	7	8	9	10
14. I have (a) clear goal(s) for my academic development.	1	2	3	4	5	6	7	8	9	10
15. When I cooperate with people of different opinion, I feel at ease.	1	2	3	4	5	6	7	8	9	10
16. I notice my prejudice on certain people/issues.	1	2	3	4	5	6	7	8	9	10
17. I am a good leader.	1	2	3	4	5	6	7	8	9	10
18. With my specialization, I can improve the livelihood of a community.	1	2	3	4	5	6	7	8	9	10

Part 4: Understanding of Service-Learning

Please indicate the extent of your understanding to the below projects, 1 = No idea at all, 10 = Fully understood

19. Definitions of Service-Learning	1	2	3	4	5	6	7	8	9	10
20. Features and effects of Service-Learning as a pedagogy	1	2	3	4	5	6	7	8	9	10
21. Roles and responsibilities in different Service-Learning organizations/ stakeholders	1	2	3	4	5	6	7	8	9	10
22. Implementation of Service-Learning	1	2	3	4	5	6	7	8	9	10
23. Reflection and its effects in Service-Learning	1	2	3	4	5	6	7	8	9	10
24. Methods to integrate curriculum and community service	1	2	3	4	5	6	7	8	9	10
25. Methods to negotiate with community organizations/ institutions	1	2	3	4	5	6	7	8	9	10
26. Administration and finances in launching Service-Learning	1	2	3	4	5	6	7	8	9	10

Information on Some of the Service-Learning Units in Tertiary Education Institutions of Asia

REGION/ COUNTRY	UNIVERSITY/ COLLEGE	UNIT	WEBSITE
Hong Kong	Lingnan University	Office of Service-Learning	http://www.ln.edu.hk/osl/
Hong Kong	Chinese University of Hong Kong	Chung Chi College	http://www.ccc.cuhk.edu.hk/
Hong Kong	Polytechnic University of Hong Kong	Office of Service-Learning	http://sl.polyu.edu.hk/
Taiwan	Fu Jen Catholic University	Service-Learning Center	http://slc.mission.fju.edu.tw/
Taiwan	Soochow University	Service-Learning and Life Center	http://vschool.scu.edu.tw/service/
Japan	International Christian University	Service-Learning Center	http://web.icu.ac.jp/slc/index_e.html
South Korea	Seoul Women's University	Institute of Teaching & Learning	http://www.swu.ac.kr/english/#
The Philippines	Silliman University	Institute of Service Learning	http://su.edu.ph/
The Philippines	University of St. La Salle	University of St. La Salle	http://www.usls.edu.ph/?page=6&
India	Lady Doak College	Centre for Outreach & Service-Learning Programmes	http://www.ladydoakcollege.edu.in/
Indonesia	Petra Christian University	Institute of Research and Community Outreach	http://lppm.petra.ac.id/ppm/cop/
Singapore	Singapore University of Social Sciences	Office of Service-Learning	http://isotope.suss.edu.sg/servicelearning/

List of Academic Journals that Encourage Publications on Service-Learning

- *Adult Education and Development*
- *American Journal of Community Psychology*
- *Australasian Journal of University-Community Engagement*
- *Change: The Magazine of Higher Learning*
- *Citizen Science: Theory and Practice*
- *Collaborative Anthropologies*
- *Community Development Journal* (Oxford University Press)
- *Community Works Journal*
- *Education, Citizenship and Social Justice*
- *eJournal of Public Affairs*
- *Engaged Scholar Journal*
- *Gateways: International Journal of Community Research and Engagement*
- *Global Journal of Community Psychology Practice*
- *Innovative Higher Education*
- *Interdisciplinary Journal of Partnership Studies*
- *International Journal for Service Learning in Engineering*
- *International Journal of Civic Engagement and Social Change*
- *International Journal of Public Deliberation*
- *International Journal of Public Participation*
- *International Journal of Research on Service-Learning and Community Engagement*
- *International Journal for Service Learning in Engineering, Humanitarian Engineering, and Social Entrepreneurship*
- *International Undergraduate Journal for Service-Learning, Leadership, and Social Change*
- *Journal for Civic Commitment* (Community College National Center for Community Engagement)
- *Journal of Community Engagement and Higher Education* (Indiana State University)

- *Journal of Community Engagement and Scholarship* (University of Alabama)
- *Journal of Community Practice*
- *Journal of Cooperative Education and Internships*
- *Journal of Deliberative Mechanisms in Science* (DEMESCI)
- *Journal of Economic Development in Higher Education*
- *Journal of Extension*
- *Journal of Higher Education Outreach and Engagement* (University of Georgia)
- *Journal of Public Scholarship in Higher Education*
- *A Journal of Regional Engagement*
- *Journal of Service-Learning in Higher Education*
- *Metropolitan Universities Journal* (IUPUI)
- *Michigan Journal of Community Service Learning* (University of Michigan)
- *Partnerships: A Journal of Service-Learning & Civic Engagement*
- *Prism: A Journal of Regional Engagement*
- *Progress in Community Health Partnerships: Research, Education, and Action*
- *Public: A Journal of Imagining America*
- *Reflections: A Journal of Public Rhetoric, Civic Writing, and Service-Learning*
- *Review of Higher Education*
- *Revista Conexão UEPG*
- *Science Education and Civic Engagement: An International Journal*
- *UNBOUND: Reinventing Higher Education*
- *Undergraduate Journal of Service Learning and Community-Based Research*

About the Contributors

CAI Ying-hui, is a researcher at Institute of Higher Education of Shantou University and director of Academic Affairs of Shantou University. Cai presides over the Ministry of Education, Humanities and Social Sciences Youth Fund project of "Future Expectations and University Freshmen's Role In Promoting Research" and the of "Research on the Setting and Management of Service-Learning Courses in Colleges and Universities" project supported by the National Social Science Foundation of China. She is also involved in the university teaching reform research projects and promotes substantial development in the quality of learning.

Alfred CHAN Cheung-ming has been both a practitioner in welfare services for older persons and an academic in social gerontology. Chan has extensive skills and knowledge in health and social care services and policy making. His academic interests include the interpretation of intergenerational relationships, aging and long-term care policies in the Asia Pacific, the development of health and social care measurements, quality of life, caring index, etc. He is also the expert consultant for the Division of Emerging Social Issues (Aging) of the UN Economic and Social Commission of the Asia Pacific. He served as the director of Asia-Pacific Institute of Ageing Studies and Office of Service-Learning, which he founded in 2006 in the promotion of liberal arts education to university students through "Serving to Learn; Learning to Serve." Currently, he serves as the chairman of the Equal Opportunities commission in Hong Kong.

Timothy CHEN Ka-kit was a lecturer in the Social Work and Social Administration Department at Beijing Normal University–Hong Kong Baptist University United International College. His research interests include the relationship between youth and families, youth social engagement, social work at the school, narrative practice, rural migrant workers in China, and NGO development in China. He is the fieldwork supervisor of Hong Kong Polytechnic University and is undergoing doctoral research related to young social workers in China.

HAN Yi-min was a lecturer and a research postgraduate in the School of History and Culture, South China Normal University. Han teaches world ancient history, historical sociology, and changes of charity and society. Han's interests are historical sociology and service practicums and has found the intersecting point of them—oral history, which serves as the main direction of his work.

HUANG Ying is an associate professor and the dean of Tourism School of Management. Huang was the Honorary President of the Zhuhai Tourist Association Guide. She is a member of the Zhuhai City Polytechnic Teaching Guide and Tour Guides National Qualification Oral Examiner. Huang teaches courses called "Communication and Exchange," "Tour Guide Business," "Organizational Management of Tourism," and "Introduction to Hotel Management."

HUO Qiao-hong is a lecturer and the deputy dean of the School of Tourism Management, Zhuhai City Polytechnic. Her teaching and interests include service-learning practice in higher vocational schools in Zhuhai and research on vocational students' responsibility in service-learning.

JIANG Ping received her bachelor's degree from Department of Finance, Lingnan (University) College at Sun Yat-sen University, in 2010.

LI Yi-ang is a professor and served as the director of the Student Affairs Office at Guangxi Medical University. She is currently the party secretary of the Nursing College and Affiliated Nursing School. Her research areas include the psychological health of undergraduate students, psychological capital education, and the ideology of work by the Communist Youth League.

LIANG Yong-feng is a lecturer and deputy director of the Student Affairs Office at Guagnxi Medical University. His research interests include the health psychology of undergraduate students and moral education.

LIN Hao-gui is a lecturer at the Tourism School of Management. Lin works for student affairs and teaches courses on service-learning and career development for university students.

Alice LIU Cheng graduated from the University of St. Andrews in Scotland, and received her master's degree in psychology at the University of Cambridge in 2012. She is the service-learning visiting tutor in the Office of Service-Learning at Lingnan University. She mainly supports the service-learning education promotion projects in Mainland China. Her research interests include service-learning student learning outcomes and different learning models in the regions. She participates in international community activities in different regions, for example, Mainland China, Hong Kong, the United Kingdom, and Tanzania.

LIU Haijuan was a PhD student of ethics in the Department of Philosophy, Sun Yat-sen University, who participated in the service-learning course. She is an assistant professor in ethics education at Shenzhen University.

LONG Zhao-hui is an associate professor in the Department of Public Finance and Taxation, Lingnan (University) College at Sun Yat-sen University. He is also a member of council of Chinese Society of African Issue Studies, a Guangdong Province charity legislation expert, a Guangdong provincial financial planners' occupation skill appraisal expert, and a researcher of the Chinese Philanthropy Research Institute of Sun Yat-sen University. LONG won an Outstanding Teaching Award at Sun Yat-sen University in 2008, an Anzijie International Trade Outstanding Works Award (China) in 2010, and a Ministerial Research Excellence Award from the Chinese Ministry of Civil Affairs in 2012.

Carol MA Hok-ka is known among academics and community practitioners as an active and passionate promoter of service-learning. She was awarded a W. T. Chan Fellowship to study and practice service-learning at the University of California, Los Angeles and was also awarded a Lingnan Foundation Scholarship to complete a research internship at the National Primary Health Care Centre, University of Manchester, UK. She is one of the founders of the Office of Service-Learning at Lingnan University, Hong Kong, and has supported the university in institutionalizing the idea of service-learning as part of its liberal arts education. After serving as associate director of service-learning and adjunct assistant professor in the Department of Sociology and Social Policy for ten years, she moved to Singapore to work as senior lecturer (common curriculum) and senior fellow (service-learning) to teach and advise the development of service-learning at Singapore University of Social Sciences. As an energetic and committed scholar, Carol has published books and articles on service-learning and aging in refereed journals and policy papers for global agencies including UNESCAP and Asian higher education institutes. She is also on the board of the directors for both the International Center for Service-Learning in Teacher Education and the International Association for Research on Service-Learning and Community Engagement.

Fanny MAK Mui-fong is a senior project officer at the Office of Service-Learning at Lingnan University. She received her bachelor's degree in social sciences from Lingnan University, Hong Kong, where she specialized in sociology. She is the program coordinator of various service-learning programs, student training and development, and service-learning education promotion projects in Mainland China.

Lily QI Li-li is a lecturer of the School of Journalism and Communication, South China University of Technology. She has taught courses on international communication, public communication, and foreign television.

WANG Shuo is an assistant professor in the Department of Philosophy, Sun Yat-sen University. She is also the vice president of School of Philanthropy at Guangzhou and the executive director of the Institute of Philanthropy Ethics in Sun Yat-sen University. Her major research interests are Chinese traditional ethical thought and philanthropy ethics. She is also a theatre artist who is devoted to applied drama and educational theatre to change the way of teaching philosophy.

WANG Yu-qing is an associate professor and currently works as the Minister of Guangxi Medical University Party Committee Propaganda Department at Guangxi Medical University. Her research areas include the ideology of work by the Communist Youth League.

XIONG Huan is an associate professor in the Department of History, Sun Yat-sen University. His major interests are in cultural heritage and museology, and ancient ceramics studies.

XU Xin-zhong was a professor of finance and the dean of Lingnan (*University*) College, Sun Yat-sen University. Prior to joining Lingnan, Xu has held positions as chair professor in finance and associate dean at Guanghua School of Management of Peking University, chair professor in finance at Lancaster University Management School, senior economist at Bank of England, and senior lecturer at Manchester Business School. Xu has extensive research experience in behavioral finance, corporate governance, and volatility modeling and currently serves as the lead investigator for a national key research project on behavioral finance.

YU Li-ren was the head of the Student Affairs Office at Lingnan (University) College, Sun Yat-sen University. His research interests include ideological and political education and youth development for university students.

Katy ZHANG Lie-ni is the lecturer of the Service-Learning Course at Beijing Normal University–Hong Kong Baptist University United International College.

ZHANG Si-lu was a master's student at the School of Sociology and Anthropology, Sun Yat-sen University, and is a part-time researcher at the School of Philanthropy, Sun Yat-sen University.

ZHU Jian-gang is an anthropology professor from the School of Sociology and Anthropology, Sun Yat-sen University, Guangzhou. He teaches anthropology and social work. He has served as executive dean of the School of Philanthropy at the university since 2011. He was a visiting scholar at Harvard University in 2007–2008 and is now a Fulbright Scholar at the IU Lilly Family School of Philanthropy at Indiana University–Purdue University Indianapolis (IUPUI). He does research in a range of fields, including civil society and philanthropy, community development, non-profit management, and social movements. His major publications are *Between the Family and the State: Ethnography of the Civil Associations and Community Movements in a Shanghai Linong Neighborhood* and *Power of Action: Cases Studies of Private Volunteer Organizations*. Besides his academic jobs, he is also the director of the Institute for Civil Society of the University, a leading resource hub and supporting center for NGOs in Southern China, and he also serves as vice director on the board of the Guangdong Harmony Foundation, the first community foundation in China.

ZI Yan-fei graduated from the School of Journalism and Communication, South China University of Technology, in 2010.